Photo essay
by John Miller

1–2 Bilbao
3 Cala San Vincente
4 Traditional paella
5 Mallorca

6 Seville

7 Old town, Ibiza
8 Villajoysa

13

9 Pollenca market   **12** Mallorca
10 Café, Jerez   **13** Nerja
11 Beach, Benidorm

15

16

14 Costa Brava
15 Mallorca
16 Olives at a local market

17 Tapas bar, Madrid

18 Puerto Pollenca
19 Palma

20 Catalonian bridge, Besalú

Harvey Holtom

Working and Living
SPAIN

CADOGANguides

Contents

About the Authors

Harvey Holtom has lived in Madrid for over 20 years, where he has worked as a language teacher, translator, photographer and writer. He has worked on all editions of the Time Out *Madrid* Guide and was correspondent for the Time Out website. For this series he co-wrote *Buying a Property Spain, Buying a Property Portugal* and *Living and Working in Portugal*.

Nick Rider is the author of *Yucatan & Mayan Mexico* and *Short Breaks in Northern France*. He writes articles on food, travel, history, music and art, and has been a guest on Radio 5's *Globetrotting*. Having lived in Spain for many years, he is currently based in London.

Jim Trevor has lived and worked in Spain on and off for about 15 years since first arriving in 1982. A language teacher, translator and freelance writer with experience in the movie industry, Jim also did Journalism Studies at the University of Berkeley and is currently finishing a novel. His contributions to this book include some of the case studies and all the information on red tape relevant to non-EU citizens – a process he knows well!

About the Updater

Christian Williams has been in and out of the USA for the past decade, including spells based in Colorado and New Jersey. He has worked as a travel writer for various publications, including the *Daily Telegraph*, and has written and co-authored several guide books, including *The Rough Guide to the Rocky Mountains, The Rough Guide to Skiing and Snowboarding*, and Cadogan Guides' *Working and Living: USA*. He has also written extensively about Canada, Tenerife and Berlin.

Second Edition published in 2007 by Cadogan Guides

Cadogan Guides is an imprint of
New Holland Publishers (UK) Ltd
London • Cape Town • Sydney • Auckland

New Holland Publishers (UK) Ltd	80 McKenzie Street	Unit 1, 66 Gibbes Street	218 Lake Road
Garfield House	Cape Town 8001	Chatswood, NSW 2067	Northcote
86–88 Edgware Road	South Africa	Australia	Auckland
London W2 2EA			New Zealand
United Kingdom			

Cadogan@nhpub.co.uk
www.cadoganguides.com
t 44 (0)20 7724 7773

Distributed in the United States by Globe Pequot, Connecticut

Copyright © Cadogan Guides 2004, 2007
"THE SUNDAY TIMES" is a registered trade mark of Times Newspapers Limited.

Cover photographs: © Taxi, Glow Images/Alamy, blickwinkel/fotototo, foodfolio, Hortus/Alamy,
Elizabeth Padilla/Avalon Word and Image, Paul Adams/Avalon Word and Image
Photo essay photographs © John Miller
Maps © Cadogan Guides, drawn by Maidenhead Cartographic Services Ltd
Cover design: Sarah Rianhard-Gardner
Editor: Linda McQueen
Proofreader: Ronald Nicholson
Indexing: Isobel McLean

Produced by **Navigator Guides**
www.navigatorguides.com

Printed in Finland by WS Bookwell
A catalogue record for this book is available from the British Library

ISBN: 978-1-86011-370-3

The author and publishers have made every effort to ensure the accuracy of the information in this book at the time of going to press. However, they cannot accept any responsibility for any loss, injury or inconvenience resulting from the use of information contained in this guide.

Please help us to keep this guide up to date. We have done our best to ensure that the information in this guide is correct at the time of going to press. But laws and regulations are constantly changing, and standards and prices fluctuate. We would be delighted to receive any comments. Authors of the best letters will receive a copy of the Cadogan Guide of their choice.

Introduction

If you are thinking of moving to Spain to live and work, or have already decided to, this is probably because you have visited the country more than once and have been seduced by some aspect or other of the Spanish way of life. Whatever your reasons for contemplating the move, there is much you should know before you uproot and take the plunge. This book aims to give you help and guidance throughout the various stages involved in moving to a new country, usually a much bigger step than most comprehend at first.

Living and Working: Spain has been prepared by a team of writers who are all former or current residents of the country. Together they have over 40 years' experience of living, working, studying and travelling in Spain. The guide is structured over eight chapters, each covering a different aspect of Spain of interest and importance to prospective émigrés. Dotted throughout are box features highlighting specific issues.

The first chapter, **Getting to Know Spain**, covers the country's climate and geography, provides a historical overview and explains the multilingual character of Spain. Spain is large, offering more variety in terms of landscape, climate, culture and cuisine than many other European countries; Chapter 02, **Profiles of the Regions**, breaks down the country into its different areas.

Chapter 03, **Spain Today**, examines the current state of Spanish politics and society, focusing on current affairs, women's issues, the media, religion, the economy, and Spain's role in the EU as well as its art, culture and cuisine.

Chapter 04, **First Steps**, has two main sections. The first part addresses the important question that all would-be settlers should think about: why do you want to live and work in Spain? This is followed by a practical guide to getting to and travelling around the country.

Bureaucratic issues concerning visas, residency, work permits and Spanish citizenship are dealt with in Chapter 05, **Red Tape**. The chapter includes a wealth of essential information, such as the addresses of ministries, embassies and consulates.

Chapter 06, **Living in Spain**, will be most helpful in the first weeks after your arrival, as it deals with a whole host of everyday aspects of living. These include learning the language(s), finding accommodation, hooking up home utilities, health and welfare, leisure and much more.

Working in Spain, Chapter 07, is a guide to all aspects of work: looking for it, getting it, losing it, contracts, workplace etiquette, freelancing, setting up and doing business and more besides.

The final chapter, **References**, is where you will find many of Spain's 'vital statistics', a short glossary of essential Castilian Spanish words, recommended further reading lists and films, telephone and post codes, and a brief guide to holidays and *fiestas*.

¡Bienvenido!

Getting to Know Spain

Spain can appear hugely familiar. In Britain, just about everyone seems to have been to some part of the country at least once, and everyone knows the Spanish stereotypes – bullfights, dark, flashing eyes, olive groves, white-washed houses, sun, flamenco dolls, twanging guitars. Stereotypes, of course, always have some roots in reality, but in Spain the clichés tell only a small part of the story. The reality is far more complex and more fascinating.

Diversity is one of Spain's fundamental features. The Iberian Peninsula is a subcontinent, separated from the rest of Europe by the great barrier of the Pyrenees. Spain has a greater variety of landscapes than anywhere else in western Europe – from the deep-green fjords of Galicia through Alpine mountains to hot deserts in eastern Andalucía – and then there are the subtropical islands of the Canaries. It is more mountainous than any other European country except Switzerland, and the city of Madrid, at 650m, is the continent's highest capital. And there are four official languages, spoken in different parts of the country.

Spain's history is unique: it has been occupied by Celts, Phoenicians, Romans and Moors and has gone from superpower status to decline. Self-contained in their subcontinent, Spain's peoples have often gone their own way in food and customs. Lately, Spain has become Europe's most fast-changing society. All this gives life here a special richness.

Climate and Geography

Geographically speaking, Spain is not one single country. If you have ever taken a flight across the country on a clear day you will have some idea of the contrasts as you move from north to south. However, the view from the air, with its flattened perspective, does little justice to the dramatic changes in the land-scape as you move about the country.

Away from the temperate north, Spain's weather patterns are extreme. Two weeks relaxing on the beach every year may not give you a true impression of what it is like to work through a Spanish summer. You will soon realise why Spain traditionally shuts up shop in August. No amount of background reading can explain the difference between a dry and a humid heat until you have actually experienced it. On the other hand, unless you are moving to southern Mediterranean Spain, don't fool yourself that you'll never need a woolly jumper again.

For more information on temperatures and rainfall, *see* **References**, p.269.

Broadly speaking, mainland Spain's 492,463 sq km can be divided into three distinct geographical and climatic zones: the Atlantic coast, the continental centre of Spain, and the Mediterranean zone.

Atlantic Spain

Atlantic Spain is formed by the regions of **Galicia, Asturias** and the **Basque Country.** To the south of these regions lie the Cantabrian mountains, including the **Picos de Europa,** which do much to create the un-stereotypically Spanish climate of this Atlantic zone.

The rain in Spain does not fall mainly on the plain but in these regions. **Santander,** for example, has rainfall of 54mm in July, the lowest monthly average, rising to 159mm in December, the highest. Temperatures are also the most similar to the UK in the country, with an average high of 23°C in August and 13°C over the winter months in **A Coruña.** This makes this area of Spain the greenest and most scenically attractive.

Inland from the large coastal towns, the combination of climate and relatively sparse population provides habitat for some of western Europe's most exotic wildlife. For those willing to look very hard, the Cantabrian mountains will reveal themselves as home to Spain's main colonies of wolves and the remaining few wild bears. This climate also explains why most of Spain's best dairy produce comes from here. Asturias alone has 28 varieties of cheese, some of them excellent.

Central Spain

Central Spain is characterised by the dry plateau 650m above sea level. Known as **La Meseta,** it is separated from coastal Spain by various mountain ranges and also contains smaller mountainous regions of its own.

The climate of this region is generally dry, with fierce summers and chilly winters. Microclimatic variations can and do occur within this extensive region. For instance, while **Madrid** bakes at an average 31°C in August, **Toledo,** barely an hour's drive south, is often two or three degrees hotter still. Conversely **Ávila,** just northeast of the capital, is a refreshing summer retreat for frazzled city-dwellers. Variations in temperature and rainfall also crop up in some unexpected ways over the course of the year. In late January and February it might be warm and sunny enough to sit out on a Madrid *terraza* during the day, while March and April could send you scurrying indoors for your umbrella and the central heating thermostat.

Winter snowfall can be heavy in the northern part of central Spain, and in the **Sierra de Guadarrama,** just north of Madrid, the snow is reliable enough for there to be a winter sports season. However, Spain's most dramatic mountain scenery – and best skiing conditions – is to be found in the **Sierra Nevada,** just south of Granada, which contains the Pico de Mulhacén (3,482m), the mainland's highest peak.

With general rainfall quite low over the year, it is noticeable how even relatively minor rivers can influence the agriculture and landscape. Higher and drier ground, when it is cultivated, is usually reserved for olive terraces, while in the valleys around rivers more demanding crops, such as melons, are widely grown. Spain's two great wine regions, Rioja and Ribera del Duero, cluster respectively around the Ebro and Duero rivers.

Mediterranean Spain

The term 'Mediterranean Spain' usually refers to its eastern and southern coastal areas between the French and Portuguese borders. This may not be literally accurate, as towns like Cadiz and Huelva actually face the Atlantic Ocean, but it is the Mediterranean which exerts its benign influence even here.

Beginning at the most northerly part of this expanse of coast, in Catalonia, the differences in climate from central Spain are already quite noticeable. Barcelona has a much higher average rainfall than Madrid and, while the summers are noticeably milder, the air can be humid in July and August. The Catalan **Costa Brava** also periodically feels the effect of the *tramontana* wind, which can go beyond the level of a refreshing breeze.

Heading south, the stretch of land that runs between Tarragona and Alicante, including the **Costa Blanca**, sees winter temperatures rise noticeably and the average rainfall drop by more than half, to somewhere around 300mm per year. This is the beginning of holidaymaker Spain, and with a winter average of around 18°C in Alicante, rising to the low 30s in the summer months, it is not difficult to see why so many refugees from the British rain choose to make their homes here.

South of Alicante the provinces of **Murcia** and **Almería** get hotter still. Here the terrain inland from the coast is naturally quite barren – it was in Almería's desert-like landscape that many 1960s 'spaghetti westerns' were shot. However, new farming techniques, using subterranean water supplies and cultivation under plastic sheeting, have meant that great areas of Murcia and Almería now produce winter vegetables for northern European supermarkets as well as for their own domestic consumption.

The **Costa del Sol**, stretching either side of Málaga in southern Andalucía, has milder winters and steamy summers. Again there are notoriously strong winds which can blow on this coast for days at a time.

Inland Andalucía endures summer temperatures unmitigated by any form of coastal breeze. The area between Córdoba and Seville, most notably the town of Écija, is fittingly referred to as the Frying Pan of Andalucía and often sees the thermometer climbing to the very high 40s. The sun may be great for the oranges and lemons which line the streets of the historic Andalucían towns, but the essential water is being piped. Indeed, much of rural Andalucía depends on irrigation canals dating back as far as the days of Moorish Spain in order to be able to produce anything from its sun-baked soil. Winters here can be delightful, though, with crisp morning air giving way to pleasantly warm afternoons.

The coast between the Straits of Gibraltar and the Portuguese border, the **Costa de la Luz**, has no significant variation in terms of temperature or rainfall, but the wind is more refreshing, and this is a popular area for windsurfers.

The **Balearic Islands** experience weather broadly similar to the corresponding part of the Mediterranean coast. **Ibiza**, the most southerly of the three main islands, enjoys the best year-round temperatures but pays for it with a generally brown terrain. **Menorca**, the most northerly, shares the force of the *tramontana* wind with the Costa Brava – the trees grow at a slant in the north of the island and some say the people, too, have a permanent stoop, as if battling against the wind. **Mallorca**, the largest of Las Islas Baleares, exhibits quite significant micro-climatic variation, with annual rainfall in the north of the island some 1,200mm compared to a mere 300–400mm in the south.

Spain's other main island group, the **Canary Islands**, has a different climate. Heat rising from the Sahara meets winds coming off the Atlantic. Both in summer and winter, average maximum temperatures are in the 20s Celsius. The islands with the highest elevation are greener, but rainfall is generally low everywhere, though particularly on Lanzarote or Fuerteventura, which gives them barren, almost lunar, landscapes.

Historical Overview

Ancient Times

The extraordinary cave paintings at Altamira near Santander, painted around 15,000 BC, are the most spectacular evidence of extensive settlement across the Iberian Peninsula throughout the late Stone Age. The peninsula's first people were the **Iberians** (*Íberos*) who arrived, possibly from North Africa, in around 2000 BC. Then there are the mysterious **Basques**, who may or may not be related to the Iberians but were probably already settled in their Pyrenean valleys well before that date. The next arrivals were the **Celts**, who came down from across the Pyrenees in around 1000 BC and integrated with the Iberians to create a new, hybrid culture, known as the **Celtiberians** (*Celtibéricos*).

The Pyrenees may historically have been a barrier to contacts from the north, but Spain was never isolated from the ancient Mediterranean civilisations. The **Phoenicians** and **Greeks** both landed on the east coast, and founded cities and colonies. Most important of all were the **Carthaginians**, who from 500 BC controlled a large area of southeast Spain, ruled from their city of 'New Carthage', now Cartagena.

This naturally attracted the attention of Carthage's great enemy, **Rome**, which by 200 BC had conquered the Carthaginian cities in Spain and went on to subdue the less civilised peoples further west. The Romans founded more cities, among them Tarraco (Tarragona), Barcino (Barcelona) and Augusta Emerita (Mérida), built roads and aqueducts, and introduced sophisticated irrigation systems into the Guadalquivir valley and Valencia. Baetica, centred on Hispalis (nowadays Seville), was one of the wealthiest provinces in the empire, and the birthplace of many great Romans including Emperors Trajan and Hadrian and the philosopher Seneca. The last centuries of Roman rule also saw the introduction of Christianity. Of the five modern languages of the peninsula (including Portuguese), all except Basque are Latin languages.

The Great Patchwork of Medieval Iberia

AD 711 saw the start of the most distinctive era of Iberian history. An Arab warrior called **Tarik** led an army from Morocco to Gibraltar (the name of which comes from the Arabic *Jebel Tarik* – Mount Tarik). After easily crushing the **Visigoths**, who had occupied Iberia after the fall of Rome, Muslim rulers would control 80 per cent of Iberia for the next five centuries as **Al-Andalús**, ruled at its height by a Caliph at Córdoba. In traditional Spanish history books this was presented as a foreign, Moorish invasion, before which all good Christians retreated into the northern mountains, to retake their lands centuries later in the so-called '*Reconquista*' (Reconquest). However, it has been pointed out that the population of Al-Andalús was far too large for the invading Arab armies to have accounted for all of them, and must have included whole communities who had been there before 711. In the highly Romanised south, many people had never been happy with the coarse and chaotic Visigoths, and welcomed the change to more educated Mediterranean rulers, converting to Islam or accepting Muslim rule. For over 200 years, the Caliphate of Córdoba was the wealthiest and most sophisticated society in Europe, and its cities – Córdoba, Seville, Almería – the largest on the continent. Ever since, the image of opulence of Al-Andalús has haunted southern Spain, especially.

All-Christian Spain, meanwhile, was pushed back into Asturias and the Pyrenees, fragmented into tiny dukedoms and kingdoms. **Castile** slowly emerged as the most important in central Iberia, although **Portugal** broke away from it in the 1140s.

One state had a different origin from the others. The mountain counties that became **Catalonia** were founded from across the Pyrenees, as the southern frontier of the empire of Charlemagne (thus Catalan's closest linguistic relative is Provençal, not Castilian). In 1137 the Count of Barcelona married the heiress of Aragon, creating a complicated entity called the '**Crown of Aragon**'. Since Aragon was a kingdom, while the Catalan ruler was theoretically only a Frankish count, the name of Aragon was often given to the whole inheritance, but its court language was Catalan, and Barcelona its centre of power.

For decades, the Christian states could do little against the power of Al-Andalús. Around 1015, though, the Caliphate broke up into small, bickering emirates, called 'taifas'. This gave the Christians their chance, even though Muslim strength revived after 1100, with the taifas reunited under two militaristic dynasties from Morocco, the **Almoravids** and **Almohads**. The decisive Christian advance did not come until after the battle of **Las Navas de Tolosa**, in 1212. The Castilians took Córdoba in 1236 and Seville in 1248, while Jaume I, 'the Conqueror' of Aragon, seized Mallorca in 1229, and Valencia in 1238. Only the mountain kingdom of Granada was left as the last Muslim foothold in Spain.

Medieval Spain was a fascinatingly diverse place. There were huge **Jewish** communities; one of the greatest eras of Jewish culture flourished in Muslim Spain. There were Christians who lived under Muslim rule, and Muslims ruled by Christians. This co-existence was attacked from both sides. The Almoravids and Almohads sought to impose strict Islam in Al-Andalús, alienating previously compliant Jewish and Christian subjects. Later, with Christianity triumphant and still greater numbers of Jews and Muslims under Christian rule, another fundamentalism gained force, as Catholic orders such as the Dominicans demanded restrictions on non-Christians. Co-existence collapsed in the 14th century: the 1390s saw vicious pogroms in Jewish communities, which brought the great age of Spanish Jewish culture to a brutal end.

In power politics, once Al-Andalús was overcome, the Catalan-Aragonese monarchs took little interest in Iberian affairs but turned seawards, to the Mediterranean. The 13th and 14th centuries were the Catalan 'Golden Age,' when Barcelona was the centre of a seaborne empire that extended to Sardinia, Sicily and Greece, and competed in Mediterranean trade with Genoa and Venice. As the 15th century began, however, both Castile and Aragon were hit by devastating civil wars, which weakened Aragon's imperial pretensions. This chaotic situation was brought to an end by a significant marriage. In 1469 **Ferdinand**, heir to the Crown of Aragon, married **Isabella** of Castile, bringing together for the first time ever the main Christian kingdoms (although each kept its own institutions for years to come). They stamped their authority on their domains, put a stop to rebellions, and became a power in European affairs. In their 'Year of Glory' of 1492 their armies finally took Granada, clearing away the last trace of Al-Andalús – and, of course, **Columbus** discovered America.

The rulers of Spain have often seen it as their role to force its diversity into a more orderly shape. The first concerted effort was under Ferdinand and Isabella. If there is one individual to whom Spain's reputation for intolerance can be traced, it is Queen Isabella 'the Catholic': intensely devout, she considered it her Christian duty not to tolerate the religious pot-pourri she had inherited from medieval Spain. 1492 saw the final expulsion of all Jews from Castile and

Aragon, and later she ordered all Muslims to convert to Christianity or leave. As so many forced converts could not be trusted, in order to enforce religious orthodoxy the Pope granted Isabella the right to set up the notorious **Inquisition**. Spain entered a new era with an expansive but authoritarian style.

Global Empire

For over 80 years after 1492, the power and grandeur of Spain increased at a prodigious pace. Vast and mysterious new territories were added to its domains – Mexico in the 1520s, Peru in the 1530s, the Philippines in the 1560s – and the discovery of gold and silver in America seemed to give the Spanish monarchy unlimited wealth. From a growing but moderately powerful European state, Spain (or rather Castile) suddenly found itself the first global power, the centre of the first empire on which the sun truly never set.

Part of this rise to imperial superpower was due to the released energies of a resurgent Castile, but it was also helped by a remarkable series of accidents, as *conquistador* expeditions blundered into control of lands they knew nothing about. Even Ferdinand and Isabella's grandson, the Habsburg Emperor **Charles V**, had only come into his vast inheritance – Spain, Austria and Burgundy, which included the Netherlands, Belgium and large parts of France – through the fortuitous, unexpected deaths of several of his relatives. For Charles and the Habsburgs, though, this, along with the continual discoveries in America, simply confirmed that they had been singled out by providence as the representatives of God on earth. This 'imperial mission' came with huge responsibilities, for as God's (Catholic) policeman Spain would have to fight continual wars, against native peoples in the Americas, against Protestants in the Netherlands, Germany and England, against Muslim Turks in the Mediterranean, and against the French, who had no religious quarrel with Spain but were dedicated to displacing it as first power in Europe.

This was Spain's '**Golden Century**'. It produced great art and literature, with painters like El Greco and Velázquez and writers such as Cervantes. In 1561 **Philip II** tired of taking the court around the country – as was traditional in medieval Castile – and settled it in the previously minor royal seat of Madrid, which 'boomed' into an exuberant, rough-and-ready capital that provided the setting for the first great age of Spanish theatre. This contrasted with an atmosphere of paranoid intolerance, as Crown and Church sought to stamp out all challenges to their authority and Catholic orthodoxy. The Spanish monarchy also had a talent for shooting itself in the foot: the aristocracy and the Church were largely exempt from tax, so the taxes to pay for endless wars fell overwhelmingly on the poorer sectors of society, which withered away. Meanwhile, the famous gold of the Americas was often spent before it could even be shipped to Europe. Religious intolerance was similarly destructive: in 1609

Impossible Empire

When the Habsburg kings acquired a worldwide empire and set about ruling it as sole authority, with the resources of the 16th century, they set themselves an impossible task. The rootless Charles V, celebrated for speaking 'French to his ministers, German to his generals, Spanish to God, Italian to his mistresses and Dutch to his horse', travelled constantly around Europe, fighting battles one year in Flanders, the next in North Africa. A sign of how hard it was to keep so many plates in the air was that in 1556 Charles abdicated and divided his inheritance, leaving Austria to his brother, Ferdinand, and Spain and Burgundy to his own son, Philip II (1556–98). Philip was a very different character from Charles, shy, precise and deeply religious. Early in life he decided he liked Castile more than any other of his dominions, and, after marrying Mary I of England and briefly wooing her sister Elizabeth I, from 1559 he never left Spain.

Philip II settled his court in Madrid, but was less interested in the new capital than in his giant monastery-residence of El Escorial to the north, where his spartan chambers can be visited today. Instead of leading armies in battle like his father, Philip tried to rule his empire from a desk as a 'magnum bureaucrat', seeing hundreds of documents a day. All kinds of matters were theoretically subject to the king's approval, but if a problem arose in Peru, for example, between the time it was referred back to El Escorial, reached the king's desk and then a reply was sent across the Atlantic, a year could have gone by, by which time a new set of problems had arisen. Officials often found it easier just to avoid making any major decisions at all.

The 17th-century Habsburgs – Philips III and IV, whose gloomy faces stare down from Velázquez' superb portraits in the Prado in Madrid – were obsessed by feelings of inferiority in comparison with their great ancestors, and preferred to rule through ministers than take on this giant task themselves. In the 1630s Philip IV's great minister, the Count-Duke of Olivares, sought to raise the king's morale by building him a giant new palace in Madrid, the Buen Retiro, the gardens of which now provide the city's main park. As problems mounted all around them, the Spanish Habsburgs could take refuge here in elaborate ceremonies and entertainments.

thousands of supposedly converted former Muslims were expelled, with disastrous economic consequences. A century after 1492, much of Spain was poorer than many of the countries it tried to rule over. The first global power would also be the first to burn out.

At the same time this was still a Castilian, not a Spanish empire. It is often said that Spain has been one country ever since the marriage of Ferdinand and Isabella, but things were far more complicated. Charles V really only inherited a union of crowns, one part of which, the 'Crown of Aragon', was itself already a union of crowns. Castile became the unquestioned hub of the monarchy because of its greater wealth and greater controllability. After a short revolt in the 1520s, the Habsburgs, as absolute monarchs, could levy taxes and raise armies more or less as they liked; in the Crown of Aragon, on the other hand, the infuriated rulers forever had to ask permission from local notables. The non-Castilian kingdoms, for their part, felt excluded: Charles V explicitly forbade Catalans from trading directly with his American colonies. In 1580 Philip II became King of Portugal, bringing the whole of Iberia under one monarch, but this would not last. As the empire's difficulties increased, the monarchy demanded taxes and troops from its non-Castilian territories, and in 1640 Portugal and Catalonia rose up in revolt. Portugal, helped by England, regained its independence; the Catalans looked for aid from France, who left them to make a separate peace after years of war.

By the 1660s the Spanish empire was exhausted. The last of the Spanish Habsburgs, Charles II, was physically and mentally disabled, and died childless in 1700. This led to the **War of the Spanish Succession**, in which Castile opted for the Bourbon dynasty under **Philip of Anjou**, grandson of Louis XIV of France, while the alternative, **Archduke Charles of Austria**, was supported by Austria, the Netherlands, Britain and Catalonia and the other former Aragonese territories, to whom he offered the return of their historic rights. By 1714 the British and Dutch had had enough and recognised **Philip V** as king of Spain, leaving the Catalans to their fate. In 1715 Philip V issued his **decree of Nova Planta**, abolishing the remaining rights of the rebellious Aragonese territories and placing the whole country under a unified administration. It is from this date that 'Spain' truly exists as a single state.

Modern Drama

In 1808 **Napoleon** kidnapped the Spanish royal family and tried to install his brother, **Joseph Bonaparte**, as king of Spain. He was shocked to find, though, that committees or juntas sprang up everywhere to offer fierce resistance, with six years of devastating war. Without their autocratic monarchs, the Spanish people discovered a new ability for self-organisation. In 1812 representatives of juntas from every region met in Cádiz to draw up Spain's first **constitution**.

Restored to his throne in 1814, however, **King Ferdinand VII** showed little gratitude for the efforts made on his behalf, and thought only of throwing aside the constitution and returning to the authoritarian methods of his youth. This was the prelude to decades of instability, as Spain withdrew from international affairs to concentrate on its own quarrels. Weak governments, coups and 'revolutions' succeeded each other. The country lost virtually all its vast American empire. Spain gained a reputation for incompatible extremes, for being divided between 'Two Spains' – one traditionalist, authoritarian, rural, inward-looking, deferential to wealth and wedded to a puritanical Catholicism; the other free-

Spain: the Movie

Images of Spain – parched earth, hot passions, clicking heels, all to an obligatory flamenco soundtrack – are peculiarly sharply etched. Just as peculiar is the fact that so many of them were first picked out and polished up by foreigners. The idea that Spain is somehow an exotic place, set apart from the rest of Europe – a place where colours were deeper, emotions more intense, where life had a stronger flavour – was a discovery of 19th-century Romantics. As northern Europe and North America began to industrialise and adopt a more practical outlook, travellers first looked on Spain as a place to find an older alternative. It was a favourite subject of early travel books. In 1829 the American Washington Irving travelled through Andalucía and wrote his *Tales of the Alhambra*, an arch-Romantic fantasy on Moorish Spain. A few years later the French writer Prosper Mérimée took a similar tour through Madrid and Seville. He detested the food, but was fascinated by the people. In 1845 he wrote *Carmen*, which became international shorthand for everything Spanish. All that remained to complete the picture was for it to be set to music by another Frenchman, Bizet, who himself never set foot in Spain in his entire life. In the 20th century Hemingway took up the baton with his bullfight fantasies.

Spanish attitudes to all these images are very mixed. There is a contemptuous word, '*españolada*', for all kinds of off-the-shelf 'Spanishness'. The Franco regime embraced clichés and for years promoted the country with the slogan 'Spain is Different', meaning, yes, that this is a place you will find things you won't find elsewhere, but with a subtext that Spaniards are so hot-blooded that they can't be trusted with things other peoples take for granted – like democracy. The Romantic clichés of Spain have overwhelmingly been drawn from Andalucía. They are most irritating, therefore, to those such as the Basques and Catalans, who don't identify with them at all and feel they have a perfectly good, different identity of their own.

thinking, liberal, believing in progress and rooted in or sympathetic to the poor. The army was the most solid part of the state, and generals intervened regularly to impose governments of one stamp or another.

However, political instability did not prevent significant economic development in some parts of Spain. Catalonia and the Basque Country entered the Industrial Revolution in the 1830s. Textile factories were set up in Barcelona and iron works in Bilbao. This was the background to the revival of Basque and Catalan national identity, seen above all in the rebirth (**Renaixença**) of Catalan language, art and literature. For Basques and Catalans, nationalism was seen as inseparable from modernity. Cultural movements aside, industrialisation created a tangible economic and psychological gulf between those regions and the poor, rural Spain that seemed impervious to change.

With the arrival of the 20th century, the pace of social change accelerated when railways, roads and electricity allowed even Madrid to become an economic centre rather than just a city of civil servants. As well as democratic and nationalist groups Spain acquired a truculent **labour movement** – which was also divided, between socialists and anarchists. This was also a time of great cultural energy, dubbed the '**Silver Age**' of Spanish literature and culture, with a string of great writers, musicians and artists such as Picasso, Manuel de Falla, Antonio Machado and Federico García Lorca.

This was the background to the **collapse of the monarchy** in 1931, and the inauguration of Spain's **Second Republic** (the first, in 1873, had only lasted a few months). It arrived amid immense popularity and with huge expectations that it would bring in sweeping reforms, and deal with problems that had festered for decades. It gave autonomy to Catalonia, and later to the Basque Country and Galicia. However, the Republic was dragged down by five years of political and social crisis, as relations polarised between the right and the left. In 1936 fresh elections were won by a united 'Popular Front' of the left; for right-wing generals, though, things had gone far enough. On 18 July 1936 they launched a military coup, and the **Spanish Civil War** began. The right wing or Nationalists – among whom General **Francisco Franco** emerged as unchallenged leader – had virtually all Spain's regular army, and the support in men and weaponry of Hitler and Mussolini; the Republic had a largely ad hoc army, the support of idealists from around the world and a few arms from the Soviet Union. In the Nationalist zone a fascist regime was set up, while in many Republican areas there was a revolution. Gradually the Republic was worn down. In spring 1939, as the rest of Europe headed towards the Second World War, Franco's forces took Barcelona and Madrid.

One of the '**Two Spains**' was triumphant, and in a vengeful mood. The Franco regime divides into two phases. For its first 20 years it was an out-and-out fascist regime. Uniformity, not diversity, was the ideal, and a dour Catholicism looking back to the Habsburg Golden Age became almost obligatory. Minority nationalities received special attention, and all publishing in, public use of or sometimes just mentioning of the Catalan and Basque languages was banned. Rigid censorship was imposed, and all political activity outside Franco's 'National Movement' prohibited. As the last survivor of the fascist regimes of the 1930s Spain was an international pariah, until in the early 1950s the USA decided the Cold War was more important and gave Franco cash and support in return for military bases. The country was desperately poor – much poorer in many areas than in the 1930s – and many older Spaniards have more traumatic memories of these 'hunger years' than of the Civil War itself.

Things began to change in 1959, when a '**Stabilisation Plan**' for the economy was drawn up by technocrats of the Catholic lay organisation Opus Dei, the 'brains' of the regime. This opened Spain up to international trade and investment; it also coincided with the Europe-wide boom of the 1960s, which provided another vital element: tourists. As more and more Europeans sought out Mediterranean beaches, money flooded in, filtering into every sector of the economy; Spain had one of the highest growth rates in the world. The regime still expected to maintain absolute political control, but an expanding society was more difficult to keep in check. In the 1960s the Basque nationalist organisation, **ETA**, began its armed campaign for independence, and everywhere else new union and opposition movements were emerging from the woodwork. Even so, the regime hung on until the old dictator died, on 20 November 1975.

The New Spain

Spanish stereotypes often celebrate tradition and the past – Moorish palaces, Gothic cathedrals, bullfights. In fact, Spain has changed more rapidly than any other country in Europe in the past 40 years. The Franco-era boom of the 1960s was followed by further economic booms after Spain gained EU membership in the 1980s, and during the 1990s. From an overwhelmingly rural country in the 1950s it has become urban, with a huge movement to the cities.

One fundamental change has been that industries of different sizes – once confined to traditional 'pockets' like Catalonia, the Basque lands and Madrid – have spread around the country. Economic imbalances between regions are still a Spanish characteristic, but are far less extreme than before 1939. Another massive transformation since 1975 has been in the position of women: previously confined to the home under a regime that allowed neither divorce nor birth control, Spanish women now work in every area of the economy, and after 1975 the birth rate has fallen from one of the highest in Europe to one of the lowest in the world (see **Spain Today**, pp.67–8).

Spain's political transition has been one of its most remarkable changes. Franco had ordained that on his death the monarchy should be restored under **King Juan Carlos**, grandson of Spain's last king dethroned in 1931, but nobody knew what he intended to do. He appointed a former Francoist official, **Adolfo Suárez**, as prime minister, and charged him with bringing modern democracy to Spain. Opposition parties were made legal, and in June 1977 the first open elections since 1936 were held. They were won by Suárez himself. It also became clear that any democratic system in Spain would have to acknowledge some of the demands of the historic nationalities, especially the Basques and Catalans. To some astonishment, Suárez offered autonomous governments and the devolvement of powers not only to these strongly nationalistic areas but also to Spain's 15 other regions. This broke with a 250-year tradition of rigid centralisation, and made negotiations between central government and the regions a constant of modern Spanish politics. It created a situation that is much less clear-cut than a fully federal system, the implications of which have had to be worked out gradually. In more nationalistic regions separatist debates continue, but – with the major exception of the Basque Country – the 'Autonomies' have provided a good framework for government (*see* pp.32–3).

For some years members of the armed forces plotted to restore a Franco-style regime. Most Spaniards, though, had little interest in re-fighting old battles. Instead Spain's transition was based on a muddy compromise, a tacit agreement between the mainstream right and mainstream left not to mention the past but to concentrate on the future. New freedoms were asserted, and previously impossible projects set in motion, such as the spectacular renovation of Barcelona. Politically, the permanence of democracy was confirmed with the election of a Socialist government under **Felipe González** in 1982. Against expectations, they gave more emphasis to modernisation – including EU membership – than radical social reform, and presided over a spectacular boom. From a country associated with repression, Spain became ultra-liberal in some areas – censorship, drugs – and the style of the 'new Spain' was a country out to enjoy itself. Towards the end of their 14 years in power the González governments became complacent and mired in corruption scandals; the deliberately hard line they adopted towards ETA also culminated in the shadowy affair of the GAL, a band of hired hitmen covertly organised through the security forces to eliminate ETA militants. However, they also had major achievements, in transport and health, where services vastly improved, and in returning Spain to the European mainstream, a process crowned by the 'Year of Spain' in 1992, with Expo '92 in Seville, Madrid's stint as European Capital of Culture, and the Barcelona Olympics.

The discrediting of the Socialists left the way open for the rise of the conservative Partido Popular (PP), a party descended from former followers of Franco, under **José María Aznar**. The rise of the PP reflected a revival in social conservatism after the liberal 1980s, and a backlash in Castilian-speaking Spain against the assertiveness of national minorities. In power from 1996 to March 2004, the PP was happy to bear the fruit of Spain's ongoing modernisation, pursuing only moderate ambitions including the successful privatisation of some state concerns, and in general enjoying moderate support from a largely disinterested public. Yet despite this the PP lost the 2004 general election, as a consequence of mishandling of several events.

The first among these was the government's proposed changes to employment law and unemployment benefit. Part of the proposals meant that people might be obliged to accept jobs at up to an hour and half's journey from their homes or risk losing their benefit. This caused a well-supported general strike in June 2002, and helped re-polarise the Spanish political scene, highlighting differences between left and right. Ultimately the government backtracked on over 80 per cent of the law's content. Later that year the government blundered the management of the sinking of the *Prestige* oil tanker off its northwest coast, which spilt some 70,000 tons of oil: by acting too slowly and making the wrong decision – towing the tanker out to sea where the slick was harder to control rather than towing it inland – the government looked impotent, particularly in the face of the dedicated work of thousands of volunteers along the coast. Foreign policy too, brought the PP under fire, particularly Aznar's unswerving support for the invasion of Iraq, which provoked outrage from all parts of Spanish society where polls showed nearly 90 per cent of the population opposed the war. Even so the PP clung on in polls until the terrorist attacks on Madrid's trains on 11th March 2004, in which 201 people died and several hundred were injured, many seriously. The attack was possibly the result of the government's Iraq policy and certainly the work of extremist Muslims with Al-Qaeda links, but the government's first reaction was to attempt to shift the blame away from itself and towards ETA, the Basque separatist group. When the truth of the suspected Al-Qaeda links came out massive, spontaneous demonstrations took place outside PP headquarters in Madrid and Barcelona to protest about the lack of transparency in the government's handling of the situation and the perceived manipulation of it in its own electoral interest. The general public echoed the sentiment within days, by polling in favour of the PSOE on the 14th March. The situation in Spain since then, its major issues and political parties, is discussed in full in Chapter 03, **Spain Today**, pp.61–76.

Spanish Languages

Castilian Spanish

¡Hola! is the greeting used by around 400 million people across the Spanish-speaking world, and Spanish is today, with English and Mandarin Chinese, one of the three foremost global languages. In its homeland it is more often known not as *Español* but *Castellano* (Castilian), in acknowledgement of the place where it originated, in northern Castile. It began life as one of several related Latin-based languages in the Christian 'fringe' north of Muslim territory; the oldest Castilian written texts date from the 970s. From there, it spread southwards with the 'reconquest' of Muslim Spain. Centuries of contact also left behind one of the distinctive features of Spanish: its many words of Arabic origin, such as the great many words beginning with *al-*, from *alfombra* (carpet) and *almohada* (pillow) to *alcalde* (mayor).

Because the language has a known origin, Spaniards have a clear idea, strange to English-speakers, of where the 'best Castilian' is spoken, and indeed, throughout Old Castile people, rich and poor, do still generally speak with remarkable clarity. Valladolid is considered to be the home of the 'most correct' Castilian. Further south, street Spanish tends to come in a variety of accents, some much stronger than others: Andalucíans, above all, are notorious for 'swallowing' the ends of words and missing the 's' off plurals.

English is widely taught in Spain nowadays but, even if only for practical purposes (understanding your own bank account, dealing with shopkeepers, official paperwork, etc.), anyone living in Spain requires a certain level of proficiency in Spanish. Fortunately, several features of Spanish make it an easy language to learn. It is a phonetic language, with (unlike English) a simple, rational spelling system so that, once you've learnt the basic rules, you can tell immediately from how a word is spelt how it should be pronounced. Basic Spanish grammar is also perhaps the simplest in all the Latin languages: in everyday conversation questions, for example, are formed not by changes in word order or use of auxiliary verbs but by tone of voice, so that the difference between *tiene mucho dinero* ('he has a lot of money', as a statement) and *¿tiene mucho dinero?* is just one of intonation, which anyone can understand (this is also why the inverted question and exclamation marks are used in written Spanish). Spaniards are appreciative when they meet someone who does try to communicate in their own language.

Other Languages

Castilian Spanish is the only language found in every part of Spain, but three others have co-official status with it in different autonomous communities – Catalan, Galician and Basque, known to those who speak them as *Català*, *Galego* and *Euskera*. Castilian became dominant with the rise of Castile itself as the hub of the Spanish monarchy, and in 1715 Philip V's Nova Planta decree imposed it as the sole language of state business.

Spain's linguistic diversity is an expression of its cultural diversity which, as has been seen above, makes the country a mosaic and means that, culturally speaking, Catalans, Castilians, Asturians, Basques, Galicians and Andalucíans have as many as or more differences than, say, English, Scottish, Welsh or Irish people, or Mancunians, Devonians and Londoners.

Over the centuries the contradictions and tensions between the regions have been expressed through centrifugal and centripetal swings, with greater or lesser degrees of freedom or autonomy for the 'historical regions' and a greater or lesser emphasis on central – and centralised rule. Franco and his regime, believing Spain to be *'una, grande y libre'* ('one, great and free') leaned heavily towards the latter, suppressing the political autonomy that had been granted to Catalonia during the Second Republic and wiping out the degrees of freedom that had also been awarded to the Basque Country and Galicia during that period. Apart from in the political sphere, this had its expression in Franco's linguistic policy, which meant that Catalan, Galician and Basque were banned from all aspects of public life, were not taught in schools and could not be used in the media, either written or spoken, the field of publishing, or the pulpit. It was Franco's hope that by thus strangling these other languages they would die a natural death and Castilian would impose itself. The fact that they survived is proof of their strength as a symbol of the cultural identity of those who speak them. Franco's regime was all-pervasive, but behind closed doors many continued speaking their own languages as they had always done.

Since the return of civil liberties in the 1970s, each of these languages has enjoyed a renaissance that has, in some cases, been spectacular. All are taught in schools, the autonomous political institutions now use them as their language of administration, there are newspapers, television channels and radio stations that use them, and it is now possible to find literature published in these languages.

Catalan (*Català*)

Catalan is spoken by over six million people in Catalonia, Valencia, the Balearics and one corner of France (Roussillon, around Perpignan) – more people than speak Danish or Finnish, which are both official EU languages. Catalan-speakers form the largest linguistic community in Europe without their own state. Catalan is another Latin-based language but, since the founders of Catalonia were from north of the Pyrenees, in some ways it is closer to French than Castilian – although its closest similarities are with Provençal, which still just survives in France. In the *Reconquista*, as Castilian spread south to Andalucía, Catalan travelled down the Mediterranean coast and out to the islands. Again, it is not hard to learn. It has a less 'melodic' sound than most Latin languages, but Catalan phonetics are actually easier for English-speakers than Spanish sounds: the Catalan 'j' has a 'zh' sound like a French 'j', instead of the guttural Castilian *jota* in *Juan*.

Catalan was the main language of the Crown of Aragon for most of its history; its decline began under the Habsburgs, but even after 1715 it remained the main spoken language in its home areas. Unlike Galician or Basque – or Welsh, for that matter – it has never been relegated to being a 'mountain language', associated only with country people. Catalan's greatest revival came between the mid-19th-century *Renaixença* (rebirth) and the Civil War, which made Franco's subsequent cultural *blitzkrieg* all the more bitterly resented.

The degree to which Catalan has reasserted itself varies from region to region. In Catalonia itself it has effectively been reinstated as the primary language of public life, including education. In small towns and the countryside it is the main everyday language, too, but Barcelona and its suburbs are still around 50 per cent Spanish-speaking. In the tourist-dominated Balearics, some would say English or German are as common as Catalan or Spanish, but Menorca and inland Mallorca are actually just as Catalan-speaking as rural Catalonia; on Ibiza and the Mallorcan coast Spanish comes more to the fore. The Valencian region is more bilingual, but still with variations, Castellón being more Catalan-speaking than Alicante. If you move to a Catalan village, learning some Catalan will be as important as learning Castilian is elsewhere; to live and work in Barcelona, you need to be able to understand and to a lesser extent use both. Most road and information signs are also in Catalan, as are official forms.

Galician (*Galego*)

This language can sound (and look) like a hybrid of Castilian and Portuguese, but it is a language in its own right, and actually the older parent of modern Portuguese. It is a Latin-based language, and until the 13th century enjoyed comparable status in the northern Christian kingdoms with Castilian, but fell back to second place long before Catalan declined in its territories. However, because Galicia has been poor and rural, producing emigrants rather than drawing Spanish-speakers in, *Galego* has remained the first language of most of its people, above all in Galicia's countless villages.

Galicia too had a cultural revival pre-1936, only with less impact than the languages of the Catalans and Basques. Since 1980 the regional government has overseen a relatively modest restoration of the language, and many place names have been converted back to *Galego* from Castilian forms.

Galicians speak Castilian with a musical lilt, due to the influence of their own language, and at times it can be difficult to tell which of the two they are speaking. For anyone with some understanding of Castilian, though, *Galego* should not be too difficult to grasp in conversation. Galicians are traditionally unassertive nationalists, but, again, if you live in any small community in Galicia you will have closer contact with people if you can handle the local language.

Basque (*Euskera*)

Euskera is spoken by nearly a million people in the three main Basque provinces of Vizcaya, Guipúzcoa and Álava and in neighbouring Navarra, and by some 80,000 more in the French Basque country. No contact with another language prepares you for Basque: decades of study have failed to establish clear links between it and any other living language. It is unquestionably the oldest in Europe. The language and the Basques themselves were already described as 'ancient' by the Romans.

Basque is a language which combines single words without change of form to express compound ideas (an agglutinating language; other examples are Finnish and Hungarian). This means that instead of prepositions and other parts of speech it has suffixes that are added on to stem-words: thus, from *Bilbo* (Bilbao), you can have *Bilbon* ('in Bilbao'), *Bilbo'ko* ('from Bilbao') and *Bilbo'koa* ('to Bilbao'), but there are many more suffixes and combinations, permitting the creation of single words of terrifying complexity. The great Bilbao-born philosopher Unamuno, a Basque-speaker in his youth, later abandoned it, saying that agglutinating languages could not express complex thought, but this has naturally been hotly contested.

Until the 19th-century nationalist revival, Basque functioned principally as an oral language. It was also split into seven dialects, and the form now taught in schools, called *Euskera batua*, is a deliberately created unified version that some older Basques find artificial. Learning Basque is of a different order of difficulty from learning any of the Latin languages. The Basque government has programmes to support the language, but they have had less impact on everyday usage than their Catalan equivalents. In Basque towns and villages, though, new arrivals will still find they need to make at least some effort with *Euskera* if they wish to integrate.

Below are a few useful phrases in all languages, so you can see both the similarities and the differences. Note that there are two ways of spelling Galician, owing, on the one hand, to its close relationship to Portuguese and, on the other, to a strong Castilian influence. The first is practically identical to Portuguese, the second is closer to Spanish and (where different) is in italics in the table. The pronunciation hardly differs.

Getting Around
* note that no Galician cities actually have a metro system.

English	Castilian	Catalan	Galician	Basque
Train	Tren	Tren	Trem, Comboio/ *Tren, Convoio*	Tren
Bus	Autobús	Autobús	Bus, Linha/*Liña*	Autobus
Underground	Metro	Metro	Metro*	Metro
Airport	Aeropuerto	Aeroport	Aeroporto	Aireportu
Train station	Estación de tren /de ferrocarril	Estació de tren	Estaçom/ *Estación* do trem/*tren*	Trengeltoki
Bus station	Estación de autobús	Estació de autobusos	Estaçom/ *Estación* dos autobuses	Autobusgeltoki
Underground station	Estación de metro	Estació de metro	Estaçom/ *Estación* do metro*	Metrogeltoki
Departure	Salida	Sortida	Saídas	Irteera
Arrival	Llegada	Arribada	Chegadas	Etorrera
Car rental	Alquiler de coches	Lloguer de cotxes	Agência/*Axencia* de aluguer de autos	Berebilak alokatzeko ajentzia
Parking	Parking/ Aparcamiento	Aparcament	Estacionamento, Aparcadoiro	Aparkalekua
Hotel	Hotel	Hotel	Hotel	Ostatu

General Terms

English	Castilian	Catalan	Galician	Basque
Hello	Hola	Hola	Olá	Kaixo
Good morning/ day	Buenos días	Bon dia	Bom dia/*Bons dias* Bo día/*Bos días*	Egun on
Good afternoon	Buenas tardes	Bona tarda	Boa tarde/*Boas tardes*	
Good evening	Buenas tardes/noches	Bon vespre/ Bona tarda	Boa noite/*Boas noites*	Arratsalde on
Goodbye	Adiós	Adéu	Adeus/*Abur*	Agur
Goodnight	Buenas noches	Bona nit	Boa noite/*Boas noites*	Gau on/Gabon
See you	Hastaluego/ Hasta la vista	Fins desprès	Até logo/Até mais ver/*Ata logo/Ata máis ver*	Gero arte
See you tomorrow	Hasta mañana	Fins demà	Até amanha/*Ata mañá*	Bihar arte
I am/My name is	Yo soy/Me llamo...	Jo sóc.../Em dic...	Eu sou...	(your name) ... dut izena
What is your name?	¿Cómo se llama?/ ¿Cómo te llamas?	Com et dius?	Cal é o seu nome?	Zein da zuri izena?
How are you?	¿Cómo estás? Or (more formal) ¿Cómo está usted?	Com estàs? Or (more formal) Com està vostè?	Como te encontras? Or (more formal) Como se encontra?	Zer moduz zaude?
Fine/Good, thanks	Muy bien, gracias	Molt bé, graciès	Bem, graças/ *Ben, gracias*	Ederki, eskerrik asko
Not well/Bad	Mal	Malament	Mal	Gaizki
Okay/ o-so	Así así	Així-així	Vou indo	Erdipurdi
Please	Por favor	Si us plau	Se fai o favor	Mesedez/Arren
Thank you	Gracias	Gràcies	Graças/*Gracias*	Eskerrik asko
Thank you very much	Muchas/ Muchísimas gracias	Moltes/ Moltíssemes gràcies	Gracinhas/ *Graciñas*	Eskerrik asko
You're welcome	De nada	De res	Nom tem de quê /*Non ten de que*	Ez horregatik
Yes	Sí	Sí	Si	Bai
No	No	No	Nom/Non	Ez
Why...?	¿Por qué?	Perqué...?	Por qué...?	Zergatik?
How...?	¿Cómo...	Com...?	Como...?	Nola?
When...?	¿Cuándo...?	Quan...?	Cando...?	Noiz?
What...?	¿Qué...?	Qué...?	Que...?	Zer?
Where...?	¿Dónde...?	On...?	Onde...?	Non?
How much is...?	¿Cuánto es...?	Quant és...?	Canto é...?	Zenbat?
I don't understand	No entiendo	No ho entenc	Nom entendo/ Non entendo	Ez dut ulertzen
Do you speak English?	¿Hablas/Habla usted inglés?	Parles anglès?	Fala o inglês/inglés?	Hitz egiten al duzu ingelesez?

Numbers

English	Castilian	Catalan	Galician	Basque
1	Uno	U, un (m), una (f)	Un (m), unha (f)	Bat
2	Dos	Dos (m), dues (f)	Dous (m), dúas (f)	Bi
3	Tres	Tres	Tres	Hiru
4	Cuatro	Quatre	Catro	Lau
5	Cinco	Cinc	Cinco	Bost
6	Seis	Sis	Seis	Sei
7	Siete	Set	Sete	Zazpi
8	Ocho	Vuit	Oito	Zortzi
9	Nueve	Nou	Nove	Bederatzi
10	Diez	Deu	Dez	Hamar
11	Once	Onze	Onze/*Once*	Hamaika
12	Doce	Dotze	Doze/*Doce*	Hamabi
13	Trece	Tretze	Treze/*Trece*	Hamahiru
14	Catorce	Catorze	Catorze/*Catorce*	Hamalau
15	Quince	Quinze	Quinze/*Quince*	Hamabost
16	Dieciséis	Setze	Dezasseis/*Dezaseis*	Hamasei
17	Diecisiete	Disset	Dezassete/*Dezasete*	Hamazazpi
18	Dieciocho	Divuit	Dezaoito	Hemezortzi
19	Diecinueve	Dinou	Dezanove	Hemeretzi
20	Veinte	Vint	Vinte	Hogei
21	Veintiuno	Vint-i-un	Vinte e um/*Vinteún*	Hogeita bat
30	Treinta	Trenta	Trinta	Hogeita hamar
40	Cuarenta	Cuaranta	Quarenta/*Corenta*	Berrogei
50	Cincuenta	Cinquanta	Cinqüenta/*Cincuenta*	Berrogeita hamar
60	Sesenta	Seixanta	Sessenta/*Sesenta*	Hirurogei
70	Setenta	Setanta	Setenta	Hirurogeita hamar
80	Ochenta	Vuitanta	Oitenta	Laurogei
90	Noventa	Noranta	Noventa	Laurogeita hamar
100	Cien	Cent	Cem/*Cen*	Ehun
1,000	Mil	Mil	Mil	Mila
1,000,000	Un millón	Un milió	Um milhom/*Un millón*	Milioi bat

Days of the Week

English	Castilian	Catalan	Galician	Basque
Monday	Lunes	Dilluns	Segunda feira, Luns	Astelehen
Tuesday	Martes	Dimarts	Terça feira, Martes/*Terza feira, Martes*	Astearte
Wednesday	Miércoles	Dimecres	Quarta feira, Mércores/*Corta feira, Mércores*	Asteazken
Thursday	Jueves	Dijous	Quinta feira, Joves/*Quinta feira, Xoves*	Ostegun
Friday	Viernes	Divendres	Sexta feira, Venres	Ostiral
Saturday	Sábado	Dissabte	Sábado	Larunbat
Sunday	Domingo	Diumenge	Domingo	Igande

Profiles of the Regions

02

Diversity is a Spanish fundamental. Not only does Spain contain nationalities with languages and entire cultural traditions of their own – Catalans, Basques, Galicians – but every regional identity is proudly maintained. Unlike countries such as the British Isles and France, where the centre of political and economic power has nearly always been in the same place (London and Paris), the Iberian Peninsula has had no such natural hub: Madrid was plucked out of obscurity to become capital of Spain in the 1560s, but until quite recently was economically less important than Barcelona or Bilbao. The great varieties in landscape have reinforced regional differences, and Spain's many mountains helped keep regions apart, so that even when they shared a language they developed strongly individual characters and traditions, from architecture to food (for most Spaniards, for example, there is no such thing as 'Spanish food', but only Basque, Catalan or Asturian cuisine, etc.). Another factor is that modernity and industrialisation hit different regions at different times, so that there could be a gulf in the whole style and pace of life between Barcelona and rural Extremadura. Modern economic developments have narrowed these divides, but their mark is still felt in the atmosphere. For anyone coming to live in Spain, this means there is a tremendous range of homs and work places to choose from.

Urban Spain, Rural Spain and the *Costas*

Whichever part of Spain you are attracted to, another distinction will be as important in choosing where to live: between urban, rural, and a third alternative, the new communities around the coast.

In spite of all the regional differences, in every area of Spain, town life has traditionally followed a similar style. D.H. Lawrence, in one of his more bad-tempered blasts at his native land, wrote that the English did not know how to build a city or how to live in one. By this he meant that the spread-out, house-and-garden English post-Victorian townscape did not match up with the Mediterranean idea of urban living. In Spanish towns and cities individual homes have generally been clustered as close together as possible, interspersed by clearly identified urban public spaces – squares or *plazas*, markets, the spaces around cathedrals, or the classic *rambla* promenades of Catalan towns. They are cities, archetypally, of apartments. Even most country towns and villages were made up of narrow streets of terraced houses, from where agricultural workers went out every day to work in fields outside the town.

The closely packed nature of Spanish town life generates many of its most seductive features – its street life, intimacy, vibrancy and accessibility. In cities like Madrid or Barcelona – which have excellent public transport – nowhere you want to go to is likely to be much more than 30 minutes away from any other

part of town. This means, for example, that urban Spaniards never feel it necessary to plan to visit someone a week in advance, as Londoners might do. The
disadvantage of this concentrated urban environment is that with more people
close together you also get more noise, and more contact with your neighbours
than you may be used to. Even locals and people who love cities sometimes
suffer from claustrophobia, hence the mass exodus at weekends and holidays,
and the premium placed on top-floor apartments (*áticos*) with roof terraces. For
people for whom a quiet, garden-sized, private space is an essential, Spanish
urban life can be all too much.

However, some significant changes have been noticeable recently. Outside the
bigger Spanish cities – to the west of Madrid, or in the hills around Barcelona –
there is now an ever-expanding number of house-and-garden developments,
advertisements for which pack the local papers' property supplements. They are
increasingly popular with young Spanish families in search of more space and
the chance of their own swimming pool, and also with foreign residents who
don't want to take on every aspect of Spanish city life. Instead of the wonderful
accessibility of Spanish city centres, though, residents often find that their main
way into town is by car, joining atrocious daily traffic jams.

In contrast to the urban concentration, rural life in Spain has always been
more truly 'rural'. Until this recent growth of residential suburbs, Spanish cities
did not straggle into a suburbanised countryside as British towns do, but came
to a clear stop, where the country began. Many areas of rural Spain maintain a
sense of remoteness that's rare in Britain. On a practical level, in isolated farms
and even in villages, basic services – water, electricity, drainage – may be more
expensive and harder to arrange than in town, and to obtain them at manageable cost it may be important to be able to do some work yourself. Village life in
remoter areas can be very quiet and very traditional. Contrary to the
Mediterranean stereotype, locals can be very reserved towards foreigners, and it
will be up to new residents to make the effort to break this down. In country
districts in regions with their own languages, it will be important to use the
local language, not necessarily Castilian Spanish, to have anything more than
formal contacts with local people.

After urban, suburban and rural, the last main alternative is the one in which
the greatest number of foreign residents in Spain now live, especially if they've
retired to Spain or initially bought a second home – the new leisure communities around the holiday *costas*. All around the Mediterranean coast and the
islands there are thousands of *urbanizaciones*, purpose-built villa and apartment developments, at every point on the scale in size and density. Some are
attached to existing towns or villages, giving residents access to markets and
everyday local life, while others are isolated and self-contained. Some have a
mixed population, others are 95 per cent British or of another nationality. In and
around the holiday towns there are also a great many individual apartments, or

The Geography of Britspain

According to the Spanish government there were 3.7 million foreign residents in Spain in 2005, though independent estimates put the figure at 4.8 million or 15.1% of total population. Based on official statistics, UK citizens form the second-largest foreign community, after Spain's half-million Moroccans, with a total population of around 300,000, up from c. 90,000 in the 2001 census.

The geography of new British settlement in Spain doesn't hold many surprises: the familiar holiday *costas* – above all the Costa del Sol and Costa Blanca – are the most popular, followed by the major cities, Barcelona and Madrid. The British have a reputation for being more conservative than other nationalities, notably Germans, in seeking out new areas, such as the Atlantic regions, or the Valencia coast north of the Costa Blanca. The autonomous regions with the most UK residents, from the 2001 census, are as follows, with current local estimates for the main regions in parentheses:

Andalucía	30,664 (45,000)
(includes Costa del Sol, Costa Tropical, Costa de la Luz)	
Valencia	27,638 (90,000)
(includes Costa Blanca)	
Canaries	11,690 (20,000)
Balearics	7,944 (11,000)
Catalonia	6,681
(includes Barcelona)	
Madrid	4,856

villas in the hills. If you live on an all-foreign development, your contact with 'Spain' is naturally pretty limited. Whether you choose to live in one, or in a village, or in a city, will depend very much on the kind of life you want.

Regional Breakdown

Rulers of Spain, especially authoritarian ones, have often seen its great diversity as an obstacle to be crushed. In contrast, the current 'Autonomy State' or Estado de las Autonomías seeks to manage regional differences rather than stamp on them. Spain has been divided into 19 autonomous regions, varying in size from Castilla y León, with nine provinces, to single-province regions like La Rioja, and the North African enclaves of Ceuta and Melilla. This can be confusing, particularly because, unlike in a true federal system, there is no uniform template as to what powers a region can have. Gradually, they have divided into two main blocks: the 'historic nationalities' and large regions like

Andalucía or the Canaries which enjoy ample powers such as control over education and health, their own police forces, and some tax-raising powers; and, in the second rank, smaller regions that function more like arms of local government.

As the Basque situation indicates, the *autonomías* have not resolved all national and regional differences, nor have they ever quite settled down into a stable system. Most recently, the PP governments in Madrid have made reaffirming the primacy of central government a key slogan, and in response not just the Basques but also mainstream Catalan politicians have called for renegotiation of their 1980 autonomy statutes. Overall, though, on a day-to-day level regional administrations are for most Spaniards an established part of the scenery. They have practical consequences for foreign residents, in that some details of tax, property law, etc. vary by region. In regions with their own language this will often be the primary language of local services and education, ahead of Spanish.

The Central Heartlands

Foreigners tend to think of Spain in terms of its coastline, but the landlocked heart of the country is really the natural place to start.

Madrid

Madrid is a city that inspires extreme opinions. Not only is it Europe's highest capital but also the one closest to high mountains, the Sierra de Guadarrama, where within an hour of the city you can find near-alpine scenery, for walking or skiing. Madrid's crystal-clear skies are celebrated, and it's also known for extreme weather, from fiery summers to icy winters.

Madrid was one of the first purpose-built capitals, like Washington or Canberra, but also probably the only one built on a whim. Before 1561 it was only a small town next to a royal palace mainly used by the Habsburg monarchs as a hunting retreat. Philip II never deigned to explain why he chose to settle his court here, giving Spain Europe's only capital not on a navigable river. Once court and aristocracy were installed, though, Madrid mushroomed. Over the centuries it would be frequently abused as a parasite on the body of Spain, a place of aristocrats, civil servants and all their hangers-on, with the trappings of power and wealth but which looked down on the mundane process of actually producing anything. Only in the 20th century, after railways and roads were built that ended the city's isolation, did a series of economic booms allow Madrid to become a major industrial centre in its own right, drawing in migrants from rural areas around. Today, with three million people, Madrid is unquestionably the country's main banking and finance centre, and the preferred base for many foreign companies operating in Spain.

Madrid also retains a very special atmosphere. Madrileños, its inhabitants, are known for being loud, and Madrid is almost certainly the noisiest and most manic of all Spanish cities. Within its traffic, though, are remarkable oases of calm. Much of local life is still concentrated within the boundaries of the 17th-century city, where everything is within walking distance. It has great art museums, vibrant theatre and music scenes, and is the primary centre for many all-Spanish arts like bullfighting and flamenco. In shops and overall style, Madrid is less hip than Barcelona, but can be friendlier. Its combination of bar life, restaurants, nightlife and easy sociability makes it one of the best places in Europe for going out, in spite of city council efforts to get locals to curb their 24-hour habits.

Madrid and its surrounding province constitute an autonomous region, the **Comunidad de Madrid**. The rest of the Comunidad is home to another 2.5 million people, spread around a surprising variety of places – both industrial-sprawl towns like Leganés and Getafe, and residential suburbs like Pozuelo. Towns in the Guadarrama such as **El Escorial** have long been treasured by Madrileños as weekend escapes, and are now popular commuting bases, with good rail links. To the south is the charming town of **Aranjuez**, with a royal palace with gardens that inspired Rodrigo's famous *Concierto de Aranjuez*.

Castilla y León

These two historic kingdoms form Spain's largest region, but one of its least densely populated, with only 2.5 million people. Spanish writers have long pondered the enigma of how and why the hub of an empire that went out to conquer the world seemed to fall off the train of history a few decades later. In the 20th century Old Castile at last acquired some industries, especially around the regional capital, **Valladolid**, and it produces many fine wines. However, thousands have left rural Castile for Madrid, and many of its old villages and towns can seem part of that Spain that feels lost in time.

The region's superb old cities – Burgos, Valladolid, León, Salamanca – contain some of Spain's finest historic architecture, from Gothic to Baroque, and outside are the castles (*castillos*) that gave Castile its name. Between them stretches the great plateau of the *meseta*, a vast, flat, leather-brown landscape of wheat fields, rocky crags and soaring skies. Its climate is continentally extreme: the temperature range in Burgos is similar to that in Warsaw. In **León**, to the north-west, the landscape is more mountainous, while to the south it rises into the Guadarrama and the Sierra de Gredos, one of Spain's most beautiful mountain ranges and home to some of its rarest wildlife. Castile is a dry region, and Castilians are known as dry people, bluff, austere and formal. In many Castilian towns life still has a conservative feel. The only city with a more cosmo-politan atmosphere – and known for nightlife – is Salamanca, home to Spain's oldest university.

Castilian food reflects its austerity. If an ingredient is good, it is regarded as best appreciated simply and with as few frills as possible. The specialities are superb meats: steak in Ávila, lamb or suckling pig (*cochinillo*) in the capital of Castilian cuisine, Segovia, slow-roasted or grilled and then served alone, with no green vegetables in sight. With strong red wine, it's delicious, but for less committed carnivores, let alone vegetarians, this diet can feel seriously limited.

Castilla–La Mancha

This large region south and east of Madrid corresponds to the historic area of New Castile. It was 'new' in that this was the first large area captured from the Muslims after the fall of Toledo in 1086. It has a similar dry, brown and empty *meseta* landscape of olive groves, wheat, vineyards and mountains, but is yet more depopulated than Old Castile, with many old villages sunk in permanent stillness. **La Mancha**, south of Toledo, was already associated with the past when Cervantes set *Don Quixote* there in the 1600s.

Of its main towns, **Guadalajara** is the least architecturally attractive, but gains in bustle from its closeness to Madrid; **Cuenca** is a spectacular old Moorish city between two steep gorges, famous for its 'hanging houses' built on top of sheer cliffs. Exceptional, though, is the extraordinary medieval city of **Toledo**, the regional capital, one of Spain's greatest attractions and a magnet for foreigners fascinated by Spanish history and tradition.

Aragón

This was the only roughly Spanish-speaking region of the medieval Crown of Aragon, but in landscape and atmosphere it has most in common with the Castilian meseta. Aragonese, once a distinct linguistic variety, dissolved long ago into Castilian except for a strong local accent. Aragón retains its share of traditions, especially the boisterous folk dance, the *jota aragonesa*.

This is the least densely populated of all Spain's regions, and two-thirds of its 1,200,000 people live in or around the capital **Zaragoza** (Saragossa in English). Spain's fifth-largest city has some fine architecture, including a Moorish fortress and one of the country's foremost Catholic shrines in the enormous Basilica del Pilar. It also has a lot of modern industry, notably car plants.

Aragón's three provinces are quite different. **Huesca** is a Pyrenean province with the highest peaks and some of the most magnificent scenery in the whole range, with winter sports resorts, national parks and ancient, slate-roofed mountain villages. **Zaragoza province**, along the Ebro valley, is a flat meseta,with important wine-producing areas. Much of Teruel consists of a rugged, rocky, empty plateau called the **Maestrazgo**, with villages that even for Spain seem outstandingly remote from the modern world.

Green Spain

The most noticeable geographical divide in Spain is between all the regions south of the Cantabrian mountains, the long ridge that runs behind the north coast from the Pyrenees to Galicia, and the much narrower strip to the north of them. Everywhere further south has a Mediterranean climate; the areas to the north, facing the Atlantic, are that much colder, that much wetter and, most of all, that much greener.

The Basque Country

Most British people who travel to Ireland soon recognise that they've arrived somewhere new. People may speak English, but they behave slightly differently. A similar sensation affects anyone used to southern or eastern Spain when they arrive in the Basque Country. Even if the surrounding conversation is in Spanish, everything else is vaguely altered: the way people eat or drink, the music, sports, even body language. The Basques have never had their own state but have a far stronger identity than many peoples, with a seat in the United Nations. Basque culture is an odd mix of ruggedness and subtlety: Basques pride themselves on being blunt, but their delicately special cooking has long been held up as the most refined in all Spain – so that the region contains more than its share of fine restaurants, and wonderful (and distinctively Basque) tapas bars.

The three Basque provinces (**Vizcaya**, **Guipúzcoa** and **Álava**) are small in area but densely populated, with an exceptionally beautiful countryside of steep-sided green valleys leading to sea cliffs and fine Atlantic beaches. A feature of the Basque cities – especially Bilbao and its suburbs, a ribbon-city spread along the narrow inlet of the River Nervión – is that even from the city centre one can see fields and farms on surrounding hills. Basques have a strong sense of rural tradition, and of the life lived in the giant stone farmhouses called *caseríos* (*etxea* in Basque). For most of the last 180 years the Basque country was also Spain's foremost centre for heavy industry – steel and shipbuilding. Industry declined in the 1980s, but the many small Basque towns still contain a wide variety of light industries.

Of the cities, **Vitoria** (Gasteiz in Basque), the official capital, is a pleasant, spacious, small city; **San Sebastián** (or Donostia) has the most charm, a great resort of the Victorian era with one of Europe's most elegant seafronts on one of its loveliest bays; while **Bilbao** (Bilbo), for decades a soot-caked steel town, has been transformed by a comprehensive clean-up, and above all by the dramatic arrival of the Guggenheim art museum, into a buzzing, busy city with a very lively bar and student scene.

The Basque government has acquired the widest powers of any of Spain's regional administrations, but this has not ended the decades-long confrontation between supporters of absolute Basque independence, including the ETA

The Basque Olympics

Spaniards love sports, but have not invented many of their own – except for the Basques. They, in contrast, have come up with a whole locker-room's worth of energy outlets and tests of strength, some of which go back centuries. Basque country sports, which feature in most village *fiestas*, are characteristically tough and macho, and competition is fierce: the most popular include high-speed wood-chopping (*aizkolaritza*), competitive grass-mowing (with old-fashioned scythes, *segalaritza*), goat-racing and, wildest of all, stone-lifting (*harri-jasotzea*), in which giant-limbed mountain farmers vie to shift solid stone blocks. Its most legendary practitioner, the awesome man-mountain Iñaki Perureía, was for years considered the world's strongest man, having picked up 315kg.

In San Sebastián and the fishing towns along the Basque coast, *fiestas* include rowing regattas, using the long, thin launches in which Basque fishermen once hunted whales all over the Atlantic. The most sophisticated and elegant Basque sport, though, is *pelota*. It's played in a three-sided court called a *frontón*, one of which exists in virtually every Basque town. *Pelota* can be played in several different ways: with the hand, with different sizes of bat or, in the most spectacular version, with a long, curving basket. Games are dynamic and exciting, and attract keen betting.

One of the most remarkable Basque sporting institutions is a game they didn't invent but took to with devotion: football. Athletic de Bilbao is one of Spain's most historic football clubs, founded in 1898 by English engineers (hence it's *Athletic*, not *Atlético*). Amid the money-mad world of modern football, the amount usually spent by Athletic on close-season transfers is precisely zero. This is because under club rules it can only play locally raised players, trained through the club's own junior sides or other Basque teams. This policy has been maintained through thick and thin, and gives the club a unique bond with its fans. Bilbao has maintained a high standard within one of Europe's biggest leagues even against mega-star teams like Real Madrid or Barcelona. It has never been relegated, and has never, ever been seen as a soft touch.

terrorists and their sympathisers, and the Spanish government and its supporters. The violence leaves its scars, notably at street level, in the polarisation between the intransigent nationalist community and those against them. Anyone living in a Basque town may find themselves obliged to take sides, even if only socially, because the two rarely mix.

One source of Basque frustration is the state of the language. Probably because *Euskera* is so fiendishly hard to learn (*see* pp.21–8), the Basque government's language-promotion schemes have had much less success in terms of city-street usage than similar programmes in Catalonia. In small towns and the countryside, though, the Basque language is very prominent.

Navarra

The large single-province region of Navarra appears Basque in many ways, but has always been a problem for Basque nationalists. Northern Navarra is heavily Basque-speaking and in some parts strongly nationalist; the south, below Pamplona on the map, is Spanish-speaking and resists any amalgamation with the other Basque provinces. Historically, while the main Basque provinces were long associated with Castile, Navarre was a separate ancient kingdom that was the last of the Christian kingdoms to come under the Spanish monarchy in 1513. Northern Navarra is a mountainous region of dairy farms, forests and magnificent Pyrenean scenery, while the south, which includes part of the Rioja, produces many of Spain's best wines, including exceptional rosés.

Pamplona (or Iruña, in Basque), Navarra's capital, is a historic, deeply Catholic city that's usually quite quiet. It's world-famous, though, for the event that makes it explode into life every July: the bull-running festival of *San Fermín*, beloved by Ernest Hemingway and nowadays by wandering backpackers and other tourists.

La Rioja

When Spain was divided into 'autonomies', some provinces became separate regions, largely because they didn't really fit anywhere else. One such region is La Rioja, tucked between Castile and Navarra and Spain's smallest autonomous region. It does not even cover the whole Rioja wine area, which extends into Navarra and the Basque province of Álava, but wine dominates local life, and La Rioja region contains the most prestigious Rioja *bodegas*, especially around **Haro** in the northwest. It's a popular place to visit for wine-lovers, but few foreigners stay on here. **Logroño**, the capital, has fine old architecture from its days as a stop on the pilgrim road to Santiago de Compostela, and is now a prosperous little city.

Cantabria

Sandwiched between two regions with strong characters – Asturias and the Basques, the one-province region of Cantabria – seems a little anonymous by comparison. Its capital of **Santander** was often regarded more as 'the port of Castile' than as a place in its own right. Later it became one of Spain's 19t-century Atlantic holiday resorts, with a lovely promenade along El Sardinero beach, and it still gets busy each summer. It's also an important port, with a ferry connection to Plymouth.

Outside Santander are more fine beaches, while the rugged green mountains inland and along the coast are superb for walking and climbing, and increasingly popular for energetic holidays, with many farmhouses available for rent. They are also quite cheap to buy.

Asturias

Although it's only one province, with a little over a million people, there has never been any doubt that Asturias is a region on its own. Its mountains are enshrined in romantic history as the last redoubt of Christian Spain, where the 8th-century hero, Pelayo, supposedly rallied resistance against the Moors. The Asturian dialect has largely blended into Castilian, but Asturians still have their own music, architecture and many other traditions, as well as distinctively robust food. Strong cider, not wine or beer, is the traditional drink, and other specialities include the pungent *cabrales* goat's cheese and rich winter stews like the bean and sausage *fabada, to* counteract the wet, chilly Atlantic weather.

Along with the Basque Country and Catalonia, Asturias was one of Spain's three old industrial centres, with coal mines in the valleys around **Oviedo** and shipbuilding in **Gijón**. The decline of these industries left considerable unemployment, but the region has lately enjoyed a mild revival. The main towns of Oviedo, Gijón and **Avilés** are not famed as beauty spots but all have attractive and well-restored old centres, with much more green space than you find in Mediterranean Spain. Asturians are also known for being sociable, with a thriving bar culture, so it can be easier to get to know people here than in more internationally famous regions. The green, wooded countryside is among Spain's most beautiful, rising up from old fishing villages and surf-swept beaches to the spectacular high mountains of the **Picos de Europa**, a magnet for hikers and climbers and home to rare wildlife such as brown bears.

Galicia

Perhaps nowhere is further from a conventional image of Spain than Galicia, in the northwest corner of Iberia. Galicians are Celts, and the country has fascinating similarities to Ireland, Brittany or Cornwall: green everywhere, grey-stone villages, folk traditions, traditional music played on bagpipes, the ever-changing and often damp weather. Galicians were sufficiently Romanised that their language, *Galego*, is Latin-based rather than pure Celtic, but it preserves many Celtic words. Until the arrival of modern roads and railways Galicia was isolated from the rest of Spain. In rural Galicia, dotted with hundreds of villages, *Galego* remains the first language of daily life, and it's also widely used in cities, helped by a relatively unemphatic regional education campaign. Closely related to Portuguese, it is not a hard language to learn.

Celebrated features of the Galician coastline are its *rías*, fjord-like inlets surrounded by fine sand beaches, green hills and pretty fishing towns. The largest *rías* contain the region's busiest cities, **Ferrol**, **A Coruña** (La Coruña, in Spanish) and **Vigo**; Galicia's 'spiritual heart,' though, is inland in the magnificent medieval city of **Santiago de Compostela**, for centuries one of the most important Christian pilgrimage destinations in Europe.

Galicia has not traditionally been known for industry but it is the base for Spain's largest fishing fleets, with modern shipyards, and since the 1980s Vigo has become notably successful as a production centre of Spain's new, hip fashion industries. Galicia also produces cider and crisp white wines (most notably Albariño and Ribeiro), and the *rías* are a prime source of the superb fish and seafood (especially mussels and octopus). Local fisheries, though, were severely hit by the devastating oil spill from the tanker *Prestige* in November 2002, the effects of which may linger.

Galicia has been a land of emigration (all Spaniards, regardless of their origin, are referred to as *gallegos* in Argentina and Uruguay) and many returning migrants, having made their money in Britain, Barcelona or elsewhere, buy houses in their home towns or around the *rías*. The main factor deterring foreigners from moving into this engaging and beautiful region has probably been its high rainfall.

Mediterranean Spain

The three large regions along Iberia's east coast – Catalonia, Valencia and the Balearic Islands – are the parts of Spain most familiar to foreign visitors. Another important thing they have in common is the Catalan language.

Catalonia

With the Basque Country, Catalonia (Catalunya) has the strongest sense of its own culture, language and identity of any of Spain's subdivisions. To Catalans and indeed many other Spaniards it feels very much a country in its own right, not a 'region' of anywhere. One difference from the Basque country is that in Catalonia, with a long history as a self-governing entity, nationalism has been more 'institutional', emphasising the restoration of its historic government, the Generalitat. This fits a stereotype of Catalans as practical people, who always like to be doing something. They have long traditions in art, architecture and music, reflected in the work of Gaudí, Miró or Dalí, each exhibiting a very Catalan mix of practical skill and wild imagination. In the Middle Ages Catalan was a vigorous literary language, and to this day Catalan-speakers sustain a high literary output. Barcelona's Liceu is Spain's premier opera house. Catalonia produces many fine wines and *cava* (sparkling wine), and Catalan food is the prime rival to Basque cooking for the title of Spain's most varied and sophisticated cuisine. Catalonia has also always been one of the most economically active parts of Spain. Today, it no longer contains 70 per cent of Spanish industry, as it did before 1936, but its continued importance and vibrancy is reflected in Barcelona's rise to become one of Europe's most fashionable cities.

Modern Catalan nationalism has been strictly constitutional, accepting 'autonomy', but lately Catalonia has been pushing at the limits of what it means to feel like a country without actually being a state, a dilemma aggravated by the tendency of PP Madrid governments to make a point of showing who's boss. Nevertheless, one of the most dramatic achievements of any regional administration has been the Catalan government's linguistic 'normalisation' programme, which has effectively reinstated Catalan as the main language of public life, including all levels of state education. 'Normalisation' has come up against limits of its own in the Barcelona area, where the linguistic split remains around 50–50. To get the most out of living anywhere in Catalonia, though, you need to be able to move between both languages, as locals do all the time. It's surprisingly easy after a while.

Barcelona itself scarcely needs any introduction. Almost too popular for its own good at times, Catalonia's sophisticated capital is a centre for the creative industries, which means that for young EU-passport-holders there is a wider range of openings in fields outside traditional expat sectors like teaching than anywhere else in Spain. Many foreigners here also run businesses. Outside the city, the Catalan countryside is rugged, rocky but greener than areas further south. North of Barcelona along the coast is the **Costa Brava**, the first of Spain's seashores to open up for tourism, but still surprisingly unspoilt in many areas, with lovely rocky coves. The coast to the south, the **Costa Daurada**, is plainer but contains some attractive beach towns such as **Sitges**, now also growing as a residential 'addition' to Barcelona.

Inland Catalonia offers a delightful landscape of green wooded valleys between rocky ridges, climbing up to the High Pyrenees. A feature of the Catalan countryside is its *masia* stone farmhouses, giant chalet-like structures often centuries old, and now in great demand as rural retreats.

After Barcelona, the two main cities of **Tarragona** and **Girona** are both very attractive, historic towns. Catalan prosperity also means that industry and business are widely spread through small towns, so that openings for foreigners are more widely distributed than elsewhere in Spain. It can be easier to find work in smaller places than in Barcelona, where English teaching, for example, is now seriously oversubscribed.

Valencia

After Andalucía, the Valencian region hosts the second-largest number of British residents in Spain, but nearly all live in just one of its three provinces, Alicante. Its coastline, the **Costa Blanca**, has been described by international reports as having the healthiest climate in the world, and this is one prime reason why its pretty old towns like **Denia** or **Altea** are a favourite of British house-buyers, especially older people looking for a sunny retirement. In the 1990s villa-building also spread down to the 'Southern Costa Blanca' below the mega-resort of **Benidorm** and **Alicante** city, around **Torrevieja**. Previously considered too arid for large-scale development, this area, boosted by artificial

Valencia Urbanisation Law

A law introduced by the Valencian autonomous government in 1994 (the Ley Reguladora de la Actividad Urbanistica de la Comunidad Valencia or LRAU), has meant that developers have been able to move on to property not owned by them. The urbanisation law allowed local developers to submit a plan and acquire rural land, frequently part of somebody's *'finca'*, or estate, at a fraction of the market value. To make matters worse, many British and Spanish owners have been forced to contribute to the developers' construction costs, which meant many faced financial ruin.

The legislation, known as the 'land grab law', was designed to cut through complex planning procedures and to pay for improvements in the infrastructure such as roads and airports, but in reality it has given property developers and speculators *carte blanche* to acquire land below the market price from owners who do not want to sell. If they refused, the local town hall could sequester their property. If they sold part of their land, they were left with properties that were practically worthless or drastically reduced in value. The result has been overdevelopment up and down the coast and the undermining of property investment security.

A long campaign led by expat and local home-owners, taken to the European Parliament, has been attempting to persuade the Valencian government to scrap the act. However, the fight is ongoing; some changes were made, but anyone interested in individual, particularly older or rural properties anywhere in the region (that is, except modern apartments, or in existing planned villa developments) should check on the development of the campaign and have the legal status of any ownership of any property checked carefully before buying.

irrigation, is now the fastest-growing zone for new leisure developments in the whole of Spain. Around these often self-contained communities are all kinds of foreign-owned businesses and expat services.

The rest of the Valencian coast north of the Costa Blanca consists mainly of one long, flat plain, the **Costa del Azahar** or 'Orange Blossom Coast', lined by mile upon mile of the citrus groves that produce the celebrated Valencian oranges.

South of Valencia city is a stretch of fertile marsh, the **Huerta**, where the best rice is grown for another famous local product, *paella*. **Valencia** itself is a stylish, imaginatively renovated city, Spain's third-largest, with considerable industry but which also boasts a nightlife to rival Barcelona's. Nevertheless, it still comes to a stop each March for the extravagant *fiesta* of the *Fallas*, when massive painted figures are set on fire all around the town.

Valencia suffers from schizophrenia. When it was captured from the Muslims its Catalan conquerors brought their language with them, although some villages were settled by Aragonese and have always been Spanish-speaking. However, relations with Barcelona are always uneasy. Some Valencians bristle at anyone calling their language Catalan, and insist that the Valenciá or Valenciano dialect is a language all on its own. In country areas, especially in Castellón (Castelló in Catalan), Valencian Catalan is the main language of local life.

The Balearics

Synonymous with modern tourism, the Balearic Islands have been the favourite Mediterranean holiday destination for all of northern Europe for 40 years. The largest Balearic property-buyers are the Germans, the British favouring the Costa Blanca and the Costa del Sol. However, there are still plenty of British property-owners around, and many residents who work in tourism. Such is the demand for Balearic properties that prices for the most desirable villas can be very high, but given the amount of building here since the 1960s there is still a remarkable range of prices on all the islands.

The statistics of Balearic tourism are staggering – with more hotel beds here than in some entire countries – but, strange as it can seem, the islands have a life of their own as well. Away from the big resorts there are characterful towns and undeveloped stretches of countryside and even shoreline. The Balearics – also an autonomous region – are another bilingual, Catalan-speaking area. In the 13th century the islands were settled by Catalans, and unlike Valencians few locals have any problem with the origins of their language. They are less linguistically demanding than Catalans, and more concessions are made to foreigners overall. The more you use local services, however, above all schools, the more useful you will find it to be able to communicate in Catalan – especially on Menorca and inland on Mallorca, where the language remains strongest.

Each island has its own character and climate. Over 90km wide, **Mallorca** is too big to be totally taken over by tourism. Its capital, **Palma**, home to over half the 600,000-plus population, is a real city with a proper life of its own, while in the middle of the island there is a rugged interior scattered with engaging small towns and villages, virtually all nowadays with some foreign residents. Put broadly, there are two sides to Mallorca. The ultra-developed package Mallorca is concentrated around the Bay of Palma; a much more refined Mallorca is found along the northwest coast, in and around old towns like **Sóller** and **Deiá**. Between these extremes you can find just about every other intermediate grade of property and tranquillity.

Menorca, northernmost and greenest of the islands, has a noticeably cooler winter climate, and is prey to powerful north winds. Though small, it has a strong character, and two attractive old towns, **Maó** (Mahón) and **Ciutadella**, and beautiful coves and beaches that are still reachable only by dirt track.

A long way further south than the other islands is **Ibiza** (Eivissa in Catalan), a burnt-brown desert island much of the year, which briefly explodes with flowers in February and March. Its popularity as a party venue is unstoppable: nevertheless, the real 24-hour Ibiza club scene is very localised, concentrated in

Ibiza Town, **Sant Antoni** (San Antonio) and along the road between them. Elsewhere there are still surprisingly secluded spots, although to have one to oneself is increasingly expensive. **Formentera**, smallest and least-known of the Balearics, is a still smaller desert island reachable by ferry from Ibiza Town.

The South

Other sides of Spain may have made an impact internationally – Barcelona's urban style, the green Cantabrian mountains – but the hot south has held its place as the most popular area for British people moving to Spain.

Andalucía

Andalucía is home to all the most classic Spanish images: flamenco, guitars, sherry, bullfights, elaborate religious festivals, whitewashed houses with metal-grille windows. It is the hottest part of Spain, and the highest temperatures ever recorded in Europe have all been here. The centuries of Moorish rule that gave the region its name (*see* p.12) left behind countless other traces, in architecture, the layout of towns, place names or food. Moorish architecture still dominates the great cities of inland Andalucía: Seville, Córdoba and Granada.

Extending through eight provinces, Andalucía is also very varied. The highest mountains in mainland Spain are here, in the Sierra Nevada south of Granada. In a relatively short distance one can travel from green, snow-peaked mountain valleys in the Alpujarra foothills of Granada to real sand deserts in Almería, where most of the really high temperatures have occurred.

Although Spanish-speaking (albeit with a strong accent), Andalucía, as one of Spain's regions with the most distinctive character, has demanded rights similar to those of nationalities like Basques and Catalans, and its regional government enjoys wide-ranging powers.

Andalucía has the most British residents of any Spanish region. Its greatest magnet is of course the **Costa del Sol**, 'Europe's California', where, as well as resorts such as **Torremolinos** and **Marbella**, there are villa developments, golf courses and other attractions for every taste and every price bracket scattered all along the 140km from **Gibraltar** to **Málaga**. There's also Spain's largest concentration of expat-orientated, foreign-owned businesses and services. In many communities along the *costa* or in the hills behind it, foreign residents make up over 50 per cent of the population. If you want to live in a self-contained British community, but with winter sunshine, and with only occasional contact with Spanish life, this will be for you; if not, maybe not. Those looking to avoid the crowds have headed further afield, into areas such as the celebrated 'white villages' of the Serranía de Ronda between Málaga and **Cádiz**, or the coast and hills east of Málaga past **Nerja** and **Almuñécar**, now labelled the **Costa Tropical**. Once relatively undeveloped, this area is catching up fast.

Other alternatives include the **Costa de la Luz** in Cádiz and Huelva provinces – facing the Atlantic, with surf beaches, and smaller, more laid-back tourist towns – the exquisite if often chilly Alpujarra foothills of the **Sierra Nevada**, discovered by hippies in the 1970s and recently made famous by Chris Stewart's book *Driving Over Lemons*, or, for the determined, the arid and still remote Andaluz interior. Andalucía's cities are fascinating to visit, and Seville, Málaga and Cádiz are probably the liveliest. Anyone living there, though, may find that to get along they need to make more effort to adapt to the many traditions of local life than would be necessary in more cosmopolitan cities further north.

Murcia

The province of Murcia was another that had no clear links with any major region, and so became a region on its own. Previously it was a land whose people emigrated to find work and were the butt of jokes elsewhere in Spain as dim bumpkins. The capital, **Murcia** itself, was founded by the Moors, who knew how to live in deserts, but, since they left, it has become a sleepy provincial city; **Cartagena**, the Carthaginians' Spanish capital, is now a Spanish naval base. Much of the landscape is the same rocky desert as Almería in Andalucía, with the same fierce heat, interrupted by oases or *vegas* that produce Murcia's famed red peppers. Murcia's most unusual feature, though, is the **Mar Menor**, a giant saltwater lagoon east of Cartagena separated from the Mediterranean by a long beach-lined strip of land, **La Manga del** (the sleeve of) **Mar Menor**.

Recently Murcia has undergone two transformations. One is that big areas of desert (as also happens in Almería) have been irrigated and covered with acres of plastic tunnels to produce vegetables year-round for Europe's supermarkets. The other is the arrival of tourism and villa-building, especially around La Manga, centred on the Club La Manga golf and sports resort famous as a winter training base for northern Europe's football teams. Murcia's tourist coast, dubbed the **Costa Cálida** or 'warm coast', blends into the southern Costa Blanca around Torrevieja in Alicante. Both are currently experiencing a massive boom, as Spain's fastest-growing area for new villa *urbanizaciones*. Most of its communities are brand new, with no connection to any existing Spanish towns.

Extremadura

The two provinces of Extremadura, **Cáceres** and **Badajoz**, contain some of Spain's most rugged scenery, from soaring *sierras* and mountain valleys to silent hills of olive groves and pine woods. This is another area with a climate of extremes, from baking summers to glacial winters. Its people are known for hardiness, and Extremadura is famous as the homeland of most of the *conquistadores* who seized the Americas for Spain (the names of towns like **Mérida** or **Trujillo** can be found all over Latin America).

A Quick Guide to Iberian Prejudices

Cut off in their subcontinent for long periods of time, the different peoples of Iberia have had plenty of time to take note of each other's habits, pick holes in them, and make fun of them. Foreigners newly arrived in Spain often marvel at just how often these stereotypes are trotted out as props in everyday Spanish conversation, even in the face of evidence directly to the contrary, such as a generous Catalan, or an Andaluz who's not the life and soul of the party. Reliance on such collective images could be said to be one thing all Spain's groups have in common. Here is a quick guide to some of the most common clichés. How each group sees *itself*, of course, will usually be quite different.

Andalucíans: A lot of fun, passionate, but don't rely on them to do what they say.

Aragonese: Rough and ready but good-hearted.

Asturians: Generous, sociable, rebellious and left-wing.

Basques: Impenetrable, always go their own way, but everyone admires their cooking.

Castilians: Dry, severe, conservative, probably religious, but everyone admires the way they speak (to Catalans in particular: unfriendly, hostile, arrogant, intolerant, they all hate us but won't admit it).

Catalans: Stingy (they feature in exactly the same kinds of jokes as used to be told about the Scots in England). Also pretentious, and believe they're better than everybody else.

Galicians: Believe in fairies (from their Celtic heritage). Slow on the uptake but not nearly so much as Murcians, and apt to answer questions evasively, with another question.

Madrileños: Loud, pushy, smart-alecky, and (especially to Castilians) they speak very badly and mess up their grammar.

Murcians: Thick.

In previous eras this was a much more prominent part of Iberia – Mérida was one of the largest Roman cities in Spain, and has some of its finest Roman ruins – but for the past 400 years it has been a backwater, with more livestock than people. Extremadura is, though, known to all Spaniards as the source of the finest of dry-cured Serrano hams, from traditionally reared, acorn-fed pigs. This is the part of Spain perhaps least affected by the modern world and mass tourism, which could be an attraction in itself.

Three Enclaves: Gibraltar, Ceuta and Melilla

Impossible to miss beside the Bay of Algeciras is that strange piece of British territory, **Gibraltar**. Space is expensive on the Rock, so few non-locals live there, but many Costa del Sol expats visit regularly on pilgrimage to the branches of Marks & Spencer and other familiar names, or to make use of the high-interest, zero-tax savings accounts offered by Gibraltar's many banks. However, residents in Spain should be aware that not to declare these accounts to Spanish tax authorities is illegal, and that they could potentially be penalised whenever they bring such money into Spain to spend it. *See* further **Living in Spain**, 'Money and Banking', pp.178–80.

Less well-known than Gibraltar is the fact that Spain owns two small towns on the coast of Morocco, **Ceuta** and **Melilla**. Both have been Spanish since the 16th century, and have mainly Spanish populations. The Spanish government rejects all parallels between their status and its own demand for Gibraltar on the grounds that, while Gibraltar is a colony, Ceuta and Melilla have been made integral parts of Spain, with parliamentary representation in Madrid, and theoretically each town constitutes an autonomous region by itself. This legal distinction is generally lost on non-Spaniards. To most outsiders, they're of interest only as cheap ferry ports into Morocco, with duty-free shops.

The Canaries

Closer to Africa than to the Iberian Peninsula, the seven Canary Islands have one overriding attraction for most long-stayers: their subtropical climate, often described as 'eternal spring'. Winter sunshine is guaranteed while, thanks to ocean winds, even midsummer temperatures rarely reach the heights of the hottest spots on the mainland, except on Lanzarote. Spread over 500km from east to west, these volcanic islands also offer an extraordinary mix of landscapes and ecology, from the deserts of Lanzarote to the laurel forests of Tenerife, and including superb beaches. Colonised from Castile and Andalucía in the 15th century, the islands developed a quirky, slow-moving culture of their own during long centuries of virtual isolation.

Nearly all the islands have some large-scale resorts, and there are sizeable colonies of foreign residents. There is also a full variety of English-speaking services, especially on Tenerife, Gran Canaria and Lanzarote. However, while all-year sunshine represents an essential draw for some, for others the Canaries' isolation and more difficult access (a three-and-a-half-hour flight from the UK) can be off-putting.

The individual islands are very different one from another. **Tenerife** is the largest and offers the greatest variety in villages, scenery and activities, and its capital of Santa Cruz de Tenerife is the most attractive of the island towns. This is also the most popular of the Canaries among British home-buyers. The sheer range of landscapes on Tenerife is astonishing, from beaches through banana fields, cactus plains and woodlands up to the highest mountain in the whole of Spain, the giant volcano of Mount Teide at 3,718m (12,198ft). The big resorts like

Playa de las Américas are all on the southwest coast; more secluded areas popular with older British residents are on the north shore. The island of **Gran Canaria** is slightly smaller but contains the Canaries' regional capital and largest city, Las Palmas. For scenery it is less spectacular, but it has better beaches. Again, Gran Canaria's big package resorts are mostly on the south side, while quieter, more upmarket developments are near the greener, cliff-lined north coast.

East of Gran Canaria towards Africa lie the Canaries' two 'desert islands', **Fuerteventura** and **Lanzarote**. Both have small populations and only a few small towns, and remain surprisingly undeveloped, since most of their tourist traffic and new villas are concentrated around just a few resorts. Fuerteventura is loved by windsurfers; Lanzarote, hottest of all the Canaries, has a bizarre, near-treeless desert landscape that makes the whole island into a geological park. Dedicated sun-lovers adore these islands, but others find the setting too arid and unbending to stay for any length of time (both can also suffer water short-ages). On the opposite side of the archipelago, the three tiny far-western islands of **La Palma**, **La Gomera** and **El Hierro** have no direct connections with the UK, and are reached by ferry or local flights from Tenerife. The greenest of the islands, they have few beaches and development is still small-scale. Most of the few outsiders who love the smaller islands do so precisely because of their atmosphere of quiet isolation.

To compensate for the economic effects of their remoteness, the Canaries have enjoyed tax privileges within Spain, and these have been transferred into the EU. They are not considered part of the EU for customs purposes and, most importantly, normal Spanish VAT is not levied here. Instead, there is a flat-rate local sales tax, the IGIC, at four per cent. Consequently, many big purchases, such as cars and large electrical goods, are unusually cheap. However, should you ever take them into the EU proper (whether mainland Spain or Britain), you are officially obliged to pay extra duty on them.

Spain touring atlas

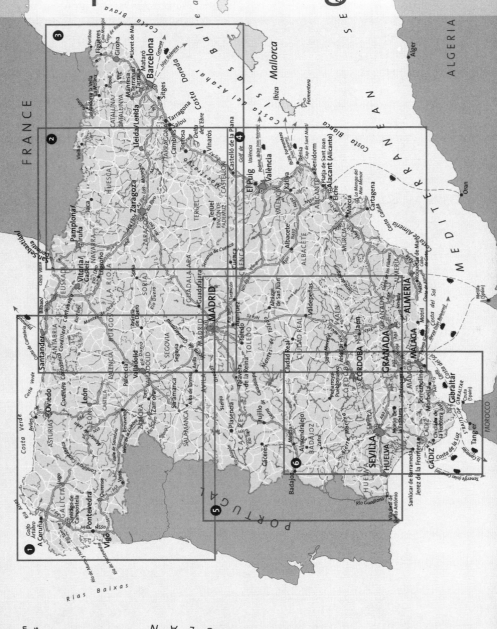

80 km
40 miles

N

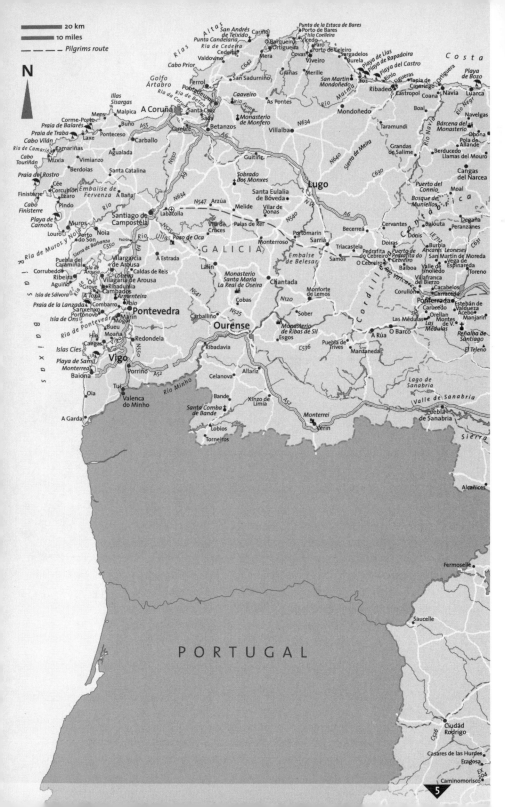

1

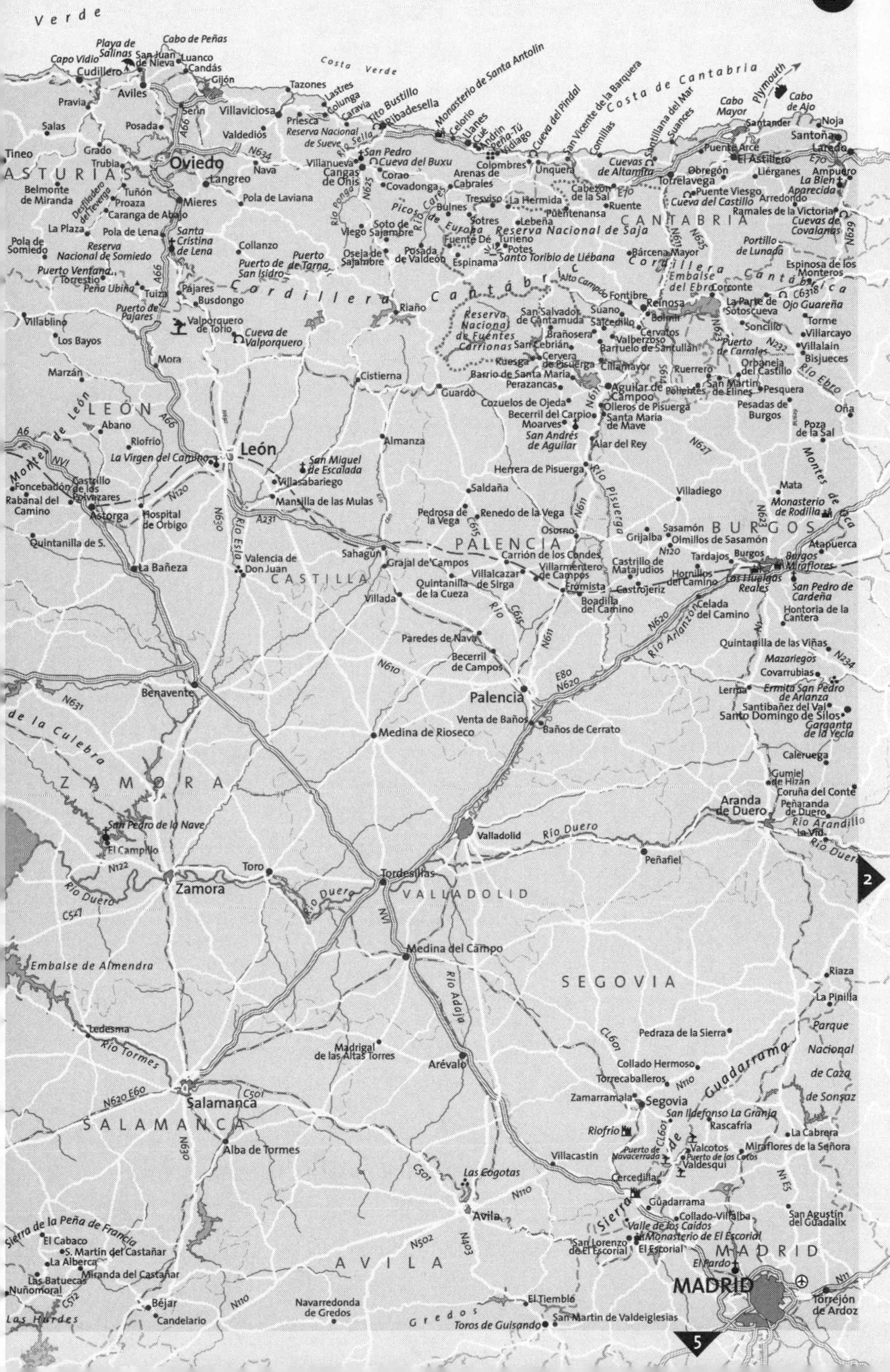

Verde
Costa Verde
Cabo de Peñas
Playa de Salinas
Capo Vidio
Cudillero
San Juan de Nieva
Luanco
Candás
Gijón
Aviles
Pravia
Tazones
Lastres
Colunga
Caravia
Tito Bustillo
Ribadesella
Monasterio de Santa Antolín
Cueva del Pindal
San Vicente de la Barquera
Costa de Cantabria
Comillas
Santillana del Mar
Suances
Cabo Mayor
Plymouth
Cabo de Ajo
Santander
Noja
Santoña
Laredo
Salas
Posada
Serín
Villaviciosa
Priesca
Reserva Nacional de Sueve
Río Sella
Celorio
Llanes
Cué
Andrín
Peña-Tú
Vidiago
Valdediós
Tineo
Grado
Trubia
Oviedo
ASTURIAS
N634
Nava
Villanueva
San Pedro
Cueva del Buxu
Cangas de Onís
Corao
Covadonga
Arenas de Cabrales
Colombres
Unquera
Cuevas de Altamira
Puente Arce
El Astillero
Obregón
Liérganes
Ampuero
La Bien Aparecida
Belmonte de Miranda
Desfiladero del Teverga
Tuñón
Proaza
Langreo
Mieres
Pola de Laviana
Caranga de Abajo
La Plaza
Pola de Lena
Santa Cristina de Lena
Pola de Somiedo
Reserva Nacional de Somiedo
Puerto Ventana
Torrestío
Peña Ubiña
Tuiza
Collanzo
Puerto de San Isidro
Puerto de Tarna
Río Ponga
N625
Picos de Europa
Río Cares
Soto de Sajambre
Viego
Oseja de Sajambre
Posada de Valdeón
Bulnes
Tresviso
Sotres
Fuente Dé
Espinama
La Hermida
Lebeña
Turieno
Potes
Santo Toribio de Liébana
Cabezón de la Sal
Puentenansa
Reserva Nacional de Saja
Ruente
Torrelavega
Puente Viesgo
Cueva del Castillo
Arredondo
Ramales de la Victoria
Cuevas de Covalanas
CANTABRIA
Bárcena Mayor
Cordillera Cantábrica
Portillo de Lunada
Espinosa de los Monteros
Embalse del Ebro
Corconte
Reinosa
Fontibre
Alto Campóo
La Parte de Sotoscueva
Ojo Guareña
Pajares
Busdongo
Puerto de Pajares
Villablino
Valporquero de Torio
Cueva de Valporquero
Los Bayos
Riaño
Reserva Nacional de Fuentes Carrionas
San Salvador de Cantamuda
Suano
Salcedillo
Bolmir
Cervatos
Brañosera
Valberzoso
San Cebrián
Barruelo de Santullán
Cervera de Pisuerga
Kuesga
Barrio de Santa María
Perazancas
Cillamayor
Ruerrero
Orbaneja del Castillo
Puerto de Carrales
Soncillo
Torme
Villarcayo
Villalaín
Bisjueces
Río Ebro
Mora
Marzán
Cistierna
Guardo
Aguilar de Campoo
Pomar de Valdivia
Polientes
San Martín de Elines
Pesquera
Pesadas de Burgos
Oña
Cozuelos de Ojeda
Becerril del Carpio
Olleros de Pisuerga
Santa María de Mave
Moarves
San Andrés de Aguilar
Poza de la Sal
LEÓN
Abano
Riofrío
A6
Monte de León
NVI
La Virgen del Camino
León
San Miguel de Escalada
Almanza
Alar del Rey
Montes de Oca
Foncebadón
Castrillo de los Polvazares
Rabanal del Camino
Astorga
Hospital de Orbigo
N120
Villasabariego
Mansilla de las Mulas
Saldaña
Herrera de Pisuerga
Río Pisuerga
Villadiego
Mata
Monasterio de Rodilla
Pedrosa de la Vega
Renedo de la Vega
A231
Río Esla
N630
Osorno
Sasamón
Olmillos de Sasamón
Grijalba
BURGOS
Atapuerca
Quintanilla de S.
Sahagún
PALENCIA
Carrión de los Condes
Castrillo de Matajudíos
Tardajos
Burgos
Miraflores
Valencia de Don Juan
Grajal de Campos
Villalcázar de Sirga
Villarmentero de Campos
Hornillos del Camino
Las Huelgas Reales
San Pedro de Cardeña
La Bañeza
CASTILLA
Quintanilla de la Cueza
Frómista
Castrojeriz
Boadilla del Camino
Villada
Celada del Camino
Hontoria de la Cantera
Río Arlanzón
N620
Paredes de Nava
Becerril de Campos
Quintanilla de las Viñas
Mazariegos
N234
Covarrubias
N610
Benavente
Palencia
E80
Lerma
Ermita San Pedro de Arlanza
Santibañez del Val
Santo Domingo de Silos
Garganta de la Yecla
N631
Venta de Baños
Baños de Cerrato
de la Culebra
Medina de Rioseco
Caleruega
ZAMORA
Gumiel de Hizán
Coruña del Conde
Aranda de Duero
Peñaranda de Duero
Río Arandilla
La Vid
San Pedro de la Nave
Valladolid
Río Duero
El Campillo
Peñafiel
N122
Toro
Tordesillas
Zamora
VALLADOLID
C527
Embalse de Almendra
Medina del Campo
Río Adaja
SEGOVIA
Riaza
La Pinilla
Parque Nacional de Caza de Sonsaz
Ledesma
Río Tormes
Pedraza de la Sierra
Madrigal de las Altas Torres
Arévalo
Collado Hermoso
CL601
Torrecaballeros
N110
Guadarrama
Zamarramala
Segovia
Salamanca
N620 E60
C501
SALAMANCA
San Ildefonso La Granja
Riofrío
Rascafría
La Cabrera
Alba de Tormes
Puerto de Navacerrada
Valcotos
Puerto de los Cotos
Valdesquí
Miraflores de la Señora
Villacastín
Las Cogotas
Cercedilla
N1 E5
Sierra de Guadarrama
Sierra de la Peña de Francia
Avila
N502
N403
Collado-Villalba
San Agustín del Guadalix
Valle de los Caídos
Monasterio de El Escorial
El Cabaco
S. Martín del Castañar
San Lorenzo de El Escorial
El Escorial
MADRID
La Alberca
AVILA
El Pardo
Miranda del Castañar
Las Batuecas
Nuñomoral
C512
MADRID
N11
Torrejón de Ardoz
Béjar
Navarredonda de Gredos
El Tiemblo
Candelario
Las Hurdes
Gredos
Toros de Guisando
San Martín de Valdeiglesias
2
5

2

20 km
10 miles
- - - Pilgrims route

N

FRANCE

NAVARRA

HUESCA

**CATALUÑA/
CATALUNYA**

ZARAGOZA

TARRAGONA

TERUEL

CASTELLÓN

Cabo Higuer
Fuenterrabía
San Marcial
Bera
Lesaka
Zugarramurdi
Urdazubi
Etxalar
Parque Natural
Señorío de Bertiz
Arizkun
Elizondo
Ituren
Zubieta
Puerto de Izpegui
Valle Bidasoa
Noam
Valcarlos
Orzanzurieta
Puerto Ibañeta
Burguete
Auritzberri
Roncesvalles
Orbaitzeta
Orhí
Pic d'Anie
Sierra de Abodi
Ochagavia
Pamplona/
Iruña
Urroz
Agoitz
Vidángoz
Isaba
Zuriza
Puerto de Somport
Candanchú
El Formigal
Valle de Astún
Sallent de Gállego
Balneario de Panticosa
Panticosa
Artaiz
Roncal
Siresa
Canfranc Estación
Hoz de Arbayún
Navascués
Echo
Canfranc
Santa María de Eunate
Obanos
Artajona
Lumbier
Sierra de Leyre
Monasterio de Leyre
Berdún
Jaca
Biescas
N260
Torla
Parque Nacional de Ordesa
Bielsa
Benasque
Pico de la Maladeta
Aneto
Cerler
Caldes de Boí
Boí
Erill la Vall
Taüll
Parc Nacional d'Aigüestortes
Boi-Taüll
Vielha
Vall d'Aran
Beret
Baqueira
Tuca-Betrén
Túnel de Vielha
Pla d'Espot
Super-Espot
Espot
Tafalla
Olite
Ujué
Sangüesa
Javier
Yesa
Embalse de Yesa
Río Aragón
Santa Cruz de la Serós
Monasterio de San Juan de la Peña
Sos del Rey Católico
Castillo de Loarre
Loarre
Ayerbe
Sierra de Guara
Alquézar
Torreciudad
Graus
Embalse de Grado I
Tremp
La Pobla de Segur
Uncastillo
Sádaba
Bárdenas
Ejea de los Caballeros
Las Cinco Villas
Esquedas
HUESCA
Huesca
Monasterio de Pueyo
Barbastro
Monzón
Río Cinca
Río el Segre
Alfaro
Corella
Cintruénigo
Cascante
Tudela
Sancho Abarca
Tarazona
Borja
Tauste
Alagón
Zaragoza
ZARAGOZA
Río Ebro
Los Monegros
Lleida/Lerida
Fraga
Bellpuig
Mequinenza
Embalse de Mequinenza
Monestir de Poblet
Cornudella
Prades
Scala Dei
Siurana
Falset
TARRAGONA
Cambrils
Miami Platja
L'Ametlla de Mar
Calatayud
Ateca
La Almunia de Doña Godina
Quinto
Cariñena
Belchite
Hijar
Caspe
Monasterio de Piedra
Daroca
Alcañiz
Móra la Nova
Gandesa
El Pinell de Brai
Castillo Miravet
Tortosa
Delta de L'Ebre
Deltebre
Parc Natural Delta de l'Ebre
Montalbán
Valderrobres
L'Ebre
Monreal del Campo
Sorita
Villarluengo
La Iglesuela del Cid
Forcall
Morella
Vallibana
Traiguera
St Carles de la Rápita
Port dels Alfacs
Reserva Nacional de los Montes Universales
Albarracín
Río Guadalaviar
Muela
Cantavieja
Mirambel
La Todolella
Teruel
La Virgen de la Vega
Valdelinares
Vilafranca
Castellfort
Benassa
Catí
Ares del Maestrat
Sant Mateu
Albocàsser
les Coves de Vinromà
Alcalà de Xivert
Castillo de Xivert
Peñíscola
Vinaròs
Benicarló
Montes Universales
Rubielos de Mora
Arc de Cabanes
Vilafamés
Cabanes
Orpesa del Mar
Castelfabib
Ademuz
RINCÓN DE ADEMUZ
Montanejos
Río Mijares
Desert de les Palmes
Benicàssim
El Grau de Castelló
Onda
Castelló de la Plana

3

4

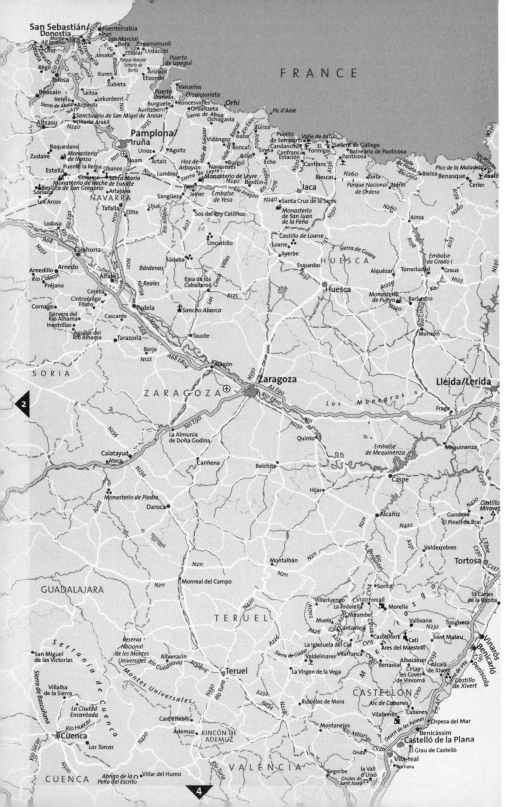

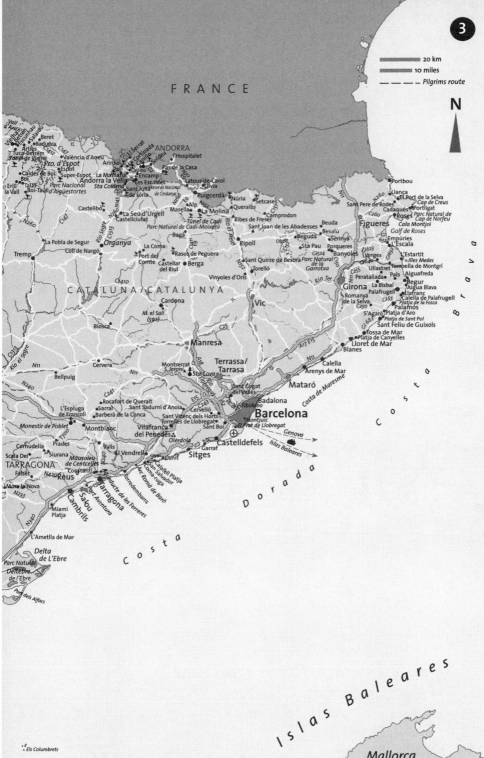

3

─────── 20 km
─────── 10 miles
– – – – Pilgrims route

N

FRANCE

Vall
d'Aran
Vielha
Escunhau
Beret
Artíes
Baqueira
Tuca-Betrén
Tónel de Vielha
Pro. d'Espot
València d'Àneu
Caldes de Boí
Espot
Super-Espot
La Massana
Boí
La Vall
Erill
Taüll
Boí-Taüll
Parc Nacional
d'Aigüestortes
ANDORRA
El Serrat
La Cortinada
Canillo
Soldeu
Arinsal
Pal
Ordino
Encamp
Sant Julià
de Lòria
Andorra la Vella
Les Escaldes
Sta Coloma
Pas de la Casa
l'Hospitalet
Latour-de-Carol
Llívia
Reserva Nacional
de Cerdanya
Puigcerdà
Núria
Portbou
Llança
El Port de la Selva
Cap de Creus
Portlligat
Cadaqués
Sant Pere de Rodes
Parc Natural de
Cap de Norfeu
Roses
Cala Montjoi
Golf de Roses
Castellbó
La Seu d'Urgell
Castellciutat
Alp
Masella
La Molina
Queralbs
Camprodon
Ribes de Freser
Sant Joan de les Abadesses
Beuda
Besalú
Figueres
Empúries
L'Escala
Illes Medes
L'Estartit
Tremp
Organyà
La Pobla de Segur
Coll de Nargó
Port del
Comte
La Coma
Rasos de Peguera
Castellar
del Riul
Baga
Berga
Ripoll
Sant Quirze de Besora
Torelló
Beguda
Serinyà
Sta Pau
Porqueres
Banyoles
Parc Natural
de la
Garrotxa
Verges
Torroella de Montgrí
Ullastret
Peratallada
Pals
Palafrugell
Llafranc
Calella de Palafrugell
Platja de la Fosca
Palamós
Platja d'Aro
Platja de Sant Pol
Aiguafreda
Begur
Aigua Blava
Girona
La Bisbal
Romanyà
de la Selva
S'Agaró
Sant Feliu de Guíxols
Tossa de Mar
Platja de Canyelles
Lloret de Mar
Blanes
Vinyols d'Oris
CATALUNA/CATALUNYA
Cardona
Vic
M. el Salí
(592)
Biosca
Manresa
Cervera
Bellpuig
Montserrat
S. Jeroni
Sta Cova
Terrassa/
Tarrasa
Sant Cugat
del Vallès
Badalona
Calella
Arenys de Mar
Mataró
Costa de Maresme
L'Espluga
de Francolí
Rocafort de Queralt
Sarral
Sant Sadurní d'Anoia
Barberà de la Conca
Cervelló
Sant Vicenç dels Horts
Torrelles de Llobregat
Sant Boi
Vilafranca
del Penedès
Olèrdola
Tibidabo
Montjuïc
El Prat de Llobregat
BARCELONA
Genova
Islas Baleares
Monestir de Poblet
Montblanc
Valls
El Vendrell
Garraf
Castelldefels
Sitges
Cornudella
Prades
Siurana
Mausoleu
de Centcelles
Constantí
Cunit
Platja
Sant Salvador
Coma-ruga
Scala Dei
TARRAGONA
Falset
Reus
Tarragona
Torredembarra
Arc de Berà
Vila-seca
Aqüeducte de les Ferreres
Móra la Nova
Salou
Port Aventura
Cambrils
Miami
Platja
L'Ametlla de Mar
Delta
de l'Ebre
Parc Natural
Deltebre
de l'Ebre
Parc dels Alfacs

Costa

Dorada

Costa

Brava

Els Columbrets

Islas Baleares

Mallorca

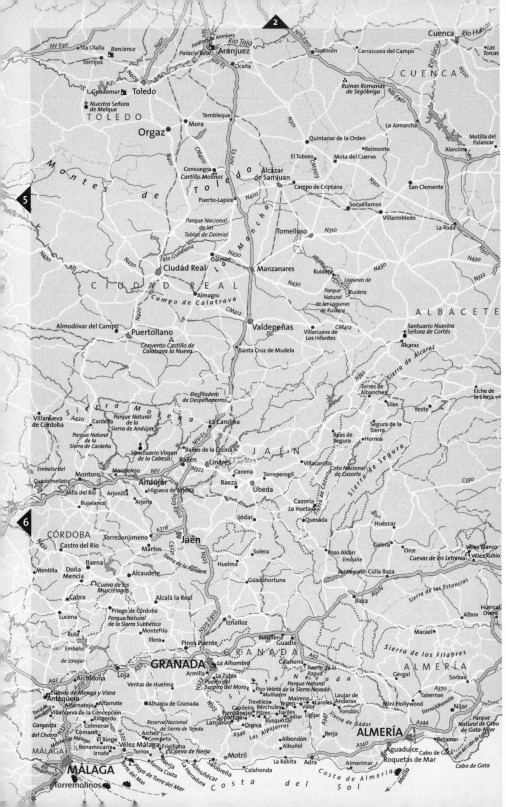

Ademuz
RINCÓN DE ADEMUZ
Montanejos
Río Mijars
Desert de les Palmes
Benicàssim
Castelló de la Plana
TERUEL
CASTELLON
CV20
El Grau de Castelló
Onda
Vila-real
Els Columbrets
Villar del Humo
Abrigo de la Peña del Escrito
Grutes de Sant Josep
Segorbe
la Vall d'Uixó
Borriana
Platja de Nules
Río Turia
N225
Platja de Xilxes
Almenara
Sagunt
El Port de Sagunt
Golf
de
València
Lliria
CV21
Utiel
El Puig
Manises
Alboraia
Platja de Malva-Rosa
València
Palma, Ibiza (Islas Baleares)
A3901
Requena
Chiva
Ego-A3
Platja de Pinedo
El Saler
Platja del Saler
L'Albufera
Platja de la Devesa
El Palmar
El Perelló
Buñol
Cofrentes
VALENCIA
Costa del Azahar
Cullera
Albacete
Cueva de la Vieja
Xàtiva
Costa Blanca
Gandia
Oliva
N430
Ibiza, Formentera (Islas Baleares)
Rugat
Dénia
Les Rotes
Cap de Sant Antoni
Almansa
El Montgó
Xàbia
Platja de l'Arenal
Cap de Sant Martí
Alcoi
Guadalest
Teulada
Moraira
N344
Parc Natural de la Font Roja
Biar
Callosa d'en Sarrià
Platja de Moraira
Penyal d'Ifac
Yecla
Villena
Ibi
Port de la l'Carrasqueta
Calp
Cova dels Canelobres
Altea
Tobarra
Sax
Xixona
Benidorm
Hellín
Jumilla
ALICANTE
Busot
La Vila Joiosa
Calasparra
Santa Fe
Platja de Mutxavista
Platja de Sant Joan
Moratalla
N330
A7-E15
Platja de l'Albufereta
Caravaca de la Cruz
Cehegín
Alacant (Alicante)
L'Altet
Golf d'Alacant
MURCIA
Elche
L'Alcudia (Ruines d'Ilici)
Santa Pola
Oran
Parque Natural de la Sierra de España
Orihuela
Illa de Tabarca
La Marina del Pinet
Guardamar del Segura
Murcia
Torrevieja
La Zenia
Platjas de Orihuela
Cap Roig
Alhama de Murcia
Sierra de España
Aledo
Monasterio La Santa
Totana
San Pedro del Pinatar
San Javier
Santiago de la Ribera
Los Alcázares
Mar Menor
La Manga del Mar Menor
Lorca
Cartagena
Los Nietos
La Manga del Mar Menor
Cabo de Palos
Mazarrón
Sierra de la Muela
Bolnuevo
Playa de la Isla
N305
Playa de Mazarró
Puerto de Mazarró
Calabardina
El Hornillo
Río Almanzor
Águilas
Costa Cálida
Palomares
Garrucha
Turre
Mojácar
Carboneras
Costa de Almería

MEDITERRANEAN   SEA

N

20 km
10 miles

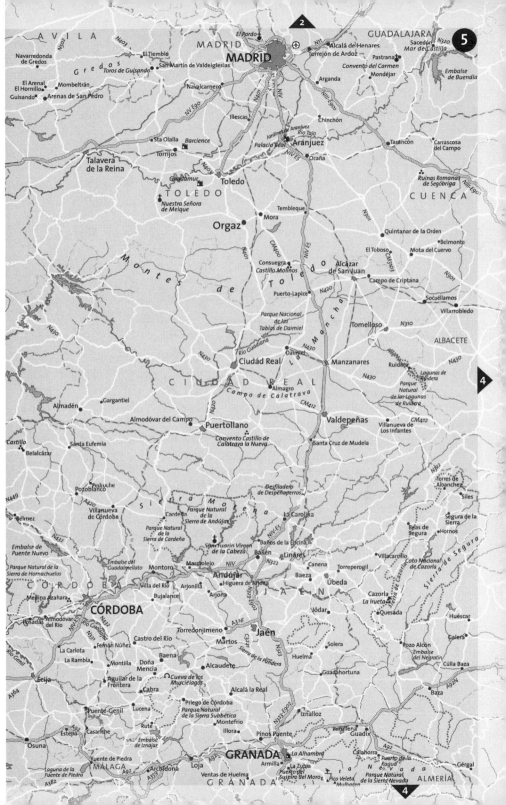

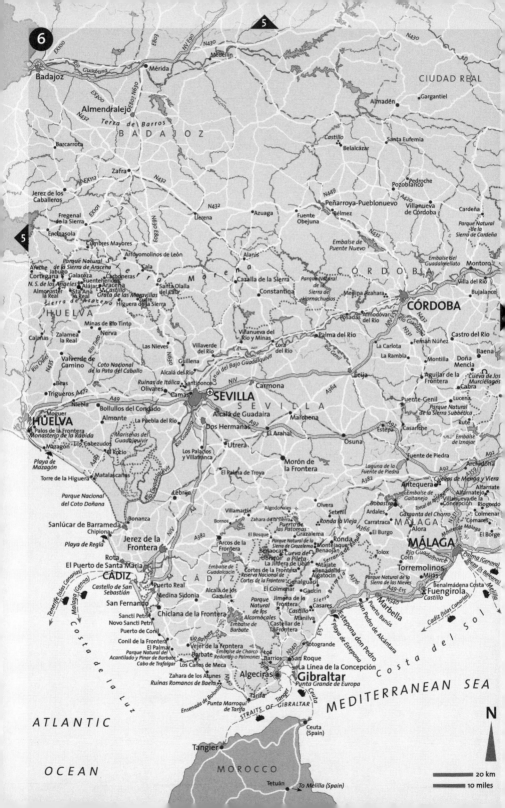

Spain Today

03

Spain is a country in flux – one that has undergone more changes than most in the last quarter-century. Many of these changes may not be so obvious to the outsider. While many of the 'typical', or stereotypical, images of the Spain that tourists know and love are still all-pervasive, the political scene, the economy, its demographic make-up and indeed its ethnic composition have all undergone profound transformations since Franco died.

The old centralist state has given way to a series of 'autonomous communities' (autonomías), some of which have considerable decision-making power and now want even more. Spain is now firmly part of the EU and its citizens enjoy full membership rights, just as other EU citizens do in Spain. Single-parent and single-child families are now frequent, as are common-law marriages, both between straight and same-sex couples: even the Guardia Civil, that bastion of the 'old Spain', now allows gay agents to live in the barracks with their chosen partners. One of the 'whitest' countries in Europe just 25 years ago, Spain now presents an increasingly multicoloured face to the world as a result of recent immigration.

Major Political Parties, Alliances and Elections

Spain's 1978 constitution created a two-chamber parliamentary democracy. Elections are held every four years, with members elected to the Congress of Deputies (Congreso de los Diputados, the lower house) on a system of proportional representation and to the Senate (Senado) on a first-past-the-post basis. The constitution also provided for a high degree of devolved power for the 17 autonomous regions. The *autonomías* or regional governments of Catalonia, the Basque Country, Galicia and Andalucía, particularly, exercise a high level of control over how these regions are run – greater, for example, than that enjoyed by either the Scottish parliament or the Welsh assembly.

The base of the pyramid of Spanish government is formed by the municipalities (*ayuntamientos*), a system of elected town councils with mayors. The mayors of even quite small villages exercise considerable powers in comparison with comparable British institutions. A village *ayuntamiento* may, for example, choose to institute a dangerous dog register without reference to national or regional law. EU citizens are entitled to vote in municipal elections, providing they are registered (*empadronado*). As might be expected, relatively small, independent parties and groupings often have a large say in the outcome of municipal elections.

Given its past, Spain's recent political history has been undramatic, not to say soporific. The transitional governments of Adolfo Suárez' UCD which straddled the 1978 constitution were followed in 1982 by 14 unbroken years of government by the centre-left **Partido Socialista Obrero Español (PSOE)** led by **Felipe González**. Winner of four consecutive general elections, the PSOE governed in a broadly centrist fashion, with a liberal bias in economic and social policy. Its achievements included taking Spain into the EU and NATO, and spearheading considerable modernisation through improvements in infrastructure. Yet, facing a seemingly unelectable opposition, the González government became complacent and damaged by a series of corruption scandals in the 1990s, which saw it voted out of office in March 1996 – see p.20. It then formed the opposition for eight years, regrouping and electing a new leader, **José Luis Rodríguez Zapatero**, in July 2000 while still struggling to articulate a coherent and credible agenda for government and suffering from occasional appearances of disunity, largely due to differences of opinion with the party's powerful regional 'barons'. In early 2004 the PSOE struggled in the opinion polls, yet the sequence of events leading up to the March 2004 election played into opposition hands and saw the party re-elected by a public looking for the lesser of two evils. However, its early moves, such as troop withdrawal from Iraq and the legalisation of gay marriage, did prove genuinely popular. Today the party has two broad wings on economic policy – liberal and interventionist – and tensions between them largely prevent the creation of a coherent reform agenda. The party has also developed a reputation for anti-clericalism and anti-Americanism, which have caused clashes with the Roman Catholic church (over gay marriage and adoption) and the USA (over Iraq and Latin American affairs) respectively.

The country's other main political force emerged as the Popular Alliance party in the 1980s, and was prey to internal divisions and, was unable to dissociate itself fully from the authoritarian Franco regime from which many of its members were drawn. In an effort to change its image, the party contested the 1989 election under a new name, the **Partido Popular (PP)**, and a new leader, **José María Aznar**, who, despite initial scepticism about his leadership qualities, transformed it into a cohesive centre-right party. The PP was elected to national government for the first time in March 1996. Despite having moved towards the centre, in its second term the PP appeared to move back towards the extremes on some issues, partly causing it to lose power in 2004. Since its return to opposition, the new leader, **Mariano Rajoy**, has struggled to give direction to the party, and the authoritarian strain within the PP has grown stronger. Yet the PP continues to oppose the government in two fundamental and traditionally right-wing areas: favoring centralisation over greater regional greater autonomy, and opposing liberal reforms with its social conservatism and devotion to the Roman Catholic church.

The third major nationwide force in politics is the much smaller Communist-led coalition, the United Left or **Izquierda Unida (IU)**, a conglomeration of

The Monarchy
The least controversial political institution in Spain today is probably the monarchy, something which would have astonished anyone with a crystal ball in 1975. Gifted with charm and a natural warmth, King Juan Carlos and his family have worked hard to make contact with every part of the country, and become genuinely popular. They have also cultivated contacts with the minority nationalities, avoiding historic prejudices, and – except maybe among the worst Basque intransigents – do not attract any of the animosity in these regions that gets directed at tub-thumping Castilian politicians.

previously separate left-wing groupings, especially the recycled Partido Comunista de España (PCE). Izquierda Unida is most important for its control of some municipal councils, but has the potential to be electorally significant at a national level.

At the level of the Comunidades Autónomas the political scene is somewhat more diverse and in some cases volatile. Each of the national parties has a separate regional party, while other regional issues also come into play.

In **Catalonia** the **Convergència i Unió (CiU)** is a federation of two Catalan nationalist groups, the populist 'Convergence' and the Christian Democratic 'Union', and has dominated the political scene since the re-establishment of Catalan regional government (Generalitat) in 1980. The CiU played a pivotal role in Spanish politics between 1993 and 2000, when it held the balance of power in parliament, until it lost influence after the PP won an absolute majority in March 2000. Following its deal with the PSOE government in early 2006 it has regained ground, though out of office in its home region. The CiU's main aim is greater autonomy for Catalonia, though its brand of nationalism is moderate and pragmatic and within the limits of the constitution. As coming from one of Spain's richest regions, the CiU is also closely identified with business interests. The **Catalan Republican Left (ERC)**, a more aggressively devolutionist party, has shared power in Catalonia with the PSOE since 2003. It has emerged in recent years as a significant force in regional politics and won eight seats in the national parliament to become Spain's fourth-biggest party.

In the **Basque Country** or Euskadi, Spain's other main ethnically and linguistically defined region, the situation is more complicated. Here, as in Catalonia, many efforts focus on squeezing the most advantageous economic and social package from the national government, but a violent element survives. The **Basque Nationalist Party (PNV)**, the largest and generally moderate nationalist party, shares many characteristics with the CiU. It has traditionally been been closely allied with the regional business community, and has played a crucial intermediary role between nationalist Basque sentiment and national Spanish politics. In recent years, however, it has adopted a more radical nationalist posture and now explicitly supports the Basque Country's right to self-determination.

Batasuna Banned

While Spanish politics may in general be quite a boring affair, this is sadly not true of the political landscape in the Basque Country, where the shadow of violence is still cast over public life.

With the region having suffered severe political and cultural repression under Franco, it was no surprise when 1959 saw the birth of ETA (Euskadi ta Askatasuna, Basque Homeland and Freedom), which took up arms in the struggle against the centralist state. It is often forgotten that in the dying years of the dictatorship ETA enjoyed considerable support in radical circles throughout Spain, and their 1973 assassination of Luis Carrero Blanco, Franco's heir apparent, was widely celebrated.

When democracy came to Spain, many thought that the Basque question would settle itself, and it is true that the Basque autonomous region, habitually governed by the constitutionally nationalist PNV, enjoys a level of independence which the Scottish and Welsh assemblies can only dream of. However, democracy and devolution saw a stepping up of rather than a diminution in ETA's terrorist campaign, provoking a shocked revulsion amongst Spain's population at large. In 1979 Herri Batasuna was born as ETA's political wing. Limited electoral successes meant that the radical nationalists were given a voice in the regional assembly, which prompted further outrage across the country.

Despite short-lived ceasefires, notably in 1997, little has changed in the way that ETA and its political wing, now known simply as Batasuna, are viewed by the rest of Spain, or indeed how they view Spain itself. In the summer of 2003, new anti-terrorist laws, introduced by Aznar's government in the wake of 9/11, were used by high-profile judge Baltasar Garzón to ban Batasuna, initially for a three-year period.

This was not an uncontroversial move even amongst the most vocal opponents of the Batasuna–ETA element in Basque politics. Many argue that it is the perfect excuse for the terrorists to mount a recruitment drive amongst young Basques, and it certainly seems to have hardened anti-Madrid sentiments throughout the region. Whether or not banning Batasuna ultimately proves to have been a wise idea, it is certain there is little prospect of a permanent peaceful solution in the Basque Country any time in the near future.

Its leader, **Juan José Ibarretxe**, has led this more radical departure in what appears to be an attempt to poach support from Batasuna, the outlawed political arm of terrorist group **Euskadi ta Askatasuna (ETA)**. Provided ETA's latest ceasefire holds, the ban on the party is likely to be lifted in 2007 (*see* 'Batasuna Banned', above).

In late December 2006 ETA broke a ceasefire, which had begun to look promising, with a bomb in Madrid airport, killing two people. As a consequence, the standing of prime minister, Jose Luis Zapatero, who had been naively optimistic about a peace process, took a severe blow. The result of the next general election, due by May 2008, now looks increasingly open; in all likelihood the PSOE will continue as the parliament's largest party, although, as now, without an overall majority.

Religion

Religion has traditionally been important in Spain, and the Catholic church was long a dominant force in society and politics. It is less so today, but it still exerts influence, with 76 per cent of all Spaniards considering themselves Catholic. This figure is probably more nominal than real, as only 19 per cent attend mass regularly, compared with 98 per cent 50 years ago. About the same proportion – 19 per cent – of the population are agnostics or atheists.

The remaining percentage of the population follow other religions, among them 350,000 Spanish Protestants, 450,000 Muslims, 50,000 Jews and 9,000 Buddhists.

The Catholic church remains influential, despite the modern constitution that made Spain secular with freedom of religion. Catholic baptisms, communions and marriages are still important as family events. Popular *fiestas*, the majority of which celebrate some religious event, are the most visible manifestation of the importance of Catholicism in Spanish culture. A further example of the Catholic church's continuing importance is that everybody must state on their tax returns if they do *not* want a percentage of their taxes to fund the Church but to be assigned to other 'social ends'. Failure to tick the relevant box is understood to mean the taxpayer gives tacit approval of the money going automatically to the Church. No other religious organisation, Protestant, Jewish, Muslim or otherwise, receives public funding.

The Catholic Church has, though, been on the defensive since 1978 and has had to accept fundamental changes in Spanish society. It has witnessed legalised divorce, contraception, abortion (not free and on-demand but available nevertheless), and a fundamental relaxation of sexual customs which has produced a visible gay community – and one that since 2005 has even been allowed same-sex marriages. On top of that, compulsory religious education was removed from the state school curriculum, which meant parents could choose whether or not their children attended these classes. In a further blow to the Church's power over the political establishment, the present government has also encouraged stem-cell research with human embryos. The Catholic Church, meanwhile, is being forced to close monasteries and convents and import priests from South America as what was once a powerful political and social force slowly declines.

The Family and Role of Women

During the four grim decades of Franco's régime, the role of women was defined as that of keeper of the home, maker of babies, demure, deferential and loyal wife. Whatever the husband did, adulteresses could be sent to prison. Women were practically chattels of their husbands or fathers, whose permission they needed in order to open a bank account, apply for a passport or get a job. The family as an institution was sacrosanct and divorce was banned, though men often abandoned their wives and left them struggling to bring up the family on their own.

Things are now very different. Even the most superficial analysis shows that the area of Spanish society that has seen most change in the last 30 years is the situation of women and, correspondingly, family structure. There are now more women than ever in the labour market, at executive levels in large companies, as entrepreneurs and in politics. In the academic world, female students outnumber their male counterparts and more women occupy lectureships and chairs. In the media and the arts, the female presence is also far greater than ever before; there have even been women bullfighters on the circuit in recent times. Female troops were among the Spanish contingent deployed in Iraq. Women's life expectancy also exceeds that of men, an estimated 83 years as opposed to men's 77.

There is still room for improvement as far as the lot of women is concerned. Women often suffer from discrimination in the workplace and are frequently overlooked in favour of male colleagues when promotion vacancies arise. Lower wages for the same jobs as those carried out by their male counterparts, and cases of pregnant women being dismissed, are not uncommon. Sexual harassment in the workplace and cases of promotion being offered in return for sexual favours are also reported in the press. As well as this, blatantly sexist advertising still persists. Most worryingly of all, domestic violence seems to be on the rise. While few agree on the causes, it would seem that the rise of women and their increasing independence represents a challenge to males in a society that has traditionally kept women firmly in their place.

Spanish women are marrying later. In addition, more and more people of both sexes are exploring and adopting other forms of sexuality: being openly gay or lesbian is now much more acceptable. The traditional Catholic Mediterranean extended family structure is one of the institutions that has changed most in recent decades. Birth rates are amongst the lowest in the world, an estimated 1.35 children per woman. There are more single-parent families than ever before, and the single child family is practically the norm. This trend is being counterbalanced by immigrant families, who tend to have more children. The effects are notable in the labour market (see 'Internal Issues in Spain', pp.73–4) and in recent changes in social legislation aimed at encouraging more births –

a *familia numerosa*, a status which entitles the parent(s) to certain benefits, is now defined as a family with three children.

Major Media

Under Franco the Spanish media was a dismal collection of controlled news sheets serving up flatly reported, adulatory accounts of official functions and radio channels offering escapism through popular, 'typically Spanish' songs, football commentary, radio soaps and prefabricated news. The arrival of television in the 1960s added just another facet of mediocrity. With little debate or discussion, the media was another victim of those culturally barren times.

Things have changed immensely. There is now a greater choice of regional, national and foreign newspapers, representing a full range of viewpoints, and more choice of TV channels and radio stations catering to all tastes. The Internet also provides access to a formerly inconceivable range of news and views. However there are still few truly national newspapers, and the most important belong to antagonistic media groups that sometimes use editorial space for mutual sniping. Readership levels are also lower in Spain than in most developed countries.

Newspapers

Nationally, the most important and widely read newspaper is *El País* (**www. elpais.es**), founded in 1976 and seen as synonymous with the country's transition to democracy. A serious paper, *El País* has a liberal, centre-left editorial line but gives space to writers and intellectuals from across the political spectrum. Printed in both Madrid and Barcelona, throughout the week it comes with various supplements covering new technologies, education, arts and music, a quality literary supplement plus a well-regarded pink-paper financial section and a glossy magazine on Sundays. A selected digest of the paper's main stories is available in English, in a pull-out section distributed with the *International Herald Tribune*. Second in circulation is *El Mundo*, also distributed nationally, which is printed in Madrid, Barcelona and the Balearics with supplements catering for other regions. In the early years of the 21st century **El Mundo** became increasingly critical of the PP government it once helped to bring about, and it is harder to pin down editorially these days. It also has an array of supplements and an online edition, **www.elmundo.es**, with free content.

Spain's third most popular newspaper is the conservative, monarchist, tabloid *ABC*, published in Madrid, Seville and Córdoba. The weekly arts supplement *ABC Cultural* is more open-minded than the main paper, with excellent book reviews, art criticism and special features. Similar to ABC is *La Razón* (meaning 'reason', as in 'reasons of state') which is opportunist, right-wing, and not above using scandal to attract readers.

Most regions also have their main dailies, some available nationally, such as Catalonia's *La Vanguardia*, or locally such as *Diario de Mallorca* or *Diari de Balears* (in Castilian and Catalan respectively) in the Balearics or *Sur*, in the Costa del Sol. Those interested in finance and economics can choose from *Cinco Días*, *Expansión* and *Diario de los Negocios*, all with company reports and daily market news.

Spain has no real equivalent of the British populist press. This is mainly because of the huge range of 'society' and gossip magazines available, such as *¡Hola!*, *Semana*, or *Diez Minutos*.

Also filling the populist gap are the sports dailies, whose sales outstrip those of the serious press, and which cover football, of course, but other sports too. *Marca* and *As*, Madrid-based, generally devote about a dozen pages to Real Madrid, several fewer to city rivals Atlético and a column or two to other teams. Printed in Barcelona, *Sport* and *Mundo Deportivo* are similarly biased.

Those only interested in **English-language newspapers** have few problems nowadays, as most major British, North American and Irish papers are available at news kiosks in major cities and expat areas, arriving around midday, or earlier where there is an airport nearby. There is also a fair smattering of locally published, often free English-language newspapers and magazines. Quality varies, and news coverage is at times superficial, but they do carry features of interest to expats. They can also be useful for finding accommodation or job offers. Look out for: *The Broadsheet* (**www.tbs.com.es**), published in Madrid but distributed in Barcelona and the *costas*; *Metropolitan* (**www.barcelona-metropolitan.com**), Barcelona's monthly magazine in English; and the glut of smaller English-language newspapers in expat hotspots like the Costa del Sol, Marbella and the main Canary Islands.

Television

The Spanish watch lots of television, despite its sometimes appalling (if improving) quality. In most parts of Spain viewers can choose from five or six open-access channels, the main ones of which are: **TVE1**, state-owned, with middle-of-the-range programming; **TVE2**, the 'quality' state channel with films, arts programmes, documentaries, etc.; **Antena 3**, a private commercial channel (though often criticised for being a mouthpiece of the government) offering safe, middle-of-the-road programming; and **Tele 5** (Tele Cinco), another private channel with game shows presented by scantily clad females, etc. but offering fairly independent news coverage. There are also various regional channels.

For more on TV and getting cable TV, *see* **Living in Spain**, 'Television', pp.178.

Radio

The Spanish radio scene consists of an extraordinary number of stations, some of them just serving one town, although the bigger ones tend to be part of four groups, the state-owned **RNE** and the private **SER**, **COPE** and the more youth-orientated **Onda Cero**. Within all this apparent diversity, programming tends to divide into just two kinds: continuous chat (phone-ins, rambling discussion-interviews) and continuous music, with few surprises in between. When you do find an interesting station, it is another way of improving your Spanish.

To get the **BBC World Service** in Spain you need a short-wave radio or broadband connection. If not listening via the web, you'll find the best frequency may change slightly through the day; the World Service website (**www.bbc.co.uk/worldservice**) has a worldwide frequency guide, and an excellent information service to help listeners get the best signal. If you have satellite radio, you can also get BBC Radios 1, 2, 3, 4 and 5 and some other UK stations.

There are also several local stations in British holiday and expat hotspots that broadcast in English for all or at least part of the day. Frequencies and even stations can change frequently, but are usually listed in the local English language press.

Economic Background and the EU

Most economic historians agree that throughout the 19th century and well into the 20th, Spain missed out on industrialisation and failed to follow in the footsteps of its European neighbours. While a truly national economy developed out of a series of local economies during the 1800s, development was unbalanced, with a much greater concentration of manufacturing industries in Catalonia (by 1900, 10 per cent of the population was responsible for around 40 per cent of all manufacturing). The metallurgical mills of the Basque provinces were the only other exception.

As the 20th century dawned, Spain was still largely rural and reliant on inefficient and undeveloped agriculture; the centre and south remained especially economically backward and impoverished. The First World War, in which Spain did not take part, was the country's great opportunity, but this chance was only seized by the already industrialised areas, and the gap between them and the rest widened. Progress was made during the 1920s, with public works schemes providing some economic stimulus, and state intervention helping mining, industry and banking. The political turmoil of the 1930s as well as the world-wide depression culminated in the Civil War, whose economic effects were devastating.

Recovery would not come until the 1950s, first with the arrival of US capital in return for the establishment of military bases and later, in 1959, with the 'Stabilisation Plan' which opened the country up to foreign investment. Throughout the 1960s, the years of *desarrollismo* and spectacular earnings from tourism, the economy grew apace and money crept into every area of the economy. This process continued until the 1970s and then gathered pace again in the '80s.

Further cycles of boom and depression have followed, but the Spanish economy is the ninth largest in the world. It has fully integrated into the EU, which accounts for over 71 per cent of exports and 63 per cent of imports. Per capita, GDP is about 60 per cent of the average of the four leading west European economies (Germany, UK, France and Italy) and is growing at 3.6 per cent per year. While slowing down, this growth rate still remains higher than that of most of its EU partners. Despite this, regional differences remain marked, with areas such as Catalonia, Madrid, Navarra and the Basque Country enjoying better rates of employment, wages and prosperity while others stagnate. Unemployment has fallen dramatically since the' mid-'90s and now stands at 7.6 per cent, but is acute in some regions.

The service sector has grown considerably in the last half-century and now represents more than 67 per cent of GDP. Particularly important in this sector are retail, banking and telecommunications and tourism – Spain is now one of the most popular holiday destinations in the world.

The growth of services has come at the expense of agriculture, forestry and fisheries, which now account for four per cent of GDP. This proportion might seem low considering Spain's important role as producer of wine, olive oil, fruit and vegetables. Fishing remains important, however; with its extensive coastline and the national appetite for fish, Spain has a modern fishing fleet and fishing industry.

Industry also now contributes proportionally less to GDP – just over 29 per cent, with vehicle production accounting for around five per cent of overall GDP. Over 80 per cent of its output is exported, and since 2000 more than three million units have been produced every year. Other important manufactured goods are textiles and clothing, especially footwear, metals, chemicals, shipbuilding and machine tools.

Construction represents, proportionally, a high percentage of economic activity, around nine per cent, and enjoyed an unprecedented boom in 1998–2001, with undeclared savings emerging to be converted into bricks and mortar before the introduction of the euro in January 2002. This boom was also fuelled by strong demand for tourist-related buildings or second homes and high levels of investment in infrastructure – not just 'buildings' but roads and railways too, a reflection of Spain's large size – and a structural shortage of quality housing.

Adios Peseta, Hola Euro *(and rounded-up prices)*

Spain was one of the first countries to be seduced by the idea of a common European currency and joined the euro zone when this was first conceived. From 1 January 1999 the euro became the currency for international transactions at a fixed rate of 168.386 pesetas. Exactly three years later, the currency itself made its début and came into circulation, initially alongside the peseta, which was then withdrawn on 30 June 2002. During the latter months of 2001 there was an ongoing public awareness campaign to help people think in euros and work out prices in their heads. Prices were displayed in both currencies and people were encouraged to think in multiples and divisions of six. Thus, 1,000 pesetas was €6; 500 pesetas was the equivalent of €3; 3,000 pesetas came to €18; a salary of 150,000 pesetas would be €900, etc.

Despite a relatively smooth transition from one currency to the other, not everybody has got used to the new money and five years on it is still possible to hear people talking in multiples of pesetas. Five pesetas was always referred to as a *duro*, 100 pesetas as *veinte duros*, 5,000 pesetas as *mil duros*, etc. A million pesetas (approximately £4,000) was known as a *kilo* and house prices, annual salaries and footballers' transfer fees are still spoken of as so many *kilos*.

Many Spaniards remain unconvinced that the change has been for the best. This is mainly owing to the 'rounding up' effect which effectively pushed prices up far more than wages. Without exception, all of the residents interviewed as case studies referred to the euro-led price hike, which was particularly noticeable in prices of small, everyday items. This may seem trifling but since most people spend most of their money on purchasing small items, a few per cent here and there all add up.

The Spanish economy faces several challenges at present, though its recent strong performance has discouraged governments from meddling even if the EU funds that considerably supported the economy are progressively being withdrawn and channelled towards new EU members from Eastern Europe. One challenge is to keep generating employment – approximately 400,000 jobs are currently being created each year. Another is to continue with the programme of privatisation; which has already affected the banking, energy and telecommunications sectors. Finally, high property prices are causing concern, and there is a risk that a downturn in the property market could cause a negative shock to the economy, which is expected to dip into a mild deficit in the coming years.

Although the economy is more robust and dynamic than, say, a decade ago, and there are job opportunities, stable employment is hard to find. The areas that foreigners typically gravitate towards – English-teaching, the tourist and catering industries, writing and translating and other services – are not ones in which 'real' jobs – with a fixed salary, holiday pay and so on – are especially abundant. On the other hand, for those who are more enterprising or determined enough to go it alone there are now more opportunities to work as a freelancer than before, and it is worth looking into possible financial help (and tax breaks) for those hoping to establish a business. For more information, *see* **Working in Spain**, pp.227–54.

Internal Issues in Spain

Spain shares many of its hottest issues, like the global Islamic terrorist threat and huge waves of immigration, with many western European countries. But to these topics the country can add some of its own long-standing problems – particularly the fate of the separatist regions and Gibraltar. But recent societal and economic changes are also bringing new issues: declining birth rates; spiralling house prices; antiquated and inflexible labour laws. The Spanish response to many of these issues tends to be hot debate followed by very little tangible action, typified by its increasingly pressing need to come to terms with its horrific, yet fairly recent past.

Immigration

With Spain now receiving unprecedented numbers of immigrants, immigration has become a key daily topic. Unlike, say, the UK, France, Germany or the USA, this phenomenon is completely new to Spain, traditionally a country of net emigration rather than the opposite. But these days Spanish television screens show daily boatloads of exhausted Africans arriving illegally in the Canary Islands (*see* box overleaf), and the scale of Spanish immigration has become such that it makes angry debates in other European countries look trivial. More than half a million foreigners have arrived every year between 2004 and 2006 – more than double any other European country. Immigrants now make up 8.7 per cent of the population – a fourfold increase in just six years. However the beleaguered Africans arriving in the Canary Islands are, at 21,000 over a year, just a detail. Most step off flights from Latin America and walk straight into jobs on building sites or as work as domestic workers or agricultural labourers.

With some 700,000 illegal immigrants granted amnesty in 2006, Spaniards now consider immigration one of their worst problems, with 60 per cent blaming their government, which in turn doesn't seem to have an answer or policy. As a result, the issue gives rise to the whole gamut of reactions. Certainly Spain has benefited in many ways. Social security receipts have increased, postponing a pensions crisis. Migrants have stoked demand, helping annual GDP growth reach 3.6 per cent. And they have kept labour costs down and even turned around the country's declining birth rate; with native Spanish couples only averaging 1.35 children.

Dire Straits

One aspect of immigration into Spain that is probably known to readers of the British press is the dramatic situation in the Atlantic waters between Africa and the Canary Islands. Around 31,000 would-be immigrants, travelling in flimsy boats, are estimated to have made the trip in 2006 alone. Considered to be as dangerous as the USA–Mexico border for those trying to cross it – with one in ten thought to drown or otherwise perish along the way – this 'water frontier' is still no deterrent, such is the desperation of the aspiring immigrants. On Spanish TV it is almost daily fare to see Guardia Civil agents fishing bodies out of the water or rounding up the 'lucky' ones who have survived the crossing, often exhausted with hypothermia and dehydration and impossible to repatriate since they have no papers and often won't say where they have come from.

The issue lies high up on the EU agenda, as hundreds more arrive daily, with discussions including the creation of a multi-national police force as well as enabling short term legal migration to divert the problem.

Racism

So many welcome the newcomers, and appreciate the cultural variety they contribute; but the racism of the far right has also begun to rear its ugly head. Racist slogans have appeared on walls and violent crimes against immigrants have increased. In February 2000, in El Ejido, Almería province, there were horrific incidents in which gangs literally went 'Moor-bashing' after a mentally disturbed Moroccan immigrant was arrested on a manslaughter charge.

Stereotyping of people according to their origin is also common, as is blaming the rise in crime rates, and organised crime especially, on immigrants. Racism certainly exists at many levels. In Madrid, a well-known, prestigious private school has a co-operation agreement with an equally prestigious British school, in which the latter provides English teachers. The Madrid school requested a new teacher to be replaced immediately when the teacher who was sent, a black Briton, turned up for class. The police do have powers to 'stop and search', and black people and those of Asian or Arabic origin can expect to come in for more scrutiny than whites. How Spain finally comes to terms with and succeeds in integrating its new population will be a measure of Spanish society's maturity and the sensitivity of its politicians.

Autonomous Regions

Another issue is that of the *autonomías*. Though some autonomous regions enjoy a great deal of autonomy, many would still like to further readdress the issue and redefine their status, feeling that the statutes drawn up in the early 1980s have now become outdated. Further autonomy, not to say something approaching self-determination, is the idea up for debate. Pasqual Maragall, a recent socialist president of Catalonia, proposed during the 'autonomous' elections the creation of an economic zone that would correspond roughly to the old Kingdom of Aragon, including the eponymous Spanish region, Catalonia itself, the Balearics and a great swath of southwest France. Juan José Ibarretxe, the Lehendakari or president of the Basque government, has also put forward the idea of Euskadi becoming a 'free-associated state', independent of but still loosely linked to Spain, and plans to hold a referendum on the issue. The issue of terrorism, of course, is related to this. The Basque conflict has claimed over 800 lives. Self-determination, some argue, would go a long way to resolving the root causes.

Centralist politicians cannot begin to entertain such proposals, arguing that the 'State of the Autonomies' has gone as far as it should and needs no more tinkering with. They certainly cannot contemplate the break-up of Spain's territorial unity, which would also, in the Basque case at least, 'pander to' the terrorists. Leaving aside the painful question of the victims of terrorism and their families, they consider Euskadi and Catalonia as much a part of Spain as anywhere else. This, Maragall and Ibarretxe would argue, is because of their neo-Francoist view of 'Spain' as a single, indivisible nation, and any challenge to that idea provokes a knee-jerk reaction.

The Civil War Past

In many countries that have suffered from dictatorships and repression – including South Africa, Argentina, Chile, and eastern European states – attempts have been made to come to terms with the horrors of the past and to heal the wounds. Not so Spain, where the political pacts that ushered in the transition effectively swept the atrocities of Franco's régime under the carpet, in part to put the squabbling of the left and right behind it and establish a successful democracy. There were no truth commissions, and Francoist officials were not tried for past excesses. An unwritten agreement, known as the 'pact of forgetting', has kept even the mere mention of the Civil War out of everything, from politics to dinner-party conversation. But, in recent years, many groups dedicated to healing the country's 'historical memory' have appeared, and in 2002 Parliament finally formally condemned the 1936 military uprising. This took some doing, as PP had an absolute majority and many of its members and deputies were the children or grandchildren of former régime figures. Now socialist prime minister José Luis Rodríguez Zapatero, whose own grandfather was shot by a Francoist firing squad, has decided that public recognition should be given to victims of the Civil War and repression. So the Spanish parliament is considering appointing a committee to name victims but not those who harmed them. The list could easily stretch into the tens of thousands, ranging from those killed by death squads operating on both sides, to political prisoners, forced labourers, children who were forced into adoption and victims of torture. In addition, volunteer groups from Spain and abroad have exhumed victims from hundreds of mass graves that for years people were too afraid to talk about. In the last couple of years there has been a flood of books and exhibitions on the subject. The question of redress, moral if not financial, is now under discussion. Even the UN has become involved: the Committee of the Disappeared recently ordered the Spanish government to answer questions about those who went missing after 1945. Certainly tackling the issue, which remains a great concern to many Spanish people who lost family members, is opening a Pandora's box of troubles yet at the same time perhaps a healthy sign that Spain's democracy is mature enough to discuss the difficult recent past.

Gibraltar

Dating back 300 years, sovereignty over Gibraltar is another long-standing issue that just refuses to go away. Spanish politicians and journalists (and a good many ordinary people) feel strongly about the existence of this British colony on a rock in mainland Spain. They also react with indignation when anyone should dare to draw a parallel with the situation of Ceuta and Melilla, the Spanish enclaves on North African soil, which Morocco claims. Both the British and Spanish governments (as important partners within the EU) would like to come to some sort of agreement, and it seems that shared sovereignty is what negotiators have in mind. Certainly recent years have marked far greater co-operation over the issue. A 2006 deal agreed that Gibraltar's airport will get a new terminal straddling the frontier, with direct flights from Spanish cities and, crucially for such a poor region, for foreign tourists. Spanish border controls are also being eased, while an outpost of Spain's Cervantes Institute will open – letting the Spanish flag fly in Gibraltar for the first time in half a century. The deal resolves many arguments over Gibraltar, but leaves the question of sovereignty on one side. Asked in a 2002 referendum if they wanted co-sovereignty, 98.97 per cent of Gibraltarians said no. Britain, while happy to share, has pledged not to concede any sovereignty against local wishes. Spain, on the other hand, with its fundamental problems over self-determination in its own regions, has always refused to accept that Gibraltar can decide its own future.

Culture and Art

Music and Dance

Ask anyone to come up with a cultural reference for Spain and it is as likely as not that they will mention flamenco. Images of twirling *señoritas* are a sort of visual shorthand, summing up why Spain is so emphatically *not* the same as the UK. It is true that flamenco remains a vital and important cultural phenomenon, one which can be almost impenetrable to the outsider.

Flamenco consists of three fundamental elements: the song, the dance and the guitar. The syncopated 13-beat rhythm which defines the latter two goes some way to explaining why so many foreigners, raised on the four-beat simplicity of rock and roll, don't get to grips with flamenco. Flamenco dance and music has its origins in Andalucía and is often assumed to owe a debt to the dances of Spain's gypsies. The truth is that the origins of flamenco (the name literally means Flemish) are somewhat obscure. Spanish literature first refers to flamenco in the *Cartas Marruecas*, written by Cadalso in the 1770s, and the first flamenco academies were born in Cádiz, Jerez and Seville in the late 18th and early 19th centuries. This dates the emergence of the form to surprisingly recently, yet these developments clearly built on a pre-existing folk art. In the 21st century, authentic flamenco exists in southern Spain and major cities in small and specialised bars. The performances here are low-key and often not advertised. The atmosphere of such sessions is rarefied and can be hostile to outsiders; woe betide those who try to talk though an impassioned song.

Current big names in traditional flamenco include José Mercé, Vicente Soto and the dynamic Niña Pastori. The flamenco guitarist Paco de Lucía generates the most excitement amongst flamenco fans. The emergence of New Flamenco has seen artists and groups like Ketama mix flamenco styles with pop and rock instrumentation. Although flamenco fusion has been commercially successful, it is often looked down on by traditionalists.

Other distinctly Spanish music styles exist. The *coplas*, sometimes unfairly derided as a sort of 'flamenco-lite', tends to have more melodic tunes and can be an easier listening experience. Moving more towards a recognisable pop style, modern Spanish *cantautores*, singer-songwriters such as Joaquín Sabina, Alex Ubago and Victor Manuel, bring together traditional Spanish rhythmic elements with more recognisable songwriting aesthetics borrowed from American folk singers. Meanwhile in Galicia there is a tradition of Celtic folk music which has many similarities with Irish and Breton traditions and is some of the most accessible indigenous Spanish music.

The *zarzuela* is a Spanish form of operetta, which has been compared to Gilbert and Sullivan but which perhaps invites closest comparison with English ballad operas of the 18th century. This is an art form which is particularly associated with Madrid, where each of the old *barrios* has its own traditional *zarzuela* piece, typically with a comic/romantic plot, and where there is a theatre devoted to the genre.

Much of what is best about Spanish music and dance can be seen when a town or village is in *fiesta* mode. Here traditional forms are often stripped of their sombre rituals and the beat takes over as everyone from toddlers to pensioners takes to the street to dance or clap through the night.

Operación Triunfo (or how to manufacture stars)

Spain's traditional music scene may be thriving, but the pop charts are quite another matter. Extremely low national sales of CDs mean that it is relatively easy for an act to hit the charts but very difficult for musicians to make a living. Superstar international acts like the Rolling Stones feature heavily, but over the last two years the story of the Spanish charts has been the success story of *Operación Triunfo*.

Operación Triunfo is a reality television programme along the lines of ITV's *Pop Idol* or *X-Factor*, but in Spain the phenomenon went way beyond the level of hype achieved in the UK. Young singing hopefuls were selected from across Spain and brought to Madrid, where they were exposed to the glare of the television cameras. With their every move filmed 24 hours a day, the public became obsessed with this *Big Brother*-meets-*Pop Idol* format. The first series produced spin-off merchandising of almost sublime banality, and at one point the entire top ten albums were by the programme's featured singers. The winner of the first series, Rosa, went on to represent Spain at the Eurovision Song Contest in Estonia, while losing contestants were forced to sing backing vocals for her. Rosa continues to enjoy success in the charts, but it is David Bisbal, the curly-haired heartthrob who was runner-up in 2002, who has gone on to achieve million-plus sales – unheard of for a domestic pop singer.

Whether you view all this as harmless fun or cynical manipulation of an artistic medium will depend on your attitude to pop music in general. What is certain is that it has been impossible to ignore *Operación Triunfo*.

Spectator Sports

Readership figures for the sports-only daily newspapers (*see* 'Major Media', pp.68–9) reveal just how enthusiastic the Spanish are about sport. Barcelona's staging of the 1992 Olympic Games gave a tremendous fillip, and Spanish sportsmen and women have achieved much over the last decade. During the same period, facilities have been built and improved throughout Spain (for more on participatory sports and leisure activities, *see* **Living in Spain**, pp.224–6). But non-participants are also well catered-for. Televised sport is abundant and fans attend a considerable range of live competitions at all levels.

Known as *el deporte rey* ('the king of sports'), **football** is followed passionately throughout Spain, and *La Liga* is as competitive as the English, German or Italian leagues. Real Madrid and Barcelona tend to have a traditional stranglehold on the league, though this has been broken in recent times by Valencia. Spanish clubs have done extremely well in the Champions' League, with both Barcelona and Real Madrid winning finals in the last five years. TV money has much to do with this, permitting Spanish teams to lure stars like David Beckham, Ronaldinho and Cannavaro.

Expat areas are fairly well served for teams. Andalucía has three first division teams: Seville's bitter city rivals Betis and Sevilla, and Recreativo de Huelva (Spain's oldest club). Up the coast are Valencia and, in Castellón, plucky little upstarts Villarreal. Catalonia, of course, has 'El Barça' and the fabulous Nou Camp stadium, though rival Espanyol, based at the Olympic Stadium, is an alternative. The Balearics have the modest but fairly successful Mallorca. Canary Island dwellers will have to put up with second division football for the time being, with both Tenerife and Las Palmas fairly mediocre at that level. Check local TV listings for televised games – you will not have to look too far.

Another highly popular spectator sport is **basketball**, second only to football. The top teams are Real Madrid, Barcelona and Málaga. *Fútbol Sala* is a five-a-side game played with a small, hard ball in an area the same size as a basketball court. The ball goes out of play so there are throw-ins and goal-kicks, and it can be very exciting to watch both live and on TV.

Handball, volleyball and especially **beach volleyball** have all grown in popularity in recent years, too.

Motor sports fans can see **Formula 1 racing** at the circuits in Jerez de la Frontera (**www.circuitodejerez.com**) and Montmeló, close to Barcelona (**www. circuitcat.com**). **Rally driving** is popular.

Motorcycle racing also has a big following, and Spanish riders such as Carlos Checa, Alex Crivillé and Fonsi Nieto, nephew of the legendary Angel Nieto, have enjoyed international success.

La Vuelta de España, Spain's version of the *Tour de France* **bicycle race**, takes place in September and has many exciting mountain stages before finishing in Madrid. Andalucía and Catalonia also have their own *vueltas*. Miguel Induraín, four-times winner of the *Tour de France*, has now retired but there are many top Spanish riders, such as Abraham Olano.

La Corrida

Bullfighting is of course one of the Spanish institutions of which everybody has heard, and on which many will have an opinion. In Spain, after a dip in interest in the 1980s, bullfighting bounced back in the '90s, and shows no sign of going away in the 21st century. For locals, star *toreros* are among the country's best-known faces, and staple fodder for the gossip industry (rising young bullfighters 'traditionally' go out with/eventually marry/break up with/have affairs with brash young singers and other names from Spain's entertainment world).

There are bullrings throughout the country, but *la corrida* is by no means equally popular in every part of Spain. In Catalonia there is a very low level of interest and the Catalan government, which actively disapproves of bullfighting, has subjected it to a series of legal restrictions so that, more than anywhere else, it survives only as a tourist attraction; Galicia, the Balearics and the Canaries, similarly, are areas with no real bullfighting tradition. Castile and

Andalucía, on the other hand, are the great heartlands of bullfighting, and the most important bullrings of all, the twin meccas of the *fiesta*, are the Plaza de la Ventas in Madrid and the Real Maestranza in Seville. The bullrings in Valencia, Alicante, Málaga and indeed most cities in Andalucía also have a high reputation among *aficionados*.

The bullfighting season lasts from about March to October, varying from place to place, with corridas in each ring usually at 5pm or 7pm every Sunday. In addition, major events in the bullfighting year are the ferias, during which fights are held every day in their traditional locations, with all the most famous bullfighters present: the April feria in Seville; *San Isidro* in Madrid, which lasts virtually the whole of May; and *San Fermín* in Pamplona in July, which is accompanied by the famous bull-running through the streets, in which a steady stream of drunken foreigners are injured each year. There are also many smaller *ferias* around the country. If you do go to see a bullfight, and don't just want to be horrified, it's advisable to read at least a little of the abundant literature available on the subject, or maybe go with someone who can explain to you at least part of the sometimes complicated rituals that will be taking place.

Film

Spanish cinema is currently enjoying a well-deserved prominence all over the world. Recognition for the new generation of Spanish film-makers began when Fernando Trueba won a Best Foreign Film Oscar for *Belle Epoque* in 1994 and, within Spain at least, gave a discernible boost to the careers of a whole generation of directors including Pablo Llorca, Enrique Gabriel, Bigas Luna, Alejandro Amenábar and Chus Gutiérrez. As a consequence the annual Spanish film awards, the Goyas, are hotly contested, with each year producing a varied crop of quality films. *See* also **References**, pp.258–9.

Many Spaniards would argue that Alex de la Iglesia, whose dark humour has been visualised in films like *El Día de la Bestia* and *La Comunidad*, is the most accomplished of the home-grown talent, but it is undoubtedly Pedro Almodóvar who attracts most attention on the world stage. Almodóvar's first feature film, *Pepi, Luci, Bom...*, was released in 1980, but it was 1987's *Women on the Edge of a Nervous Breakdown* that earned him his first Academy Award nomination. Almodóvar can also take most of the credit, or blame, for projecting Antonio Banderas towards a Hollywood career. The new millennium saw Almodóvar finally awarded the Best Foreign Film Oscar for *Todo Sobre mi Madre* (*All About my Mother*), a film which also swept 2000's Goyas. Almodóvar's current standing in the world industry is indicated by the fact that in 2002 he was able to break out of the Academy's foreign film ghetto and was awarded the Best Original Screenplay Oscar for the almost balletic *Hable con Ella* (*Talk to Her*).

Of Spanish actors it is only really Penelope Cruz who has matched Banderas' achievement of being cast in major English language films, but Javier Bardem's performance in *Before Night Falls* (*Antes de que Anochezca*) alongside Johnny Depp earned him a 2001 Oscar nomination, and his rugged Spanish good looks are likely to see him in demand over the Atlantic in coming years.

Whether it is going to see Spanish-made films or the latest Hollywood blockbuster, the cinema features in a big way in Spanish life. Saturday and Sunday nights are particularly popular times for the weekly *ciné* outing and most major towns will have late-night showings for those unable to drag themselves from their work or their homes in the early evening. In cities and coastal areas you should have no problem finding cinemas which specialise in showing films in *versión original*, the original-language subtitled version, though in more provincial areas, and most of the multiplex cinemas, foreign films are only available in the dubbed (*doblado*) format.

Literature

Spain's literary heritage is astoundingly rich. The country can make an irrefutable case for being the birthplace of the novel, and the Golden Age of Spanish literature produced writers such as Cervantes and Lope de Vega who are on a par with Shakespeare. Cervantes' *Don Quixote*, published in 1604, is a text that all Spanish people are familiar with whether or not they have actually read the book – in the same way that *Hamlet* is part of the common cultural currency in England. Similarly the Spanish picaresque novels such as *Lazarillo de Tormes*, which predate Cervantes, had a major influence on world literature as well as laying a foundation stone for modern Spanish culture.

However, on arriving in Spain it is quite likely that you will be unable to name a single living Spanish writer. English language publishing houses seem to have neglected Spain's contemporary novelists in favour of the superstars of Latin American fiction. In part, the low profile of recent Spanish literature can be put down to the schism in Spanish society caused by the Civil War, with many writers abandoning Spain for South America in 1939.

Camilo José Cela was Spain's most recent Nobel laureate, and his novels, the most famous of which is *La Colmena* or *The Hive* (1951), gave birth to a school of writing known as *tremendismo* which is typified by a darkly oppressive realism. Yet even after his death in 2002 he is not exactly a household name outside Spain. His association with the Francoist forces during the Civil War also means that his memory is not universally loved at home.

Benjamin Prado's *Not Only the Fire*, winner of the 1999 Premio Andalucía de Novela, is one recent book that did make it to English translation and publication, but this remains the exception. Of the recent winners of the Premio Planeta, Spain's most prestigious and lucrative literary prize, Carmen Posada's

Little Indiscretions was published in the autumn of 2003, five years after it won the Planeta.

None of this is any reflection on the quality of fiction being published in Spain, rather on the vagaries of what is considered fashionable in the UK and the USA. For those moving to Spain who can read in Spanish there is plenty to read which will help them understand and enter into the local culture. Cities and some larger towns may have *tertulias*, discussion groups, which meet in bars and cafés to discuss literary subjects (there are also *tertulias* that discuss politics, art, etc.). If you feel your Spanish is up to it, this would be a perfect way to get into the Spanish literary scene.

Theatre

Spanish theatre suffers similar difficulties in reaching out to become known beyond the Pyrenees. An inherent love of spectacle means that many of the nation's big stages are taken up with Spanish language franchises of crowd-pleasers like Disney's *The Lion King* or *We Will Rock You*. The regional nature of much arts funding also means that resources are scattered rather than being focused on one or two national institutions. Meanwhile the fringe struggles to forge an identity, and the lack of any big-selling, quality listings magazine for any of the major cities does not help public awareness.

The one innovative Spanish theatre company to achieve a world profile is Barcelona's *La Fura dels Baus*, whose epic style came to prominence when it took part in the opening ceremony of the Barcelona Olympics. Their reworkings of the Faust myth, with theatre and film productions, were *the* Spanish theatre events of the 1990s.

Visual Arts

The visual arts of course suffer none of the need for translation and are as accessible to foreign residents as to the Spanish. Madrid alone has three world class museums, the Prado, the Reina Sofía and the Thyssen, while Bilbao has the stunningly futuristic Guggenheim. Artistic endeavour is also very much in evidence across Spain on a more low-key level. Towns of any size will usually have a municipal gallery and at least one commercial one. Art also flourishes with exhibitions in bars and cafés, and Madrid's annual ARCO fair provides an art marketplace on a grand scale.

Art is important to many Spanish people. Ask them if they have a favourite painter and it's quite likely that they will have one – it's almost equally likely that it will be either Goya or Velázquez. As in many things, the Spanish tend to favour home-grown talent, and in the case of visual art their national pride is certainly justified.

Apart from the great court painters of 16th and 17th-century Spain, the country produced three of the great figures in 20th-century avant garde art. The work of Dalí, Miró and Picasso may have become commonplace now, losing much of its original shocking novelty, but the artists still represent an astonishing explosion of talent from one geographical area.

The housing of Picasso's *Guernica*, on show in Madrid's Reina Sofía, represents *the* ongoing controversy of the Spanish art world. The vast canvas was painted to commemorate the German Luftwaffe's 1937 destruction of the Basque town of Guernica. Picasso himself famously refused to allow the painting to be exhibited in Spain while Franco was still in power, and it only arrived in the country in 1981. Since then there has been a significant body of opinion which has demanded that the painting be housed closer to the town of Guernica, and since the building of the Bilbao Guggenheim these voices have only become more vociferous. While it is extremely unlikely that any such move will take place, the issue, touching as it does on both the Civil War and regionalist tensions, tells us a lot about the important fault lines in Spanish society.

The work of the current generation of young Spanish artists generally acknowledges its debt to the 20th-century moderns, working within that identifiable tradition. Paint and canvas remains the medium of choice, but there's no conceptualist movement comparable to the headline-grabbing excesses of BritArt.

Crafts

Although in most ways Spain is a thoroughly modern country, it is still possible to get the feeling that it is more in touch with the ways of the past. Away from the big cities and tourist traps the old ways are not so much preserved as continued because they still serve their purpose. While there has been a tremendous population shift to the cities since the early 20th century, some people do stay in the town or the village where they were born, often working with their parents, and this helps the sense of continuity. What in northern Europe might be self-consciously *craft* may just be an ongoing small-scale industry.

Andalucía, among other regions, is renowned for its pottery. The cheap and gaudily coloured pots which hold extravagant displays of geraniums are likely to have been made only a short distance from where they are used. The ceramics of the Fajalauza area of Granada are legendary, and across Andalucía a Moorish influence is evident in the intertwined geometric patterns that decorate wall and floor tiles. All forms of ceramics are comparatively cheap across Spain, and the industry also supplies functional necessities such as plain terracotta flower pots, roof tiles or the water jugs (*albañiles*) used by construction workers on hot summer days.

Mallorca is internationally famous for the quality of its leatherwork, producing shoes, bags and accessories which can be bought at excellent prices. Madrid is still home to the production of the dog-tooth-pattern trousers and jackets which make up the traditional *castizo* dress, and Toledo has artisans working steel like no one else in the world.

The one craft industry which flourishes above all others is the manufacture of nylon-strung, classical or Spanish guitars. Guitar-makers (*luthiers*) exist in vast numbers and produce instruments which range from concert models worth many thousands of pounds to student guitars for less a £100. So many artisan guitar-makers exist because there is a genuine domestic market, and they make their instruments by hand because this is the best way to achieve a fine guitar. Production values are higher and prices lower than the Far Eastern imports that dominate the market in other countries, and if you had ever thought of taking up the guitar then Spain is the place to do it.

Architecture

Spanish architecture tends to be either exceedingly good or horribly bad. The residential areas of old towns manage to organically connect the life of the home with the life of the street. The typical truncated balconies give town-dwellers just enough space to peer down into the street and keep an eye on what their neighbours are doing. Patios are associated with Andalucía but common all over Spain, and provide an oasis of shade and calm where dinner can be eaten and plants tended.

Given how attractive all these old buildings are, it comes as something of a disappointment to discover how many Spanish people would rather live in modern blocks of flats or faceless new developments. The truth is, of course, that many of the old dwellings are baking in the summer and freezing in the winter, with very little natural light in some of the rooms. The Spanish are often portrayed as sentimental, but, when the choice is between a house with character and one with air-conditioning, they will typically be on the side of progress.

The downside of the love for new buildings is that many Spanish towns and cities are experiencing a doughnut effect, with inhabitants creeping outwards in ever-increasing circles and sucking the life right out of the old town centres. At the utilitarian, town-planning level of Spanish building this represents a potential crisis.

On the more exalted architectural plane Spain has the Guggenheim in Bilbao, or the sullenly aggressive leaning twin towers of the Puerta de Europa at the top of Madrid's Paseo de la Castellana, but above all it has the works of Antoni Gaudí. Although Gaudí died nearly 80 years ago and almost all his work was concentrated in and around Barcelona, he remains a national treasure. Gaudí's fantastic work on the Sagrada Família cathedral or in the Parc Güell in the Catalan capital remains the benchmark of what public architecture can and should be. There is apparently a move to have Gaudí, who was a devout Catholic, canonised. This may be because he designed the most recognisable modern church building in the world, but in fact all his work seems touched by the divine.

Food and Wine

Food

Nobody who has spent any time in Spain can be in any doubt how important food is to Spanish people. Indeed, talking about food, shopping for food, preparing and then consuming food, always of course with wine, could be said to be *the* activities which structure the Spanish way of life. From the humblest *menú del día* to the extravagant creations of superchef Ferrán Adriá at El Bulli, in the Catalan province of Girona, you never have to travel far to find food prepared with care and pride.

The pride comes from an emphasis on local ingredients and regional traditions which transcends the idea of a uniform Spanish cuisine. The Spanish culinary landscape is as diverse as its physical one.

Any breakdown of regional Spanish cuisine has to begin with the Basque Country. Basque culture is often disparaged by natives of other parts of Spain but even the most hardened centralist will concede that Basque food is the jewel in Spain's gourmet crown. Perhaps most significantly, it was early Basque fishermen who were responsible for introducing salt cod (*bacalao*) into Spain. Cod steak slowly cooked in garlic-flavoured olive oil (*bacalao al pil-pil*) is as traditional as you can get, while *bacalao a la vizcaína*, literally Basque-style cod, adds chillies and sweet peppers to the mix. It should also be noted that El País Vasco, situated in San Sebastián, run by top chef Juan Mari Arzak, is widely considered to be the best restaurant in Spain.

Galicia gives the Basque Country a close run for its money when it comes to folk-food heritage. Again the emphasis is on fish and seafood; a good Galician octopus (*pulpo gallego*) served with olive oil and paprika should overcome the scruples of the most squeamish diner. Galicia is also home to the trade in goose barnacles (*percebes*) which are collected from the rocks of the Galician coast. Sadly this rare delicacy was hit hard by the *Prestige* oil tanker disaster, and the crop is only just beginning to recover.

Also in the north, Asturias offers a more hearty peasant food tradition. *Fabada* is a stew of white beans, sausage and pork which has become a popular dish all over Spain, while *cabrales*, a very tangy blue cheese wrapped in maple leaves, was traditionally cured in the caves outside the town of the same name.

Catalonia's culinary offerings are more refined and subtle, perhaps a little more French-influenced than those of the rest of the country but with some wonderful original dishes. Sausage with haricot beans (*botifarra amb mongetes*) char-grilled large spring onions (*calçots*), a dish of grilled peeled peppers, onion and aubergine (*escalivada*) and a salad of marinated salt cod, onions, olives and tomato (*esqueixada*) are just a few. Rice dishes, such as *arròs negre*, seafood rice cooked in squid ink, are also good in Catalonia.

Which brings us to *paella*. Viewed from outside, nothing could be more Spanish than a large pan of saffron-coloured rice heaving with shellfish. Paella is traditionally associated with Valencia, although its origins have been traced to the village of El Palmar just down the coast. In truth, restaurant *paella* can be variable in quality. Remember to try the variations on the classic *paella* theme – that pan of black rice might look as if it has been burnt but, coloured and flavoured with squid ink, it can be an unexpected treat. Above all if you get the chance to eat *paella* with a Spanish family, then jump at it. You'll see just how obsessive the Spanish are about their food.

In central Spain the emphasis moves away from seafood towards meat. If you visit Segovia you will have the chance to sample suckling pig or lamb, roast in massive wood-burning ovens and so tender that it can be carved with the edge of a plate – it is a carnivore's delight. Toledo emphasises game birds, particularly partridge, while Madrid's hearty winter dish is the *cocido madrileño* (chickpeas stewed with meat, pig's trotters, *chorizo*, *morcilla*, cabbage, leeks, turnips, onions and noodles). A true *cocido* is served in three courses, first the broth and noodles, then the chickpeas and finally the meat. Offal also figures large in Castilian cuisine, Madrid's second most-typical dish is *callos a la madrilène* – tripe.

Food in Spain is not just about finished dishes that you might order as a main course in a restaurant. Single ingredients are revered, and the *tapas* culture has raised the concept of the snack to heights usually reserved for the world of fine dining and Michelin stars. The Spanish attitude to ham (*jamón*) is the most obvious example of this. The distinctions that are made between different types of cured ham – the breed of pig, the area it comes from, the diet of the animal, the length of the curing – can leave the uninitiated quite bewildered. Every bar you go into will have a ham sitting ready to be sliced, and it is not at all unusual to enter a delicatessen with upwards of 200 hams hanging from the ceiling. The most prized of all hams comes from the black *ibérico* pigs which have been fed on acorns (*bellotas*). This tender, sweet-tasting delicacy is viewed with as much respect as any vintage wine, and prices can be astronomical.

It is also difficult to ignore the Spanish enthusiasm for the sausage in its various forms. The most famous of these is *chorizo*, a cured sausage flavoured with paprika, usually served cold, and thinly sliced *morcilla* is the Spanish version of black pudding; when it contains rice and is deep-fried it becomes a delightful, and surprisingly light, starter. *Sobrasada* is Mallorca's contribution to the world of the Spanish sausage – finely chopped meat is mixed with fat and various spices before being left to cure and take on a distinctive pâté-like consistency. *Butifarras* are white sausages which are particularly favoured in Barcelona, while you will also find sausages made from wild boar (*jabalí*) and from venison (*ciervo*) across the country.

For anyone moving to Spain from the UK, one of the most startling things is the use of olive oil in the Spanish kitchen. We may all now know about the flavour and health benefits of the first pressing of the olive, but the rate at which the Spanish consume olive oil still comes as a surprise. In the shops it is not unusual to pay a premium if you are misguided enough to want to buy corn or sunflower oil, and the quantities of extra virgin which are demanded by some traditional Spanish dishes can be mind-boggling. Butter is all but unheard of in the vast majority of Spanish kitchens, nor are you likely to have much success if you ask for it to accompany your bread in restaurants. You may find that your palate takes time to adjust to the ever-present tang of what remains a luxury ingredient in the UK, but this is the very taste of Spain.

The truth is that once you are in Spain, every day becomes an education in food. From the humble *tortilla española* (potato and sometimes onion omelette) to home-produced *foie gras*, everything Spanish is cherished.

Wine and Other Spanish Tipples

Wine has been made in Spain ever since the Romans paid the country a visit 2,000 years ago. It's quite possible that you will have read how wine is becoming less popular with young Spanish people – that in fact more beer is consumed across the country. This may be true, but it misses the point that wine production is still so important in Spain because almost everyone has some connection to it. Most Spanish families have a piece of land somewhere near their village or home town (*pueblo*), and if they're not growing olives on it then they're growing grapes. Consequently, wine is produced and consumed all over Spain. Indifferent local wines will be drunk at lunchtime mixed with lemonade (*gaseosa*) or perhaps transformed into *sangría* in the summer.

This *vino del pueblo*, however, bears little relationship to what might be termed proper Spanish wines. The quality of Spanish wines is generally acknowledged to have increased dramatically over the last 20 years, and there are now many truly fine wines at very affordable prices.

Geographical distinctions between wines are made by the existence of some 40 different Denominacións de Origen (DO; *see* box, overleaf), which offer the guarantee that the wine contains only grapes from one region. The DO is the source of classifications such as Rioja or Ribera del Duero and is the basic way of distinguishing between wines of different characters.

The most common divisions of quality within a single DO are *Crianza*, *Reserva* and *Gran Reserva*. *Crianza*, when referring to red wine, can be applied to any

Do the DO

With some 40 different DOs and some perfectly drinkable wines not awarded a DO, this is only a brief selection.

Rioja: Spain's most famous wine region, situated in north central Spain. Made chiefly from the tempranillo grape, the reds have a distinctive oaky flavour but are quite light. Opinion is more divided about the quality of white Riojas.

Ribera del Duero: A region in the north central portion of Spain. Its red wines are again based on the tempranillo grape, but the wines from this region are typically 'bigger' or rich to the palate.

Alella: The smallest DO in Spain, located just north of Barcelona. Known for fresh crisp white wines and excellent *cavas*.

Albariño: Fresh, crisp white wine from Galicia. Also the name of the primary grape in these wines.

Toro: A less celebrated neighbour to the Ribera del Duero DO. Toro reds have a characteristic intense cherry colouring and hearty flavour.

Rueda: This DO based around Valladolid produces excellent-value white wines, dry and refreshing in the Spanish summer. Their characteristic taste is because of the verdejo grape used in Rueda more than in any other region. Lately, some vineyards have been producing some splendid wines with a noticeable cabernet sauvignon presence too.

Madrid: An example of how much Spanish wine has improved in general. Madrid wines used to be something of a joke, but new grape varieties and techniques have meant that the area round the capital now produces some more than acceptable wines.

wine that has an age of two years and has spent at least a year maturing in the barrel. *Reserva* indicates that a given year's wine has been judged to be suitable for long ageing. *Gran Reserva* wine is considered to be of an exceptional vintage which will take five years to arrive in shops and restaurants.

These classifications should only be used as a general guide. In fact you might come across wines which are made just outside the boundary of a prized DO, thereby sharing the soil and climate that make a famous wine but not the price premium. Similarly a young wine, that has not even a *Crianza* classification, may appeal more than its exalted siblings. The good news is that the price of Spanish wines in Spain allows you to experiment and decide on your own preferences.

Spain also produces large quantities of **sparkling wine** (*cava*). To be classed as cava the wine must be produced using the traditional champagne method, borrowed from the French. The main *cava* labels are Cordoníu and Freixenet, and these two vie for market dominance at Christmas and New Year. Available across the range from brut through extra-dry to sweet, *cava* often challenges French champagne on quality while beating it hands down on value for money.

Of the other Spanish-produced alcohols, **sherry** has the longest connection to

Britain. Most sherry comes from southern Andalucía, around Cádiz, Sanlúcar and Jerez de la Frontera. The generic name for sherry is *Jerez* but in a bar the Spanish will order by the type of sherry. *Fino* is pale and extremely dry and probably the most consumed sherry in bars across Spain. *Manzanilla* is similarly dry but originates from Sanlúcar de Barramada, while *amontillado* is more golden and a heavier drink. If you associate sherry with a rather genteel maiden aunt, then think again. In Spain, and especially in Andalucía, sherry is a working man's drink. Drunk cold, it can be a refreshing accompaniment to a *tapas* session.

Spain also produces **brandy**, often of quite remarkable quality, and any other number of **spirits**, sometimes quite undrinkable. *Patxarán* is a spirit made from sloe berries and favoured as a morning livener across the country, while in Asturias there is a long tradition of **cider**-making. As with Spanish food, drinking customs vary from region to region, but any time spent in a small local bar will tell you what the norm is where you are.

Most Spanish **beers** are fairly standard lagers, although there are variations, such as the dark, more ale-like and more satisfying Bock-Damm produced by the Damm brewery on the east coast. The most prominent brands vary by region: Cruzcampo in Andalucía, Mahou in Madrid and the centre, the Damm brewery's Estrella in Catalonia and Valencia. Draught beer is usually served in a small glass called a *caña*, or a larger mug or *jarra*. The name used for the standard 33cl beer bottle is yet another thing that changes by region, as it can be a *botella* in the south, a *tercio* in Madrid and a *mediana* (or *mitjana*, in Catalan) in Catalonia. Bottled beers are more expensive than draught, and often not as cold; imported beers such as Heineken or Guinness are pricier still, but this does not stop a legion of Irish and British theme pubs doing a roaring trade around Spain, with a mainly expat or local clientele depending on where they are located.

Coffee, Tea and Soft Drinks

Coffee can be ordered as a *café solo*, a small, black espresso, a *café con leche*, with plenty of milk and served in a glass or largish cup, or a *cortado*, an espresso with just a shot of milk. A *carajillo* is a *solo* with a shot of spirits, either brandy (a *carajillo de coñac*, the most common version), rum (*de ron*) or anything else you feel like trying. If you order **tea** (*te*) in bars, even in many touristy areas, it will often arrive as just a teabag in a glass of hot water, clouded with a little milk; frankly, it's not worth bothering, although in these same places you can nearly always find British-run bars that make the real thing with imported tea. Better, in ordinary Spanish bars, are **herbal teas** (*infusiones*), such as *manzanilla* (camomile) or *menta* (mint).

Considering how many oranges Spain produces, it is a continuing mystery how rare it is to find decent **orange juice** in the country. If you ask for a juice (*zumo de naranja*) it will often come out of a carton, even in Valencia, unless you insist on *un zumo natural* (usually very expensive!). Another soft drink well worth trying, though, is **horchata** (or *orxata* in Catalan), another speciality of Valencia, which has a milky texture and is made by crushing a type of nut called a *chufa*. It curdles quickly once made, and so has to be bought fresh, from a specialist shop-café called an *horchatería* (*orxateria*), and is only available from Easter to November. Ignored by most foreigners in Spain, *horchata* is a bit of an acquired taste, but is wonderfully refreshing.

The quality of mains **water** has improved everywhere in Spain in the last 30 years, and it is always safe to drink. However, it often has a quite strong taste and, for preference, most people drink bottled mineral water (*agua mineral*). This is what you will automatically be served if you ask for water in restaurants, unless you specify *agua del grifo* (tap water). Still water is *agua sin gas*, sparkling water *agua con gas*.

First Steps

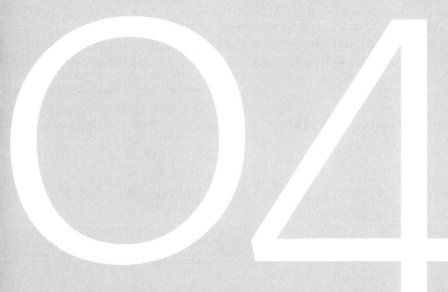

04

This chapter is an overview of what the would-be settler in Spain can expect in terms of lifestyle, what you gain by moving to Spain and what you might have to forgo. The section entitled 'Why Live and Work in Spain' conveys the impression that living in Spain is more enjoyable than living in the countries that the residents interviewed for the case studies left behind. This is despite having to reduce earnings expectations and career prospects.

Two case studies are included. One is a young woman who finished her business studies degree at a university in Madrid and then did not find the world of work to be all that she had expected. Nevertheless she has stayed on, as she feels the life she has compensates for her inability, so far, to get into the world of business. The other looks at a couple who are happy with their life in a Barcelona satellite town and with the way their daughter is growing up trilingual.

The other main part of the chapter, 'Getting to Spain', assesses the multiple options for travelling frequently and inexpensively (or not) between the UK, Ireland and Spain. It contains useful information on airlines, charters, ferries, trains and road travel.

Why Live and Work in Spain?

Spain has never been more accessible for foreigners, or at least those who enjoy EU citizenship, chiefly as a result of two factors: ever-cheaper air travel, and the gradual abolition of bureaucratic obstacles to taking up residence and working there (*see* **Red Tape**, pp.111–24). Given these factors, a growing number of Britons particularly, but also Irish and nationals of other northern European countries, are drifting towards Spain. The official figure of just over 300,000 British residents (*see* **Profiles of the Regions**, 'The Geography of Britspain', p.32) is certainly well below the real mark. Expectations are that this number will continue to grow in the coming years.

A Laid-back Lifestyle

Everybody has their own reasons for making the move to another country, but, broadly speaking, people move because they want to get away from their home country, principally because they no longer find life there satisfying and feel that greater satisfaction – or a challenge or just more fun – is to be found elsewhere. In the case of Spain there are many factors that make it a highly attractive country to move to. Most of the residents interviewed for the case studies had good things to say about the laid-back Spanish way of life and how favourably it compares with the more uptight, oppressive atmosphere they felt they had escaped from in Britain, especially, and Ireland. This is certainly a

Case Study: The Business Graduate

Salma Rashid, 35, came to Madrid from London in 1993 to complete her degree in European business administration. On finishing, she decided to stay in Madrid and see what she could accomplish. She enjoyed the social life and had Spanish relatives on her mother's side.

How did you end up working in your current job?

I thought getting a job would be easy, with three languages, qualifications from the Spanish business school ICADE, and some experience in three multi-nationals: Citibank, Iberia Airlines and Marks & Spencer. But with unemployment at 15 per cent, starting wages on offer were very low. I began giving English business training courses and then moved into the administrative and organisational side.

How is working different from at home?

In English companies, things usually run more smoothly, and tasks are more clearly defined and demarcated.

What are the pros and cons of working and living here?

As far as daily life is concerned, it's hard to be alone. Spaniards are friendly, sociable and thrive on being outdoors. They love street life, in contrast to the Brits' love of the great indoors. The British aren't entirely to blame for this; the climate and low-density urban set-up distances people. In Spanish cities, a 30-minute stroll means passing about a thousand people and dozens of cafés and bars. A similar walk in London would take you past about 20 people and two pubs! The downside? Apathetic, incompetent bank clerks, civil servants, receptionists, sales assistants, etc. who just don't have the concept of customer service. But fighting against it is a losing battle – don't bother.

What advice would you give to someone who's thinking of coming to live in Spain?

If you are working in teaching English as a foreign language (TEFL) but fancy doing something else, use the contacts you make teaching. You meet lots of people from many different fields. In Spain getting on depends greatly on who you know. Having a little cheek is advantageous. One thing I regret is not taking advantage of important contacts I made through teaching by passing on my CV or letting drop that I was interested in and qualified for a challenging job within their company. A training colleague of mine got on famously with her Siemens-Fujitsu students and within two months she was working there as a personal assistant. I also met a personnel manager who had previously taught her human resources director. One of my best friends works for the lift manufacturer Otis, and admits that almost half the staff has at least one other family member working there. So, if you have a chance to do any string-pulling, or know someone who can, don't hesitate.

Case Study: Brits in Catalunya

Val Weston and Chris Nash, both English, have lived in Terrasa, a medium-sized town close to Barcelona, since 1989. They moved there after a few years in Madrid and both hold responsible positions in the local branch of International House. Their nine-year-old daughter, Catherine, speaks English, Castilian and Catalan, the language she is educated in.

How did you go about finding work initially?

We both came over with a lot of illusions and very little money. Val had done a certificate course in TEFL in London before coming and Chris did one in Madrid six months after moving here. We both worked as freelance teachers on a semi-legal basis and after about six months got into language schools where we gained legal status and work contracts.

Tell us about working in Spain.

It depends greatly on the job, but in general salaries are lower and hours are quite spread out: often you start work around 9am, take a long lunch break and finish at 7.30pm. Language teachers work unsociable hours: evenings, mainly, plus Saturday mornings – fine if you are into bars and clubs but difficult to fit around young children.

What do you think the pros and cons of living here are?

Obviously we like it: the climate, the long opening hours of shops, bars, etc., the importance of the family, the food, the long holidays (as teachers), the

factor that attracts many to Spain. Many commented on the more relaxed attitude to rules and regulations, greater personal freedom, friendly people, long lunches (and better food), longer nights out – all at good prices and in a more benign climate.

Cost of Living

The cost of living is certainly another factor, as it is quite easy to enjoy a laid-back lifestyle when it is not costing an arm and a leg. But when looked at analytically life in Spain is not that much cheaper than elsewhere. True, it is possible to eat a *menu del día* practically anywhere in Spain for €8–12, and if you are feeling extravagant you can eat extremely well for just a few euros more. Food and drink is generally of excellent quality and available at prices that would be laughable in the UK. Most everyday items in the shopping basket are cheaper than at home, and transport is noticeably cheaper, especially buses and metros in larger cities. But other items are not cheaper, especially computer hardware and electrical or electronic goods. House prices have also taken an enormous hike in the last decade, to the extent that many areas of Madrid and education our daughter is getting. Bureaucracy can be infuriating, and involves endless queues. Newcomers may have problems getting mortgages and hire purchase without a guarantor.

Do you live mainly in the expat community or have you integrated?
We live between the two. Most of our colleagues are English-speaking, so we mix with them outside work, but many have been here for years and are mixed Spanish/Catalan-English couples. We also have many friends in our local community, neighbours, friends from our daughter's school and people we know through sports clubs, weekends away, etc.

How have you dealt with your child's schooling?
Catherine went to a local nursery from six months to three years and since then has attended the local primary school. Her first language at school is Catalan, but her school teaches several subjects in Castilian. She speaks English at home and does some elementary English at school. She is effectively tri-lingual and jumps between languages easily, which is something that would never have happened if we had stayed in the UK.

And how did you go about learning the language?
We took some basic Spanish classes when we arrived in Madrid and then gained confidence and fluency by going out with Spanish friends, watching TV, etc. We followed a similar pattern with Catalan.

Barcelona have become unaffordable (which affects lower-paid Spanish people). Salaries are also much lower than at home.

Residents have the sensation that their money goes further, which is possibly more important. Given that for many people who settle in Spain the type of life they can enjoy is more important than 'making it' (financially or professionally), then the cost of living to lifestyle ratio becomes a more significant factor. A good many residents, in terms of their working lives, are probably aware that they might have enjoyed greater career success back home than they have in Spain. But for many this is of less importance. 'Serious' career opportunities are fewer and further between (though not non-existent), but that is probably the price to pay for enjoying a better lifestyle. There are a good many graduates and other highly talented individuals who, if they had been prepared to accept the rules of the rat-race, might have done great things in their home countries. But many are content with working in lower-key jobs teaching, translating, serving pints or whatever – and feel that life in Spain offers them a certain compensation for having eschewed a more ambitious lifestyle at home. None of the people interviewed for this book feels a 'failure'. Foreign residents can and do succeed in many fields, or at least obtain a certain level of job satisfaction.

Anybody who is enterprising and dynamic can and will get on in their chosen field. Most people in Spain work in order to live, not the other way around, and live they do, with great gusto. This is something that does not escape the attention of foreign residents, who quickly adapt to and adopt the Spanish *joie de vivre* mentality.

The Weather

The weather, of course, does help. Apart from the worst extremes of heat and cold found in central Spain, the Manchester-like levels of rain that fall in the north and the sweltering summers found on the Mediterranean coasts, the climate is more agreeable than that of northern Europe. More hours of sunshine annually, and the absence of damp, are what foster the lively Mediterranean lifestyle that many who settle in Spain find so attractive.

Family Life

Other residents find Spain a better, healthier environment in which to bring up children. This is not without its problems, of course. The Spanish education system has improved immensely in recent years, and those who can afford it also have the opportunity of sending their children to a bilingual school. As important as education is the attitude to children in general. While the Spanish themselves are having fewer children than ever before, children are still welcome everywhere, seen *and* heard, and enjoy more freedom than their counterparts in northern climes. Whatever type of school they go to, children usually end up bilingual and, by extension, bicultural.

In short, moving to Spain is, for most people, a lifestyle choice. Climate and cuisine, siesta and *fiesta*, more open space and 'quality of life' (a more subjective concept than many think) convince many to go – and stay.

Getting to Spain

Spain is one of the easiest countries in Europe to get to, with flights from many airports around Britain and Ireland. Some Spanish regions, though, have far fewer flight connections than others, and ticket prices are not equally low to different parts of the country.

If you are thinking of living in Spain, accessibility could be an important factor in your choice of where to head for – particularly if you may need to go back and forth between there and the UK (of course, if you're really looking to get away from it all, you might feel the remoter the better). Ease of access will also take on much greater importance if you hope to let out your property to foreign clients, or run a bed-and-breakfast or small hotel. Plus, it's very likely you will want to drive to your new home a few times – especially when moving in – so how close it is to main road and ferry routes will also be something to consider.

By Air

Madrid and Barcelona have Spain's two biggest airports, and are the main hubs of Iberia's domestic network, with connections to every part of the country. There are also regional airports of near equal size, and many more local airports that the low-cost airlines have been discovering. While there's a big choice of flights from the UK to all the main holiday areas, there are far fewer direct links with anywhere away from the Mediterranean coast (*see* 'Spanish Airports with Direct Scheduled Flights from the UK and Ireland', pp.101–105).

The arrival of the no-frills budget airlines in the late 1990s transformed the ease of travel to Spain, and the first trailblazers were soon joined by locally based UK operators. The downsides of no-frills airlines have been well publicised – the long check-in times, more likely delays and the minimum of back-up should services be disrupted. Also, the low-cost airlines are not always as cheap as their advertising sometimes suggests. Fares for each airline vary enormously on the same route, according to when you travel and how far in advance you book; the real rock-bottom deals are only available online and generally for seats on very early-morning, early-in-the-week flights, and on the most popular routes (such as to Barcelona), while you might get a price of £30 for a 6am Monday flight, the same route can cost £140 or more on a Friday evening. Because of this constantly changing price system it is important to note that no-frills airlines are not always the cheapest. Airpost taxes, also, can easily double the cost of what seems at first to be a bargain.

One of the benefits of the no-frills revolution was in the concessions it soon forced on the older mainstream carriers (British Airways, Aer Lingus and Iberia, between the UK, Ireland and Spain). Obliged to compete, they have responded with well-priced flight offers, online booking with discounts, and one-way fares. The distinction between main-carrier and no-frills flights is increasingly blurred in other ways as well: from 2004 Iberia, for example, started charging for meals in tourist class, and cut other perks such as free newspapers. Overall, the rule to follow is always check around all the airlines operating on any specific route, and to airports nearby, and always compare budget prices with those of the main airlines and charters.

Scheduled Airlines between Spain, the UK and Ireland

The airline market is highly changeable these days – airlines get taken over, and routes change frequently – so always check current routes and future plans on websites and in the travel press.

- **Aer Lingus (t** 0818 365 000 in Ireland, **t** 0870 876 5000 in the UK; **www. aerlingus.com).** From **Dublin** and **Cork** to destinations including Alicante, Barcelona, Bilbao, Madrid, Málaga, Palma de Mallorca, Santiago de Compostela, Seville, and Tenerife.

- **Air Scotland (t** 0141 848 4990; **www.air-scotland.com).** From **Aberdeen** to Barcelona and Palma; from **Edinburgh** to Alicante, Barcelona, Málaga and Palma; and from **Glasgow** to Barcelona, Palma de Mallorca and Tenerife.

- **bmibaby (t** 0870 264 2229; **www.bmibaby.com).** Low-cost offshoot of British Midland, with flights from **Birmingham** to Alicante, Barcelona, Murcia and Palma de Mallorca; from **Cardiff** to Alicante, Málaga and Palma; from **East Midlands** to Alicante, Málaga and Palma de Mallorca; and from **Manchester** to Alicante and Málaga.

- **British Airways (t** 0870 850 9850; **www.britishairways.com).** Direct flights from **Birmingham** to Barcelona and Madrid; from Manchester to Madrid; from **Edinburgh** to Madrid; from **London Heathrow** to Barcelona, Bilbao and Madrid; from **London Gatwick** to Barcelona and Madrid. *See* also 'GB Airways'.

- **British Midland (t** 0870 6070 555; **www.flybmi.com).** Full-service flights from **London Heathrow** to Alicante and Palma de Mallorca.

- **easyJet (t** 0871 244 2366; **www.easyjet.com).** No-frills flights from **Belfast** to Alicante, Ibiza, Málaga and Palma de Mallorca; from **Bristol** to Alicante, Barcelona, Ibiza, Palma de Mallorca, Mahón, Madrid, Málaga, Murcia, Valencia and Palma de Mallorca; from **Edinburgh** to Alicante, Madrid and Palma; from **Glasgow** to Alicante, Ibiza, Málaga and Palma de Mallorca; from **East Midlands** to Alicante, Ibiza and Málaga; from **Liverpool** to Alicante, Barcelona, Ibiza, Madrid, Mahón, Málaga and Palma de Mallorca; from **London Gatwick** to Alicante, Barcelona, Bilbao, Madrid, Málaga and Palma de Mallorca; from **London Luton** to Alicante, Barcelona, Ibiza, Madrid, Málaga and Palma de Mallorca; from **London Stansted** to Alicante, Almería, Asturias, Barcelona, Bilbao, Ibiza, Madrid, Málaga and Palma de Mallorca; and from **Newcastle** to Alicante, Barcelona, Málaga, Ibiza, Palma de Mallorca and Mahón. Services on Ibiza and Palma de Mallorca routes are less frequent in late October–March.

- **flybe (t** 0871 700 0535; **www.flybe.com).** From **Exeter** to Alicante, Málaga and Palma; from **Norwich** to Alicante and Málaga; and from **Southampton** to Alicante, Málaga, Murcia and Palma de Mallorca.

- **FlyGlobespan (t** 08705 561 522; **www.flyglobespan.com).** From **Aberdeen** to Alicante, Barcelona, Palma and Tenerife; from **Durham Tees Valley** to Alicante, Ibiza, Mahón, Málaga, Palma and Tenerife; from **Edinburgh** to Barcelona, , Palma and Tenerife; from **Glasgow** to Alicante, Barcelona, Ibiza, Málaga, Málaga, Palma and Tenerife; from **Liverpool** to Tenerife; and from **London Stansted** to Tenerife.

• **GB Airways** (**t** 0870 850 9850; **www.gbairways.com/www.ba.com**). Formerly Gibraltar Airways, this airline operates as a franchise subdivision of British Airways (bookings can be made through the BA website and telephone). It flies to many Spanish destinations: from **London Heathrow** to Málaga, and from **London Gatwick** to Alicante, Gibraltar, Málaga, Menorca, Palma de Mallorca and, in the Canaries, Gran Canaria, Lanzarote and Tenerife.

• **Iberia** (**t** 0870 609 0500 in the UK, **t** 0818 462 000 in Ireland; **www.iberia.com**). Direct flights from **Birmingham** to Madrid; from **Dublin** to Barcelona and Madrid; from **London Heathrow** to Barcelona, Madrid, Seville and Valencia; from **London Gatwick** to Madrid and Barcelona; and from **Manchester** to Madrid. Iberia can also provide onward connections from Madrid or Barcelona to every local airport in Spain, and has code-sharing agreements with Aer Lingus and British Airways.

• **Jet2** (**t** 0871 7226 1737; **www.jet2.com**). From **Belfast** to Barcelona, Ibiza, Málaga, Murcia, Palma de Mallorca and Tenerife; from **Blackpool** to Alicante, Málaga, Murcia, Palma de Mallorca and Tenerife; from **Edinburgh** to Murcia; from **Leeds-Bradford** to Alicante, Almería, Barcelona, Ibiza, Lanzarote, Mahón, Málaga, Murcia, Palma de Mallorca, Tenerife and Valencia; from **Manchester** to Alicante, Barcelona, Ibiza, Málaga, Palma de Mallorca and Valencia: from **Newcastle** to Almería, Málaga, Mahón, Murcia, Palma de Mallorca, Tenerife and Valencia.

• **Monarch Airlines** (**t** 08700 40 50 40; **www.flymonarch.com**). Monarch's scheduled routes run from **Aberdeen** to Málaga; from **Birmingham** to Alicante, Almería, Ibiza, Lanzarote, Málaga, Mahón, Murcia, Palma de Mallorca and Tenerife; from **London Luton** to Alicante, Almería, Gibraltar, Gran Canaria, Ibiza, Lanzarote, Málaga, Menorca, Palma de Mallorca and Tenerife; from **London Gatwick** to Alicante, Granada, Ibiza, Lanzarote, Málaga, Murcia and Tenerife; and from **Manchester** to Alicante, Almería, Barcelona, Málaga, Menorca, Palma de Mallorca and Tenerife. Monarch also operates many charters to Spanish airports, some of which can also be booked online (**www.monarchcharter.com**) on a flight-only basis (*see* 'Flight-only Charter Tickets', p.100).

• **MyTravelLite** (**t** 0870 1564 564; **www.mytravellite.com**). From **Aberdeen** to Almería, Alicante, Ibiza, Menorca, Lanzarote and Tenerife; from **Birmingham** to Alicante, Almería, Gran Canaria, Ibiza, Lanzarote, Málaga, Murcia, Palma de Mallorca, Reus and Tenerife; from **Bournemouth** to Gran Canaria, Palma de Mallorca and Tenerife; from **Bristol** to Alicante, Fuerteventura, Gran Canaria, Ibiza, Lanzarote, Málaga, Menorca, Palma de Mallorca and Tenerife; from **Cardiff** to Alicante, Almería, Fuerteventura, Gran Canaria, Ibiza, Lanzarote, Málaga, Menorca, Palma de Mallorca and Reus; from **Doncaster** to Ibiza and Palma de Mallorca; from **Durham Tees Valley** to Almería, Ibiza,

Lanzarote, Menorca and Palma de Mallorca; from **East Midlands** to Alicante, Almería, Fuerteventura, Gran Canaria, Ibiza, Lanzarote, Málaga, Menorca, Palma de Mallorca and Tenerife; from **Edinburgh** to Alicante, Gran Canaria, Lanzarote, Málaga, Menorca, Palma de Mallorca and Tenerife; from **Leeds Bradford** to Alicante, Fuerteventura, Gran Canaria, Ibiza, Lanzarote, Málaga, Menorca, Palma de Mallorca, Reus and Tenerife; from **London Gatwick** to Alicante, Almería, Fuerteventura, Gran Canaria, Ibiza, Lanzarote, Málaga, Menorca, Palma de Mallorca, Reus and Tenerife; from **London Luton** to Alicante, Fuerteventura, Gran Canaria, Lanzarote, Málaga, Menorca, Palma de Mallorca and Tenerife; from **Manchester** to Alicante, Almería, Fuerteventura, Gran Canaria, Ibiza, Lanzarote, Málaga, Menorca, Palma de Mallorca and Tenerife; from **Norwich** to Alicante, Fuerteventura, Gran Canaria, Lanzarote, Málaga, Palma de Mallorca and Tenerife; and from **Newcastle** to Alicante, Fuerteventura, Gran Canaria, Ibiza, Lanzarote, Málaga, Menorca, Palma de Mallorca, Reus and Tenerife.

• **Ryanair** (**t** 0871 246 0000 in the UK, **t** 0818 30 30 30 in Ireland; **www. ryanair.com**). From **East Midlands** to Girona, Granada, Madrid, Murcia, Reus, Santiago de Compostela and Valencia; from **Dublin** to Almería, Fuerteventura, Girona, Madrid, Málaga, Murcia, Reus, Seville, Tenerife and Valencia; from **Glasgow** to Girona; from **Liverpool** to Alicante, Girona, Murcia, Palma de Mallorca, Reus, Seville, Santander and Santiago de Compostela; from **London Stansted** to Almería, Fuerteventura, Girona, Madrid, Málaga, Murcia, Reus, Santander, Santiago de Compostela, Seville, Tenerife and Valencia; from **Shannon** to Girona, Madrid, Málaga and Murcia.

Flight-only Charter Tickets

Low-cost flights have monopolized press attention, including recently being blamed for their contribution to global climate change, but there are still a great many charter flights between the UK and airports all around Spain, which usefully fill in gaps left by scheduled services. In principle, of course, most charter seats are booked as part of package holidays, but all the recent changes in the airline industry have also blurred the lines between charter and scheduled flights. Flight-only tickets are now available on most routes, and can often be booked direct, online or by telephone, rather than through agents. The chief remaining difference between charters and scheduled flights is that charter tickets are usually issued for a fixed minimum period, generally of seven days, 14 days or any other multiple of a week, with little flexibility. Another possible disadvantage is that many charters only operate during the Easter–October season. The best way to find flight-only charters is through ticket operators like **Avro**, but charter tickets on Excel and Monarch (see p.99) can now be booked direct on the airlines' websites, as with scheduled airlines. Good places to find other booking services are the classified pages of travel magazines and newspaper travel supplements.

- **Air Flights** (t 0800 083 7007; **www.airflights.co.uk**). This is a good booking service.

- **Avro** (t 0871 622 4476; **www.avro.com**). The largest UK operator offering flight-only charter tickets to Spain: flights from many UK airports (Birmingham, Bristol, Cardiff, East Midlands, London Gatwick, Glasgow, Leeds-Bradford, London Luton, Manchester, Newcastle, London Stansted) to a wide range of Spanish destinations (Alicante, Almería, Girona, Gibraltar, Ibiza, Málaga, Menorca, Murcia, Palma de Mallorca and, in the Canaries, Gran Canaria, Tenerife, Lanzarote and Fuerteventura).

- **Dialaflight** (t 0870 333 4488; **www.dialaflight.com**). Reliable ticket-bookers, for scheduled and charter flights.

- **Excel Airways** (t 0870 998 9898; **www.xl.com**). In many ways Excel seems like a scheduled airline – seats can be booked online – but it continues to operate as a charter airline, so returns are usually for a minimum of seven days, and there is full service on board. Prices, though, are competitive. The schedule changes by season, but Excel flights operate from Birmingham, London Gatwick, Manchester and Newcastle to destinations such as Alicante, Barcelona, Bilbao, Ibiza, Madrid, Málaga, Menorca, Palma de Mallorca, Reus (near Tarragona), Santiago de Compostela, and Fuerteventura, Gran Canaria, Lanzarote and Tenerife.

- **Flightline** (t 0800 541 541; **www.flightline.co.uk**). A wide range of options.

Spanish Airports with Direct Scheduled Flights from the UK and Ireland

The Central Heartlands

Madrid

From Birmingham: British Airways, Iberia
From Bristol: easyJet
From Cork: Aer Lingus
From Dublin: Aer Lingus, Iberia, Ryanair
From East Midlands: Ryanair
From Edinburgh: British Airways, easyJet
From Gatwick: BA, easyJet, Iberia

From Heathrow: British Airways, Iberia
From Liverpool: easyJet
From Luton: easyJet
From Manchester: British Airways, Iberia
From Shannon: Ryanair
From Stansted: easyJet, Ryanair

Green Spain: The Atlantic Coast

Asturias

From Stansted: easyJet

Bilbao

From Cork: Aer Lingus
From Dublin: Aer Lingus
From Heathrow: British Airways

From Gatwick: easyJet
From Stansted: easyJet

Santander

From Liverpool: Ryanair

From Stansted: Ryanair

Santiago de Compostela

From Cork: Aer Lingus
From Dublin: Aer Lingus
From East Midlands: Ryanair

From Liverpool: Ryanair
From Stansted: Ryanair

Mediterranean Spain: Catalonia, Valencia, the Balearics

Alicante

From Aberdeen: FlyGlobespan,
  MyTravelLite
From Belfast: easyJet
From Birmingham: MyTravelLite, bmibaby,
  Monarch
From Blackpool: Jet2
From Bristol: easyJet, MyTravelLite
From Cardiff: bmibaby, MyTravelLite
From Cork: Aer Lingus
From Dublin: Aer Lingus
From Durham Tees Valley: FlyGlobespan
From East Midlands: bmibaby, easyJet,
  MyTravelLite
From Edinburgh: Air Scotland, easyJet,
  MyTravelLite

From Exeter: flybe
From Gatwick: easyJet, GB Airways,
  Monarch, MyTravelLite
From Glasgow: FlyGlobespan, easyJet
From Heathrow: British Midland
From Leeds-Bradford: Jet2, MyTravelLite
From Liverpool: easyJet, Ryanair
From Luton: easyJet, Monarch,
  MyTravelLite
From Manchester: bmibaby, Monarch, Jet2,
  MyTravelLite
From Newcastle: easyJet, MyTravelLite
From Norwich: flybe, MyTravelLite
From Southampton: flybe
From Stansted: easyJet

Barcelona

From Aberdeen: Air Scotland, FlyGlobespan
From Belfast: Jet2
From Birmingham: British Airways,
  bmibaby
From Bristol: easyJet
From Cork: Aer Lingus
From Dublin: Aer Lingus, Iberia
From East Midlands: easyJet
From Edinburgh: Air Scotland,
  FlyGlobespan

From Gatwick: British Airways, easyJet,
  Iberia
From Glasgow: Air Scotland, FlyGlobespan
From Heathrow: British Airways, Iberia
From Leeds-Bradford: Jet2
From Liverpool: easyJet
From Luton: easyJet
From Manchester: Monarch, Jet 2
From Newcastle: easyJet
From Stansted: easyJet

Girona

From Dublin: Ryanair
From East Midlands: Ryanair
From Glasgow: Ryanair

From Liverpool: Ryanair
From Shannon: Ryanair
From Stansted: Ryanair

Ibiza

From Aberdeen: MyTravelLite
From Belfast: easyJet, Jet2
From Birmingham: Monarch, MyTravelLite
From Bristol: easyJet, MyTravelLite
From Cardiff: MyTravelLite
From Doncaster: MyTravelLite
From Durham Tees Valley: FlyGlobespan, MyTravelLite
From East Midlands: easyJet, MyTravelLite

From Gatwick: Monarch, MyTravelLite
From Glasgow: easyJet, FlyGlobespan
From Leeds-Bradford: Jet2, MyTravelLite
From Liverpool: easyJet
From Luton: easyJet, Monarch
From Manchester: Jet2, MyTravelLite
From Newcastle: easyJet, MyTravelLite
From Stansted: easyJet

Mallorca

From Aberdeen: Air Scotland, FlyGlobespan
From Belfast: easyJet, Jet2
From Birmingham: bmibaby, Monarch, MyTravelLite
From Blackpool: Jet2
From Bournemouth: MyTravelLite
From Bristol: easyJet, MyTravelLite
From Cardiff: bmibaby, MyTravelLite
From Cork: Aer Lingus
From Doncaster: MyTravelLite
From Dublin: Aer Lingus
From Durham Tees Valley: FlyGlobespan, MyTravelLite
From East Midlands: bmibaby, MyTravelLite
From Edinburgh: Air Scotland, easyJet, FlyGlobespan, MyTravelLite

From Exeter: flybe
From Gatwick: easyJet, GB Airways, MyTravelLite
From Glasgow: Air Scotland, FlyGlobespan
From Heathrow: British Midland
From Leeds-Bradford: Jet2, MyTravelLite
From Liverpool: easyJet, Ryanair
From Luton: easyJet, Monarch, MyTravelLite
From Manchester: Monarch, Jet2, MyTravelLite
From Newcastle: easyJet, Jet2, MyTravelLite
From Norwich: MyTravelLite
From Southampton: flybe
From Stansted: easyJet

Menorca

From Aberdeen: MyTravelLite
From Birmingham: Monarch
From Bristol: easyJet, MyTravelLite
From Cardiff: MyTravelLite
From Durham Tees Valley: FlyGlobespan, MyTravelLite
From Edinburgh: MyTravelLite

From Gatwick: GB Airways, MyTravelLite
From Leeds-Bradford: Jet2, MyTravelLite
From Liverpool: easyJet
From Luton: Monarch, MyTravelLite
From Newcastle: easyJet, Jet2, MyTravelLite
From Manchester: Monarch, MyTravelLite

Reus

From Birmingham: MyTravelLite
From Cardiff: MyTravelLite
From Dublin: Ryanair
From East Midlands: Ryanair
From Gatwick: MyTravelLite

From Leeds-Bradford: MyTravelLite
From Liverpool: Ryanair
From Newcastle: MyTravelLite
From Stansted: Ryanair

Valencia

From Bristol: easyJet
From Dublin: Ryanair
From East Midlands: Ryanair
From Heathrow: Iberia

From Leeds-Bradford: Jet2
From Manchester: Jet2
From Newcastle: Jet2
From Stansted: Ryanair

The South

Almería

From Aberdeen: MyTravelLite
From Birmingham: Monarch, MyTravelLite
From Cardiff: MyTravelLite
From Dublin: Ryanair
From Durham Tees Valley: MyTravelLite
From East Midlands: MyTravelLite

From Gatwick: MyTravelLite
From Leeds-Bradford: Jet2
From Luton: Monarch
From Manchester: Monarch, MyTravelLite
From Newcastle: Jet2
From Stansted: easyJet, Ryanair

Gibraltar

From Gatwick: GB Airways

From Luton: Monarch

Granada

From East Midlands: Ryanair

From Gatwick: Monarch

Málaga

From Aberdeen: Monarch
From Belfast: easyJet, Jet2
From Birmingham: Monarch, MyTravelLite
From Blackpool: Jet2
From Bristol: easyJet, MyTravelLite
From Cardiff: bmibaby, MyTravelLite
From Cork: Aer Lingus
From Dublin: Aer Lingus, Ryanair
From Durham Tees Valley: FlyGlobespan
From East Midlands: bmibaby, easyJet,
  MyTravelLite
From Edinburgh: Air Scotland, MyTravelLite
From Exeter: bmibaby, flybe
From Gatwick: easyJet, GB Airways,

Monarch, MyTravelLite
From Glasgow: FlyGlobespan
From Heathrow: GB Airways
From Leeds-Bradford: Jet2, MyTravelLite
From Liverpool: easyJet
From Luton: easyJet, Monarch,
  MyTravelLite
From Manchester: bmibaby, Jet2, Monarch,
  MyTravelLite
From Newcastle: easyJet, Jet2, MyTravelLite
From Norwich: flybe, MyTravelLite
From Shannon: Ryanair
From Southampton: flybe
From Stansted: easyJet, Ryanair

Murcia

From Belfast: Jet2
From Birmingham: bmibaby, Monarch,
  MyTravelLite
From Blackpool: Jet2
From Bristol: easyJet
From Dublin: Ryanair
From East Midlands: Ryanair
From Edinburgh: Jet2

From Gatwick: Monarch
From Leeds-Bradford: Jet2
From Liverpool: Ryanair
From Newcastle: Jet2
From Shannon: Ryanair
From Southampton: flybe
From Stansted: Ryanair

Seville

From Cork: Aer Lingus
From Dublin: Aer Lingus, Ranair
From Heathrow: Iberia

From Liverpool: Ryanair
From Stansted: Ryanair

The Canaries

Fuerteventura

From Bristol: MyTravelLite
From Cardiff: MyTravelLite
From Dublin: Ryanair
From East Midlands: MyTravelLite
From Gatwick: MyTravelLite
From Leeds-Bradford: MyTravelLite

From Luton: MyTravelLite
From Manchester: MyTravelLite
From Newcastle: MyTravelLite
From Norwich: MyTravelLite
From Stansted: Ryanair

Gran Canaria (Las Palmas)

From Birmingham: MyTravelLite
From Bournemouth: MyTravelLite
From Bristol: MyTravelLite
From Cardiff: MyTravelLite
From East Midlands: MyTravelLite
From Edinburgh: MyTravelLite

From Gatwick: GB Airways, MyTravelLite
From Leeds-Bradford: MyTravelLite
From Luton: Monarch, MyTravelLite
From Manchester: MyTravelLite
From Newcastle: MyTravelLite
From Norwich: MyTravelLite

Lanzarote

From Aberdeen: MyTravelLite
From Birmingham: Monarch, MyTravelLite
From Bristol: MyTravelLite
From Cardiff: MyTravelLite
From Durham Tees Valley: MyTravelLite
From East Midlands: MyTravelLite
From Edinburgh: MyTravelLite

From Gatwick: GB Airways, Monarch, MyTravelLite
From Leeds-Bradford: Jet2, MyTravelLite
From Luton: Monarch, MyTravelLite
From Manchester: MyTravelLite
From Newcastle: MyTravelLite
From Norwich: MyTravelLite

Tenerife

(Note that the island has two airports, Tenerife-Norte and Tenerife-Sur)

From Aberdeen: FlyGlobespan, MyTravelLite
From Belfast: Jet2
From Birmingham: Monarch, MyTravelLite
From Blackpool: Jet2
From Bournemouth: MyTravelLite
From Bristol: MyTravelLite
From Cork: Aer Lingus
From Dublin: Aer Lingus, Ryanair
From Durham Tees Valley: FlyGlobespan
From East Midlands: MyTravelLite
From Luton: Monarch

From Edinburgh: FlyGlobespan, MyTravelLite
From Gatwick: GB Airways, Monarch, MyTravelLite
From Glasgow: Air Scotland, FlyGlobespan
From Leeds-Bradford: Jet2, MyTravelLite
From Liverpool: FlyGlobespan
From Luton: Monarch, MyTravelLite
From Manchester: Monarch, MyTravelLite
From Newcastle: Jet2, MyTravelLite
From Norwich: MyTravelLite
From Stansted: FlyGlobespan, Ryanair

By Road

If you're moving to Spain it will be much easier to buy a Spanish car than to register a vehicle brought from the UK (*see* **Living in Spain**, 'Transport', p.201) – over and above the drawbacks of having a right-hand-drive vehicle on Spanish roads. For shorter trips, though, it can be handy to bring your own car, and once you have a home in Spain it's very likely that at some point you'll want to take over more things than it's ever practicable to take as airline baggage.

It's possible to get from the Channel ports across France to the Spanish border in about 17 hours, and then through Spain to the Costa del Sol in another 18. However, for non-masochists it's better to make a trip of it, and allow three or four days. Also, to get down through France and Spain quickly, you have to travel on motorways (*autoroutes* in France, *autopistas* in Spain), which in both countries carry substantial tolls: tolls from Calais to the Spanish border, for example, can add up to around £50. If you take more time, stay on minor roads and sleep a couple of nights in hotels you might find that the extra costs are not much more than you would spend on tolls if you drove straight through.

At the Spanish border most traffic gets funnelled into two roads, one at the Atlantic end of the Pyrenees via Irún, and the other, the most popular, on the Mediterranean side along the motorway that runs south from Perpignan to cross the frontier at La Jonquera (European route E-15; in France it's the A-9, and in Spain the A-7). This can be a bottleneck in summer. The routes in between, through the Pyrenees, are very scenic but more winding, so that they provide a longer, more leisurely drive. In midwinter these Pyrenean routes become very slow and are closed at times because of snow.

Some websites worth consulting (both available in English) are **www. autoroutes.fr**, for the French motorway system and current toll rates, and **www. bison-fute.equipement.gouv.fr**, the site of the French National Traffic Centre, which has useful information on traffic conditions across France. The similar official website for Spain is not as wide-ranging but has current Spanish toll rates; *see* **www.dgt.es** (also in English).

The Complexities of Ferry and Tunnel Fares

Technology is supposed to make life easier, but this isn't always apparent with cross-Channel fares. Prices on all ferries and the Channel Tunnel vary considerably by season, day of the week and time of day of travel, so finding the best price available at any time demands research. All the companies now suggest you book online, and no longer list fares in brochures. However, their fare structures are so complicated that the websites generally fail to present them clearly. When you key in a given date-time combination, as you are required to do, there's no way of telling whether you could travel for less just a day or so earlier or later. Hence, it's more effective – and saves time – to telephone and persist long enough to get through to a person, to whom you can ask the magic question, 'What is the cheapest fare available that week, and when would I have to travel to get it?' In general, night and early-morning crossings are the cheapest. Two websites that do list current fares more straightforwardly are those of Eurotunnel and Transmanche Ferries.

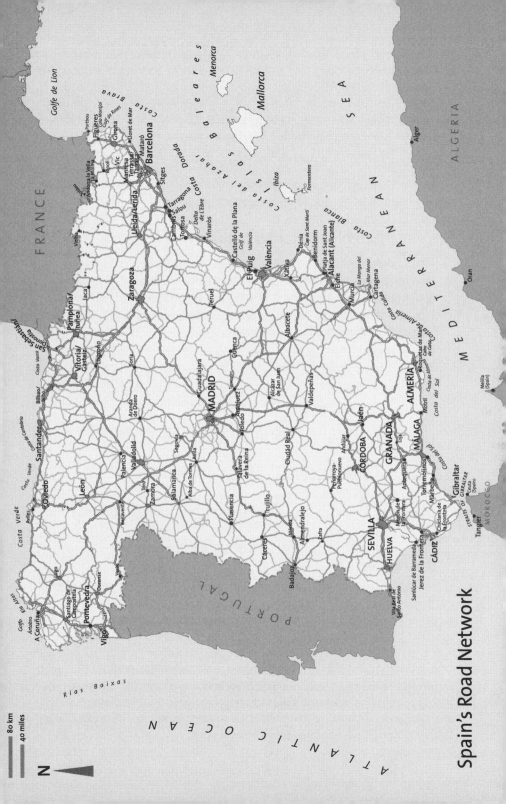

Spain's Road Network

Cross-Channel fares are discouragingly high, especially for standard returns (usually any trip of over five days); the more generous special offers are generally only available for short breaks. Fares vary at all times, though, so it's always worth checking around for cheaper deals (compare prices on **www.ferrybooker.com**); one online agencies that offers discount Channel crossings is **www.cross-channel-ferry-tickets.co.uk**.

Each company also offers a complicated range of special offers, discounts for advance booking and loyalty schemes for frequent travellers. These range from points systems, like supermarket reward cards, to more generous packages aimed especially at owners of homes abroad.

Ferry and Tunnel Companies to France and Spain

- **Brittany Ferries (t** 08709 076 103 in the UK, **t** (021) 427 7801 in Ireland; **www.brittanyferries.com**). Cork–Roscoff, Plymouth–Roscoff, Plymouth–Santander, Poole–Cherbourg, Portsmouth–Caen, Portsmouth–St-Malo.
- **Condor Ferries (t** 0870 243 5140; **www.condorferries.co.uk**). Poole/Weymouth–St-Malo, Portsmouth–Cherbourg.
- **Eurotunnel (t** 0870 535 3535; **www.eurotunnel.com**). Folkestone–Calais: car shuttle through the Tunnel, with three or four departures each hour.
- **Irish Ferries (t** 0818 300 400 in Irish Republic, **t** 08705 17 17 17in UK, **t** 0818 300 400 in Northern Ireland; **www.irishferries.com**). Rosslare–Cherbourg, Rosslare–Roscoff.
- **Norfolkline (t** 0870 145 0608; **www.norfolkline-ferries.com**). Dover–Dunkerque.
- **P&O Ferries (t** 08705 20 20 20; **www.poferries.com**). Dover–Calais, Portsmouth–Bilbao.
- **SeaFrance (t** 08705 711 711; **www.seafrance.com**). Dover–Calais; often has the cheapest deals.
- **Speed Ferries (t** 0870 220 0570; **www.speedferries.com**). Dover–Boulogne.
- **Transmanche Ferries (t** 0845 644 2737; **www.transmanche.tbreaks.com**). Newhaven–Dieppe.

By Sea

There are two direct ferry services between Britain and northern Spain. **P&O Ferries** has sailings every three days between Portsmouth and Bilbao. Journey time is about 27hrs. **Brittany Ferries** has two sailings weekly between Plymouth and Santander (Plymouth–Santander, Sun, Wed; Santander–Plymouth, Mon, Thurs). Journey time is a little less, at around 21hrs.

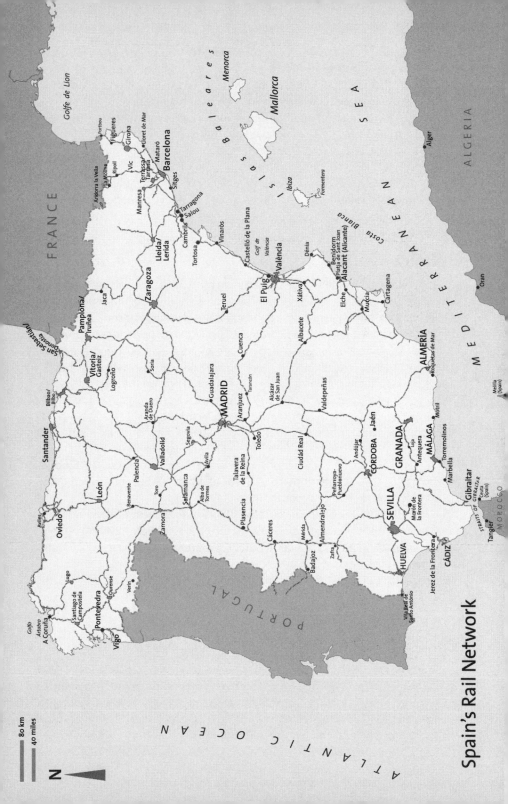

Spain's Rail Network

Since this is an ocean crossing, both companies try to give the trip the leisurely feel of a cruise rather than just a car ferry. The ships are larger and more comfortable than Channel ferries, with a wider choice of restaurants, entertainments and other amenities. Fares – although they too vary according to when you travel – are accordingly quite high, around £840 for a standard (over five days) return for a car and four people in summer. Also, if your destination in Spain is on the Mediterranean coast you still have 10–18hrs driving ahead of you when you arrive. Even so, these routes are very popular with Spanish property-owners and need to be booked well in advance in summer. Both companies have frequent-traveller loyalty schemes aimed at home owners abroad, and P&O gives bigger discounts on Bilbao sailings than on its French routes.

By Rail

It is of course still possible to get to Spain all the way from Britain by train, but nowadays this is nearly always more expensive than flying – a return from London to Alicante by Eurostar (**t** 08705 186 186, **www.eurostar.com**) and high-comfort, high-speed sleeper trains from Paris will cost around £300 in summer, although it is possible to get cheaper fares by travelling on more everyday trains, and there are also special-offer fares. It naturally takes much longer (around 24hrs), but as compensation you see much more on the way.

After getting to Paris Gare du Nord by Eurostar, for western Spain or the Costa del Sol you need to get a train from the Gare d'Austerlitz in Paris down towards the Basque border at Irún, continuing through Spain via a change in Madrid; for the Mediterranean coast, travel from Paris's Gare de Lyon towards Barcelona.

To buy tickets online for London–Paris–Spain routes, contact **Rail Europe** (**t** 08708 371 371, **www.raileurope.co.uk**). Look at **www.seat61.com**, an incredibly useful independent train travel website.

Spain's railways were built to a broader gauge than the rest of the European rail network. Hence, except for a few luxury trains, which have adjustable wheels, trains cannot cross the border, and you have to get off your French train and transfer on to a Spanish one at frontier stations.

See p.109 for a map of Spain's main railways.

Red Tape

05

Red tape in Spain is often excessive and is characterised by long queues, unhelpful officials, snail's-pace processing and a strong urge to bang your head against a wall – even if you get there in the end. All residents interviewed for this book mentioned time-consuming, Kafka-esque bureaucracy as one of the downsides of living in Spain. Whether you are dealing with the employment authorities, the tax office, the legal system, the health service or the traffic police, the general advice is to expect the worst and imagine that whatever you aim to do will take longer than you thought. Learn to live with it; it is as much a part of life as constant drizzle and grey skies in Britain. You might be pleasantly surprised when it does not take as long as you expect.

This chapter looks principally at red tape in so far as it affects becoming a resident and working in Spain. Applying for Spanish nationality is also covered. It should be stated that, for EU citizens at least, things are not nearly as onerous as before, as they now no longer need a work permit or even a residence card in order to work as employees, ply their trade as freelancers, set up in business or study. Non-EU citizens, on the other hand, can expect a rather rougher ride.

Visas, Permits and Other Paperwork

Residence Cards for EU Citizens

The good news for EU citizens who wish to establish themselves in Spain and work, either as employees, freelancers or usiness-owners, or to be a student, is that in 2003 Spain took a major step forward in reducing bureaucracy, by removing the obligation for such people to apply for and carry a residence card, enabling foreign nationals to use their passport to prove identity when voting in elections. To quote the legislation in translation:

> *A valid passport or the equivalent of a Spanish National Identity Document will suffice for any dealings or transactions such as the purchase of property, the issuing of a driving licence or a simple bank transaction. Furthermore, possession of a valid passport, or the equivalent of a Spanish National Identity Document, is sufficient for the EU resident to be included on the electoral roll and participate in municipal elections and those for the European Parliament.*

Though it does cut down a lot of bureaucracy, this ruling does make it harder to actually prove you are a resident. To do this you should go to your local town hall with your address and ask to be included on the *padrón* – the list of all inhabitants in the municipality which effectively forms the electoral roll. This step (*empadronamiento*) means you are considered a resident.

Dealing with Bureaucracy – Using a Gestor

When you first move to a new country, there are so many new things to come to terms with that, on a bad day, you can feel as if you've taken on a mountain to climb. In Spain, this is compounded by local officialdom's inordinate love of form-filling, certificates, official stamps and all forms of paperwork in general. Apparently straightforward procedures require three or four different pieces of paper, all with lots of small print, and fees that have to be paid at separate counters – many bureaucratic procedures can only be done over the counter at the relevant department, not by phone, post or, even less, online. Many departments will only have one office in each province, in the capital, so if, for example, your new home is in Ronda, having to travel to Málaga to spend a whole morning waiting in line can be seriously annoying.

Left to themselves to face the baffling demands of bureaucracy, foreign residents often wonder whether Spaniards are driven mad by having to deal with such a system all the time. The answer is, they don't. Instead, they turn to the very Spanish institution of the *gestor*, a word with no English translation since the job doesn't exist, although it could be rendered as 'administrative services'. The fundamental role of the *gestor* is to take away the burden of bureaucracy by handling things for you. You can go to *gestores* with anything and everything that might involve permits, licences, insurance or similar issues, and they will be able to explain what procedures you need to follow, and point out time- and money-saving shortcuts that you would never discover on your own. They will also have blank copies of many forms. Armed with a letter of authorisation signed by you, they can also go to present the papers at the relevant departments in your place. One standard procedure for which many foreign house-buyers use *gestores* is that of applying for Spanish residency. They can do many other useful things for you as well, such as acting as accountant, bookkeeper and small business adviser. Many Spaniards routinely use a *gestor* in all small-scale dealings with the state – such as renewing a passport – in a way that would be completely unheard-of in English-speaking countries.

A good *gestor* can be an invaluable asset, and is near-indispensable if you are working or, above all, setting up any kind of business in Spain. Regarding them as a luxury and insisting on doing everything yourself, as some expats do, is a recipe for spending much of your time feeling angry and frustrated rather than enjoying what brought you here in the first place. It is as worth building up a good, ongoing relationship with a *gestor*, to whom you can turn whenever you need a problem solving. *Gestores* are much less qualified than full lawyers, but should still have an official licence; there will be a choice of small *gestorías* (the offices of *gestores*) in any town. In areas with significant foreign communities, there will probably be several who speak English. *Gestores* are, of course, paid for their services, but fees are generally reasonable and, once you realise how much stress you've avoided, you won't begrudge the expense.

Get In Form

The application form for a residence card is in Castilian, so here is an at-a-glance guide and unofficial translation of the relevant terms.

Section 1)

• *NIE*	Foreigner's identification number
• *Datos Personales*	Personal details
• *1er Apellido*	First surname
• *2° Apellido*	Second surname, if appropriate
• *Nombre*	First name
• *Fecha de Nacimiento*	Date of birth
• *Lugar de Nacimiento*	Place of Birth
• *Sexo H/M*	Sex M/F
• *Estado Civil*	Marital status
S/C/V/D	Single/Married/Widow(er)/Divorced
• *País de Nacimiento*	Country of birth
• *País de Nacionalidad*	Current nationality
• *Nombre del Padre/de la Madre*	Father's/mother's name
• *Domicilio en España C./Pl.*	Address in Spain street/square, etc.
• *Tel.*	Telephone
• *Localidad*	City/town
• *CP*	Postal code (five digits)
• *Provincia*	Province

Section 2)

Datos del Familiar que da Derecho a la Aplicación del Régimen Comunitario: Details of the family member entitled to residency under the EU regime. It refers to children and dependants of the applicant.

• Same details as in Section 1) except for *Parentesco* (Relationship to the Applicant)

Section 3)

• *Datos Laborales*	Job details
• *Nombre o Razón Social*	Company name or registered name
• *CIF o NIF*	Company Tax Identification Code
• *Actividad de la Empresa*	Company's business

Another problem with the ruling is that everybody in Spain (Spanish or foreign) must, by law, carry some valid form of identification. Spanish citizens all carry a **DNI** (*documento nacional de identidad*). For foreigners, until recently, the residence card was sufficient for all dealings with banks, credit institutions, the administration and to show to the police on request. The ruling states that a passport or some form of official identity document is now sufficient, but since

- *Ocupación o puesto de trabajo*   Job or post held
- *Domicilio*   Address
- *Localidad*   City/town/village

Section 4)

Residencia Superior a Tres meses e Inferior a un Año:
Residence for a period greater than three months and less than a year

- *Tiempo de Duración de la*   Length of time to be spent in Spain
  Residencia en España

Section 5)

Tarjeta de Residencia Solicitada: Type of residence card applied for

- 1 *Tarjeta de Residente Comunitario (no lucrativo)*
  EU Residence Card (non-lucrative, i.e. for persons not planning to work)

- 2 *Tarjeta de Residente Comunitario (lucrativo)*
  EU Residence Card (lucrative, for persons planning to work or engage in business)

- 3 *Tarjeta de Residente Comunitario (estudiante)*
  EU Residence Card (student)

- 4 *Tarjeta de Residente Comunitario (derecho a residir con carácter permanente)*
  EU Residence Card (with right to reside permanently)

- 5 *Tarjeta de Familiar de Residente Comunitario*
  EU Family Member's Residence Card

- 6 *Trabajadores Fronterizos*
  Frontier Workers

- 7 *Renovación de Tarjeta Anterior (márquese con X el cuadro 1 al 6 que proceda)*
  Renewal of previous card (indicate, with an X in the box from 1 to 6, the card applied for)

Section 6)

Domicilio a Efectos de Notificaciones:
Address to which correspondence should be sent

UK and Irish citizens do not own identity cards, they must carry a passport as ID. Not everybody likes to do this, as losing a passport, or having it stolen, is much more traumatic (and expensive) than losing the old residence card. If you want get around this problem you can apply for a **'voluntary' residence card** (*tarjeta unificada de extranjero*, **TUE**). The process for getting it is the same as that outlined below for those who still have to apply for a residence card. It may seem strange, insisting that the authorities issue you with a document that technically you do not need, but it may save trouble in the long run.

EU Citizens Still Obliged to Obtain a Residence Card

The new ruling does not apply to everyone. 'Inactive' persons must still apply for a residence card. 'Inactive' persons are pensioners (EU or non-EU) who receive their pension from their home country, and persons of independent means. Cards are usually granted provided you can prove that you have sufficient means to live on (a pension is generally enough) and 'independent means' is understood to be an income equal to or higher than the official minimum salary. Any full EU state pension will be sufficient.

First Step: Getting Your NIE

Whether you need a residence card or not, if you live in Spain and undertake any form of work or business activity, file tax returns, etc., you must have a foreigner's identification number (*número de identificación de extranjero*, **NIE**). This also applies to non-residents such as second or holiday home-owners. The process is simple: all you have to do is go to your nearest foreigners' office or police station that deals with foreigners' affairs, take your passport and a photocopy of the important pages, fill out an application form and you will be sent your number by post. When using the number you do not need to show any document as such, just memorise it or have it copied on a slip of paper. Once this number has been obtained, you can begin the application process for a residence card if you need to (or want to). The application process is the same for non-EU citizens once they have entered the country with the correct visa.

Getting a Residence Card

Whether you are applying voluntarily or under obligation, the process is now relatively simple.

The first step is to go to your local foreigners' office, or police station that deals with foreigners' matters, and ask for an application form (*solicitud de tarjeta en régimen comunitario*) which is printed only in Castilian (*see* previous page).

This form, once completed, is then handed in along with your passport (which will be returned to you after the officials have photocopied the relevant pages), three recent passport-size colour photographs (taken against a white background) and, if expressly asked for, a health certificate.

Family members and dependants of persons who are exempt from the need to apply are also exempt, but if the head of the family is applying voluntarily then it makes sense for the whole family to get a TUE.

Dependent family members of those who do have to apply for a card are also obliged to apply. This is in any case applicable to all family members who are themselves nationals of third countries, regardless of whether their spouse, parents or guardians are exempt or not. As well as this, they must have previously obtained an entry visa in order to be in Spain. Documents accrediting the familial relationship will be asked for.

Depending on your place of residence, the card should be issued within a relatively short time or may take up to several weeks. Expect the latter in larger cities such as Madrid or Barcelona. You will be notified by post that the card has been issued and can be collected. In the meantime you are given a document stating that your application is being processed. This document *should* (though this is not always the case) serve when dealing with any official red tape.

Contacts

Contact the **Interior Ministry (t** 900 150 000) for all residency enquiries but do not expect to talk to an English-speaker. For more information, in Castilian, go to the ministry's website, **www.mir.es**, which has a complete index of foreigners' offices and police stations where residency questions are dealt with.

Residence Cards for Non-EU Citizens

While this book is aimed principally at EU citizens, non-EU readers will want to find out about the steps to be taken to obtain resident status and work legally in Spain. Here are the basic criteria which are applied.

For non-EU citizens it has become increasingly difficult to work in Spain, as they must first be offered a **contract** and then it must be shown that every effort had been made to find a qualified Spaniard or other EU citizen to fill the position. Persons with specialised knowledge or skills will, though, have fewer difficulties.

Once the contract has been offered, the process is difficult. **The paperwork** *must* **be initiated in your home country**. Even if you are in Spain when the job offer is made, you must still return to begin the process and then re-enter Spain having obtained a **residence visa** (*visado de residencia*). Only then can you begin the process of applying for a **work permit** and **residence card**. The following documents must be submitted along with the official application form:

• **a photocopy of a valid passport.**

• **a police certificate from your home city stating that you have no prison record (this must be translated into Spanish by an official translator).**

• **an official medical certificate (obtained upon arrival in Spain).**

• **three passport photographs.**

• **where applicable, documents proving why you are more capable of performing the job than a Spaniard or EU citizen.**

• **proof that you have the qualifications or training required for the job.**

The initial work permit for non-EU citizens lasts one year, the second for two, the third for three. After five years you will be granted a permanent work permit which is valid indefinitely, although it must be renewed every five years. To work as a freelancer you must demonstrate that your activity is unique and will be of benefit to the country.

To start a business, you must demonstrate that your project will contribute to developing Spain's economic, technological or employment situation. This involves supplying:

- **a project report on the business or activity to be carried out.**

- **proof that the authorisations or licences necessary for the setting up and running of the business have been applied for.**

The necessary authorisations have to be granted before the work permit can be issued. More detailed information in Castilian is to be found on the Interior Ministry's website (**www.mir.es**).

Acquiring Spanish Nationality

Given the now privileged position in which EU citizens find themselves and the wide-ranging rights enjoyed, there seems little point in taking out Spanish citizenship, as there is not really much to be gained from doing so. However, if you wish to, you *can* get Spanish nationality. Non-EU citizens may have more pressing reasons to follow the process, as obtaining residence status is tedious and a lengthy stay outside the country may mean losing it. For Americans, Canadians, Australians or New Zealanders, applying for and obtaining citizenship is an option that may prove to be a definitive solution if your aim is to stay permanently.

As this book is aimed chiefly at English-speaking readers, what follows is not a comprehensive look at all the situations in which nationality may be applied for, as the criteria depend on who you are and your origin (for historical reasons, citizens of Latin American countries and other former Spanish possessions can obtain citizenship more easily than people from Anglophone countries).

All foreigners who have resided for 10 years in Spain may apply. This is reduced to just one year in the following cases: those born within Spanish territory (i.e. children of residents); those born outside Spain but who can accredit to having one Spanish parent or grandparent; persons who are married (including by common law) to a Spanish citizen and who are not legally separated; widows or widowers whose spouse was Spanish and who were not separated from them at the time of their death. Applications may also be made by anybody who has been legally the ward of or adopted by a Spanish person, or who has been in the care of a Spanish institution.

'Residence', effectively, is taken to mean legal, unbroken (i.e. without any period of residence in another country) presence continuing up to the date of

Case Study: Gwyneth Box the Entrepreneur

After living in California and teaching English to illegal Mexican immigrants, Gwyneth Box decided she'd like to travel in Latin America. She decided to come first to Spain to learn the language before travelling. Fifteen years on she is running Tantamount – a small bilingual graphic design, web and editorial company – with her Argentinian partner.

What did you do when you first got to Spain?

I came over armed with the RSA Prep. Certificate and an English-teaching contract. That's probably still the easiest way to make the move unless you are certain of what you want to do and how to go about it. As an English teacher you can usually devote part of your flexible time to following leads in your other chosen area.

How did you end up starting your own business?

I met my partner here and it became apparent that my programming and systems analysis experience could complement his graphic design and publishing skills. There was even room in the arrangement for me to develop my interest in writing and translation. So I reduced my class hours and dedicated more time to the work which Tantamount was to do. I then went freelance, which gave me better control over my schedule. Even so, it took nearly 10 years before I dared abandon teaching and a regular salary.

How do you find dealing with the red tape in Spain? Has it got any easier?

It helps having experience in general office administration and payroll. I file the receipts, monitor the bank accounts and talk to bank managers. But, even with 15 years of Spanish, I still feel at a disadvantage when dealing with *funcionarios*. Fortunately, I have an *asesora* who does the company paperwork and takes care of the official side of the accounts. She also dealt with all the details of setting up the company for us. I have attended a couple of (free) courses for entrepreneurs run by the Madrid local council, which has helped me understand the jargon, but I still prefer to rely on a native speaker to deal with officialdom.

How are things going?

I never intended to stay in Spain, nor to run my own company; it just happened as a natural progression of what I was doing. We are coming up to the end of the second year of trading and are content with the company's performance. I have yet to reach South America.

the application for citizenship. Application may be made by the interested party, or on their behalf in the case of minors or persons who are in some way incapacitated.

Applications must be made to the local Civil Registry and, as might be expected, endless documents are needed: in general:

• an application form to the Ministry of Justice.

• a certificate of prison record (*certificado de antecedentes penales*) issued by the Spanish Ministry of Justice; effectively this is certification that the applicant has not spent time in prison and has no criminal record.

Case Study: Brendan Murphy, the Pub Manager

Brendan Murphy, 50, left his job as a commercial artist in Dublin and moved to Madrid in 1984 with little money and even less Spanish. Initially, he hoped to work in advertising, but with no Spanish and no papers he turned to English teaching, for which he had no training or experience. Answering an advertisement, he found himself facing an old school friend, the director of the school. He was promised work pending completion of a training course. Brendan eventually entered the Irish bar business and currently co-manages the largest Irish bar in Madrid.

How far have you integrated into Spanish life and how much connection do you have with the expat community?

Settling into Spanish life and making friends takes time but I got to know a lot of interesting people, some quite well, through TEFL (teaching English). Expats were usually business people, who kept to themselves and considered the English-teaching community as wandering bohemians. With the advent of the Irish bar this changed somewhat. With the opening up of Spanish markets and the arrival of multinationals, a lot more people found themselves living in Madrid with no local knowledge. Irish bars filled this gap.

How do you find dealing with red tape in Spain? Has it got any easier?

A bureaucratic attitude pervades Spanish life. These days I only have to do basic paperwork, but early on I could have used a course in the processes of getting a medical card, ID, car documents, etc., because if you don't know you find it can take days to get the simplest piece of paper (the Civil Service shuts at 2pm). All of this pales into insignificance when faced with the public health service: a simple thing like a blood test can take several visits and about three weeks, and woe betide you if they find anything wrong because the consultant side of things can take months, even before a diagnosis!

How has Spain changed, for better or worse, since you first arrived?

I arrived as *la Movida* was petering out and there was a great feeling of liberty. Madrid had a provincial air to it, which you still find, thankfully. Accession to the EU has brought improvements in infrastructures and a lot of urban renewal. Another interesting change due to Spain's new wealth has been an increase in immigrants, from South America, Eastern Europe, China, Africa, etc. Some districts now have an ethnic flavour and new shops catering to different peoples – it improves the spice rack! Considering how quickly this has happened, I think the Spanish have adapted quite well.

• a birth certificate, original copy, accompanied by a sworn translation if the original is not in Castilian.

• a certificate of prison record from the applicant's country of origin; if this cannot be obtained, a document from the consulate attesting to good conduct should suffice.

• a certificate of registration (*certificado de empadronamiento*) from the applicant's municipality.

• certification of unbroken residence from the police, accrediting the time the applicant has lived legally in Spain.

• proof of means of subsistence (pay slips, tax declarations, savings, etc.).

• original and photocopies of the current residence card and NIE.

• photocopy of the relevant pages of the passport.

• birth certificate(s) of parent(s) and/or grandparent(s) in the case of having been born outside of Spain but claiming Spanish origin.

• a marriage certificate proving matrimony to a Spaniard or, in the case of common-law couples, a joint certificate of registration in the municipality and the spouse's birth certificate.

• a marriage and death certificate in the case of widows and widowers formerly married to Spaniards, as well as the deceased's birth certificate.

Once the application and documents have been handed in, the applicant is cited to appear before the judge in charge of the local Civil Registry. The judge will interview the applicant in order to ascertain the applicant's adaptation to Spanish culture and way of life. In the case of those married to a Spaniard, the spouse will be cited also. A decision will then be made on whether or not citizenship is to be granted. Successful applicants must, within 180 days of the decision being made, swear loyalty to the Spanish king and obedience to the constitution as well as giving up their previous nationality.

Useful Addresses

Spanish Embassies and Consulates in the UK and Republic of Ireland

Spanish Embassy: United Kingdom
39 Chesham Place, London SW1X 8SB
t (020) 7235 5555
f (020) 7259 5392
embespuk@mail.mae.es
http://spain.embassyhomepage.com

Spanish Consulate General: London
20 Draycott Place, London SW3 2RZ
t (020) 7589 8989
f (020) 7581 7888
conspalon@mail.mae.es

Spanish Consulate: Manchester
Suite 1A, Brook House, 70 Spring Gardens, Manchester M2 2BQ
t (0161) 236 1233
f (0161) 228 7467
conspmanchester@mail.mae.es.

Spanish Consulate: Edinburgh
63 North Castle Street, Edinburgh EH2 3LJ
t (0131) 220 1843
f (0131) 226 4568
cgspedimburgo@mail.mae.es

Spanish Embassy: Ireland
17 Merlyn Park, Ballsbridge, Dublin 4, Republic of Ireland
t (01) 269 1640
f (01) 269 1854
www.mae.es/Embajadas/Dublin/es/home

Spanish Embassies and Consulates in Other Countries

Spanish Embassy: Washington, USA
2375 Pennsylvania Avenue N.W., Washington, D.C. 20037-1736
t (202) 452 0100
f (202) 833 5670
embespus@mail.mae.es
spain@spainemb.org
www.spainemb.org/ingles/indexing.htm
www.mae.es/embajadas/washington/es/home

Spanish Embassy: Ottawa, Canada
74, Stanley Avenue, Ottawa, ON K1M 1P4
t (613) 747 2252/7293
f (613) 744 1224
embespca@mail.mae.es
www.docuweb.ca/SpainInCanada
www.embaspain.ca

Spanish Embassy: Toronto, Canada
Simcoe Place, 200 Front Street West Oficina 2401
P.O.Box 15, Toronto, ON M5V 3K2
t (416) 977 1661/3923/4075/4705
f (416) 593 4949
cgspain.toronto@mail.mae.es

Spanish Consulate: Melbourne, Australia
146A. Elgin St, PO Box 1119, Carlton, Victoria 3053
t (03) 9347 1966/1997
f (03) 9347 7330
conspmel@mail.mae.es

Spanish Consulate: Sydney, Australia
Level 24, St. Martins Tower, 31 Market Street, Sydney, New South Wales 2000
t (02) 9261 2433/2443/1321
f (02) 9283 1695
cgspainsydney@mail.mae.es
consulspain@smartchat.net.au

Spanish Embassy: Canberra, Australia
15, Arkana St, Yarralumla. ACT 2600
or PO Box 9076, Deakin, ACT 2600
t (02) 6273 35 55
f (02) 6273 39 18

United Kingdom Embassy and Consulates in Spain
British Embassy in Madrid
C/ Fernando el Santo 16, 28010 Madrid
t 915 249 700
f 915 249 730
madridconsulate@fco.gov.uk
www.ukinspain.com

For a full listing of British consulates in Spain, see **www.ukinspain.com**.

Republic of Ireland Embassy and Consulates in Spain
Embassy of Ireland
Ireland House, Paseo de la Castellana 46, 4°, 28046 Madrid
t 914 634 093
f 914 351 677
embajada@irlanda.es

Honorary Vice-Consul: Barcelona
Gran Vía Carlos III 94, 08028 Barcelona
t 934 919 021
f 934 900 986

Other Foreign Embassies and Consulates in Spain

Australian Embassy
Plaza del Descubridor Diego de Ordas 3, 28003 Madrid
t 913 536 600
f 913 536 692
www.spain.embassy.gov.au

Canadian Embassy
C/ Núñez de Balboa 35, 28001 Madrid
t 914 233 250
f 914 233 251
www.canada-es.org

New Zealand Embassy
Pinar 7, 3rd floor; 28006 Madrid
t 915 230 226
f 915 230 171
embnuevazelanda@telefonica.net
www.nzembassy.com/home.cfm?c=27

US Embassy
C/ Serrano 75, 28006 Madrid
t 915 872 200
f 915 872 303
www.embusa.es

Living in Spain

Spain's integration into the EU has made moving there to live and work much easier. Bureaucratic restrictions have eased to the extent that many EU citizens no longer even need apply for residency. With cheap travel options available, a new phenomenon has developed: Spain-residing, UK-working commuters. An increasing number of professionals choose to live in Spain, fly home and work for a few days and then return to their Mediterranean homes at weekends. Many who do so find the cost and time involved is not significantly greater than, say, living in Norfolk and working in London. Still more people are choosing to relocate permanently, to work or retire.

So many northern Europeans now regularly visit Spain that the country is much less of an unknown quantity. But still it remains different, with its own way of doing things. If you are thinking of relocating, there are many aspects of living in Spain, both cultural and practical, that you should be aware of, to help you enjoy the best that the country has to offer. The following sections offer some important pointers on settling in.

Learning Spanish

There are many powerful arguments in favour of learning the language of any country in which you hope to live and work. In Spain there are three co-official languages apart from 'Spanish' (more accurately referred to as Castilian): Catalan, Galician and Basque. In an area where another language is spoken, it is advisable to be able to communicate in both Castilian and that one too, since this is likely to be the locals' first language (see pp.21–8).

Unless you work in a completely English-speaking environment, you cannot expect to get ahead in the workplace without speaking Spanish, but equally there are many other aspects of daily life for which speaking in the local language is vitally important – getting a drink, ordering a meal, having a medical check-up or a haircut or dealing with repair people. In emergencies it may even be critical. Without some knowledge of the local language, your social life could also be very restricted, unless of course it is limited to socialising exclusively with fellow expats. On the other hand, speaking the language (however clumsily) will earn you the respect of the locals as it shows courtesy and a commitment to the community in which you've settled.

Getting Started

You can begin learning the language before setting off or once there, but arriving with a certain level of fluency will get you off to a good start. In the UK and Ireland there are many options for studying Castilian, a popular language nowadays, but fewer for Catalan, Basque or Galician. If you look hard, though, you will find a centre where they are taught.

Attending Classes

The classic way of learning a language is to attend a course, either at evening classes in the local further education college or at a private institution. Evening classes are generally inexpensive, usually coincide with the academic year and may be aimed at students hoping to take GCSE or A Levels. There may also be less structured, conversation-based classes. These can range from 'survival' level to groups for advanced speakers. It is best to do some structured learning before embarking on a conversation course.

To find out about courses, contact your local education authority or FE college, or look in the *Yellow Pages* to find a private school. Private courses usually cost more than local authority-run evening classes. Most levels, from beginners to advanced, are catered for, though demand often determines what is available at any given time. For a price, some schools may tailor courses to your specific needs. Many schools are small, local outfits which may offer just what you need, but there are also several large language-teaching organisations that offer courses in Castilian Spanish in the UK and Spain:

- **Berlitz; www.berlitz.co.uk.** Centres in Birmingham, Brighton, Bristol, Edinburgh, London, Manchester and Oxford.
- **Inlingua**, Rodney Lodge, Rodney Road, Cheltenham GL50 1HX, **t** (01242) 250493, **f** (01242) 250495; **www.inlingua-cheltenham.co.uk**
- **Cactus Language; www.cactuslanguage.com.** Lets you select courses by place, level and duration all over the Spanish-speaking world but in ten UK cities too.

Self- and Online Study

You can also learn through self-study. Methods usually consist of a course book and cassettes or CDs for listening and pronunciation, and nowadays increasingly incorporate videos and/or CD-ROMs for interactive practice.

Much self-study is done via online courses. Look at **www.spanishlanguage. co.uk/online.htm** for a list of such courses. The BBC offers some good courses on its website (**www.bbc.co.uk/languages/spanish**). 'Spanish Steps' is a self-contained introductory course, and 'Talk Spanish' is a lively topic-based course also aimed at beginners. *'Sueños'*, a second course, builds on the language acquired in 'Talk Spanish'. All these courses come with accompanying materials, books, cassettes or CDs.

Private Teachers, Language Exchanges and Language Clubs

You could also hire a private teacher, but expect to pay £15–30 per hour depending on his or her experience and qualifications. Language exchanges with locally based speakers of the language, who wish to learn English or improve their level, provide a cheaper alternative, as well as a good way of

With Friends Like These, Who Needs Enemies?

Castilian Spanish has many cognates which look like English words and mean much the same. For example, during the *transición* from Franco's *dictadura* to the current *democracia*, complete with *elecciones*, Spain drew up a *constitución* which offers all its citizens the *garantía* of certain basic *libertades*. Easy, isn't it? To a certain point. Many words can catch you out, though. Despite looking like an equivalent English word, they mean something completely different and are what linguists call 'false friends'. Used incorrectly, they can cause misunderstanding or embarrassment. Some common ones are:

Actual/actualmente: Adjective and adverb referring to things which are **current, at the present time.** The English sense of 'actual' is *real* or *verdadero*.

Aplicar/aplicación: You do not *aplicar* for a job, you *solicitar* it or send in a *solicitud*. *Aplicar* does mean apply if you are talking about a theory or a cream for mosquito bites.

Asistir: This verb means **to attend**, a meeting or a football match. *Atender* is the verb for to serve, take care of or attend to customers or problems. To assist/help is *ayudar*.

Carpeta: Not something from Persia or Axminster but a **file or folder** in which you carry documents. Also applies to computers. A carpet is an *alfombra*.

Constiparse/Constipado: Also written **costiparse** and **costipado**, the verb means **to catch a cold**, the noun is a **cold**. If you are constipated, you are *estreñido*.

Contestar: Means **to answer** (a question, the telephone). If you wish to contest an allegation or a decision, you *protestar*.

making friends. To find a private teacher or someone for an exchange, try advertising in the local press or putting up a notice in a local college, corner shop or online. Local language clubs can also be informal, friendly and inexpensive, and again are best sought out locally.

Useful Contacts

The **Instituto Cervantes** (**www.cervantes.es**), a government-backed institution promoting Spanish language and culture abroad, offers a range of courses throughout the year. The Instituto may also provide information on courses elsewhere, and the noticeboards usually have lots of useful ads from private teachers, conversation clubs, or possible exchange contacts.

• **London:** 102 Eaton Square, London SW1W 9AN, **t** (020) 7235 0353, **f** (020) 7235 0329; **www.londres.cervantes.es**.

• **Manchester:** 326/330 Deansgate, Campfield Avenue Arcade, Manchester M3 4FN , **t** (0161) 661 4200, **f** (0161) 661 4203; **www.manchester.cervantes.es**.

• **Leeds:** 169 Woodhouse Lane, Leeds LS2 3AR, **t** (0113) 246 1741, **f** (0113) 246 1023; **www.leeds.cervantes.es**.

Decepción: Is not deception but **disappointment**. To deceive someone is *engañar*; advertising may be *engañosa*.

Desgracia: Is a **misfortune**, something disgraceful is *una vergüenza*.

Disgusto: Means **displeasure** or an **upset**. Something disgusting is *asqueroso*.

Embarazada/Embarazo: Means **pregnant/pregnancy**. Embarrassment or feeling embarrassed is expressed by *vergüenza* or feeling *avergonzado*.

En absoluto: Actually means **absolutely not!**

Ilusión: Usually means **hope** or a feeling of **expectation**.

Introducir: Can mean **to introduce** in the sense of to begin as in new laws, but also means to put something (like a diskette) in a slot. To introduce people, use the verb *presentar*.

Molestar: No sexual connotations here, this means **to bother** or **to annoy**.

Preservativo: A **condom**; preservatives, in foodstuffs, are *conservantes*.

Pretender: This verb means **to try/aim for/aspire to**. To pretend, say *fingir* or *simular*.

Realizar: Means to **carry out/make something real** (a plan or project). To realise something (mentally) is *darse cuenta de...*

Recordar: Means **to remember** or **to remind**. To record on a cassette or paper, use *grabar* or *anotar* respectively.

Sano: Means **healthy physically**; somebody who is sane is *cuerdo*.

Sensible: Is **sensitive**. Somebody sensible is *sensato* or *razonable*.

Sopa: **Soup**, not soap, which is *jabón*.

Suceso: An **event**, a **happening**. Success is *éxito*. The exit is *la salida*.

- **Dublin**: Lincoln House, Lincoln Place, Dublín 2, t (01) 631 1500, f (01) 631 1599; **www.dublin.cervantes.es**.

Also useful for London-based students is the **Hispanic and Luso–Brazilian Council** (**www.canninghouse.com**). This organisation runs classes and provides information on where to study Castilian in London, other UK cities and in Spain.

Learning in Spain

Whether or not you begin learning before moving to Spain, there are many options available once you get there. Information about schools and courses is available both from the Instituto Cervantes and Canning House (*see* above). Otherwise, look in the *Yellow Pages* under *academias de idiomas*. There are literally dozens in the larger cities, and plenty to choose from in areas with a large concentration of expats. English-language publications carry advertisements for language institutions, mainly in Barcelona or Madrid.

The **Escuela Oficial de Idiomas (EOI)**, the Official Language School, is cheaper than private schools and has centres throughout Spain. EOIs are now run by the Autonomous Communities but the central school at Calle Jesús Maestro, s/n,

28003 Madrid (**www.eoidiomas.com**), will provide information about all regional schools. The UK-based Open University also offers structured courses in Castilian, either as part of a degree or just for personal satisfaction (OU co-ordinator in Madrid, Calle Serrano 26, 3º, 28001 Madrid, t 915 777 701).

Whether you are studying Castilian, Catalan, Galician or Basque, and whatever method you choose, it is important to be patient and accept that you will make mistakes. Do not aim for perfection from the word go but immerse yourself in the language, surround yourself with it, put yourself into situations where you are exposed to it and have to use it. Watch the TV – news programmes with topics you know about are very useful – read newspapers, listen to the radio, chat to your neighbours. Above all – do not be afraid!

Spain's Other Languages

While both Catalan and Galician have much in common with Castilian, they are languages in their own right, not dialects. Basque, unrelated to any other Indo-European language, is another story. No previous language-learning experience will help you here. *See* pp.21–8.

Catalan (*Català*)

Catalan language and literature may be studied in many UK universities, generally in a sub-department of the Spanish or Hispanic Studies departments. Contact the relevant department at your nearest university.

In Catalonia itself, many are options available. The **Escuela Oficial de Idiomas** (*see* above) offers Catalan throughout the whole of Spain, and in Catalonia is called (in Catalan, naturally) **La Escola Oficial d'Idiomes**. The main branch is at Avinguda Drassanes s/n, t 933 292 458. Alternatively, go to the **Centres de Normalització Lingüística**, central office, Carrer Pau Claris 162, t 932 723 100. It is cheap, covers all levels and offers intensive summer courses. Many private language schools also offer courses.

Galician (*Galego*)

Opportunities for studying Galician outside Galicia are scarce. Some UK universities do have Galician lecturers within the Hispanic Studies depart-ments. Contact the Hispanic Studies Department at the **University of Birmingham** (**www.hispanic.bham.ac.uk/GalicianStudies**) which can also facil-itate Galician links elsewhere.

Courses are offered at the **Escuela Oficial de Idiomas** all over Spain and in Galicia. The main branch is at Calle Pepín Rivero, s/n, 15011 A Coruña, t 981 279 100; **http://centros.edu.xunta.es/eoicoruna/index.htm**. At the **Universidade de Santiago de Compostela** is the Departamento de Filoloxía Galega, Avenida de Castelao s/n, 15705 Santiago de Compostela; **www.usc.es/fgsec/doc/xeral.html**.

Basque (*Euskera*)

Basque is not taught widely outside Euskadi but if you live in Erresuma Batua ('Great Britain' in Basque), however, contact the Institute of Basque Studies within the Department of Languages, **London Guildhall University** (**ibsqueries@euskalerria.org**). There is also the Basque Association Abroad, the **Basque Society** (Euskal Elkartea), Oxford House, Derbyshire Street, Bethnal Green Town, London E2 6HD, **t** (020) 7739 7339, **f** (020) 7739 0435; **london@euskaledge.fsnet.co.uk**.

Courses in Basque are offered at **Escuelas Oficiales de Idiomas** throughout Spain – in Euskadi itself there is one in every province. In the Basque capital the address is Calle Nieves Cano 18, 01006 Vitoria, **t** 945 138 760. Online Euskera resources can be found at **www.euskara.euskadi.net**.

Finding a Home

Renting a House or Flat

There are many good reasons to rent a home instead of buying one, at least initially. If you are not sure that your stay is indefinite, then renting is certainly a sensible option. Even if you do not intend to leave, you will usually have to spend some time in rented accommodation before committing yourself to buying a property.

Finding rental accommodation in Spain is not much different from looking elsewhere, though there are some things to bear in mind. Spain has the smallest rental market in Europe; only about 13 per cent of all housing stock is rented compared with an average of 40 per cent across the continent. Spaniards prefer to buy and consequently the housing market has gone mad. Property prices have spiralled and this is reflected in the cost of renting; *see* 'How Much to Pay?', pp.136–8.

The most common search method is through the **print media**, or their online versions. It helps to be *au fait* with the language of adverts (*see* 'Housing Jargon', pp.134–5). *Segundamano* is a classifieds magazine published three times weekly (similar to *Exchange and Mart*). Although published in Madrid and sold only in central Spain, *Segundamano* does have property ads for the whole country, organised by Autonomous Communities and price band. The online version for rentals all over Spain is **www.segundamano.es**. The same publishing group also distributes two freesheets in Catalonia, *Claxon* and *Revenda*. The major dailies also have classified property ads. There are some English-language publications offering flatshares (often from Spanish people looking for an English-speaker) or you can advertise there yourself. For some of the major English-language publications, *see* **Spain Today**, 'Major Media', pp.68–9.

Case Study: Frances Sullivan

Frances Sullivan, 39, from London, a graduate in English Literature from London University, came to Barcelona six years ago. She works as a freelance journalist for British and American publications.

How did you sort out accommodation when you first arrived?

I stayed in a friend's flat until we were booted out, then an overpriced room in a shared flat, followed by an overpriced 'flatlet' from the newspaper. Eventually we bought somewhere – which worked out cheaper than renting.

How did you find your first job? Was it easy?

I already had work and contacts set up from the UK.

How do you find working here compares with working at home?

Difficult to answer as a freelance. Tax and social security conditions are not brilliant for *autonómos*.

The pros and cons of working and living here?

It's a beautiful city, small, manageable but with lots going on. Unlike London there are no great distances to travel, and public transport is cheaper and more efficient, so social life tends to be more spontaneous. The climate makes life more fun for more of the year.

How did you find dealing with red tape?

Not always as bad as the rumours say. To get an NIE is actually very quick and straightforward. With this, everything becomes easier.

Agencies (*agencias inmobiliarias*) are to be found on practically every major street. They charge a fee, usually a month's rent on whatever acceptable property they find you. (This is in addition to any deposit payable to the landlord.) Most agencies specialise in buying and selling property. Rentals may represent only a small percentage of their work, and not all provide as good a service as they claim, so talk to people who have used their services. Above all, do not let yourself be bullied into accepting anything you're not completely satisfied with.

Those with time to spare may prefer to **search independently**, pounding the streets looking for '*se alquila piso/apartamento*' signs. This can produce results, especially since many landlords who advertise this way include razón portería (contact the caretaker) in the advertising poster, which means you can view the flat without making an appointment. If you choose this method, go armed with patience, pre-prepared questions if your language skills are not too good, and a comfortable pair of shoes!

Word of mouth can also be useful. Once you get to know people, this is probably the most reliable and least stressful way of finding somewhere to rent. If for example you are taking a job at a company or in a language school, you may

Do you live mainly in the expat community or have you integrated? Or is your life a bit of both?
We spend more time among *guiris* (the affectionate term for foreigners) for a couple of reasons – not only the shared cultural backgrounds (I can make a Brit laugh, but when I make a Catalan laugh it's generally by accident), but also because of shared immigrant status. I probably know as many South Americans as I do Spaniards. Catalans have generally lived in the city all their lives, so they already have a solid circle of friends, most of whom they've known since childhood. It's not easy to break into that.

How did you go about learning the language?
I already spoke a reasonable level of Spanish. I make occasional ineffectual attempts to have *intercambios* with Spanish-speaking friends. For Catalan, the Generalitat runs free or dirt-cheap Catalan courses, which are a good introduction. You need a bit of both here.

How do you find the prices?
Barcelona is more expensive than other Spanish cities (including Madrid, I think), and becoming more so. Accommodation is still comparatively cheap for Brits or Americans, however.

Any tips for would-be residents?
Try and get some work set up before you arrive and approach companies from your own country. Be aware that the working methods of Spanish companies can seem very hierarchical, with less regard for workers' rights than at home. But the holidays are great!

well get better results through your new colleagues than through more traditional channels.

However you choose to look, certain times of the year are better than others. Spring to early summer is good, since many students leave rented accommodation to go home for the summer. August can be tough, as many landlords are on holiday. September is worse as the students flock back. Christmas and New Year can also be a slow period.

When viewing flats, have your 'spiel' ready if you are not yet confident in the language. If your level is really basic, take someone along to do the talking. You may have to be more convincing than locals if you are a foreigner, as some landlords are wary of renting to *extranjeros*. Remember to dress well and appear trustworthy. It also helps to have some cash ready to put down as a **partial deposit** (*seña*) if the property is just what you are looking for. This is common practice and avoids the landlord letting to the next person who comes along. It need not be a full month's rent and will be deducted from the actual full deposit paid on signing the lease. Do not be rushed into renting the first thing you see; rather have a clear idea of what you are looking for and when you see it, grab it!

Housing Jargon

Frequently employed abbreviations, as often seen in classified ads, are in brackets after the full word.

a estrenar	brand new
aire acondicionado (a/a)	air-conditioning
alquilar/se alquila	to rent/for rent
(el) alquiler	(the) rent (i.e. what you pay)
amueblado	furnished
armario empotrado	built-in wardrobes
ascensor	lift/elevator
aseo	small bathroom usually with just a toilet and washbasin
ático	roof or attic apartment/flat
aval or *aval bancario*	bank guarantee equivalent to a letter of credit
bajo	ground floor apartment
balcón	balcony
baño completo	full bathroom
bien comunicado	well located for public transport
buhardilla	loft or attic apartment, usually with sloping ceilings
calefacción central (c/c)	central heating
calle (c/)	street
chimenea	fireplace
cocina americana	integrated kitchen (generally in an open-plan kitchen-diner-cum-living room)
cocina amueblada	kitchen complete with pots, pans, utensils, etc.
cocina independiente	separate kitchen (from the living room)
(gastos de) comunidad	community expenses such as rubbish collection or cleaning of common areas (stairwells, lobby, etc.) that may or may not be included in the monthly rent
dormitorio	bedroom
dúplex	maisonette (duplex apartment in US English)
electrodomésticos	kitchen appliances, e.g. fridge, microwave, food mixer
entresuelo	mezzanine
estudio	studio apartment

exterior (ext)	exterior (i.e. looking on to the street)
fianza	deposit paid to landlord (usually one or two months' rent)
garantías	guarantees (financial)
gas ciudad/natura	piped gas (many apartments do not have this, using bottled butane – butano – gas instead)
habitación (hab)	room (can also mean bedroom)
hall	hallway
hipoteca	mortgage
interior (int)	looking on to an interior patio
luminoso	bright, with lots of sunlight
luz	electricity (literally 'light')
moqueta	wall-to-wall/fitted carpet
nómina	salary/wage slip (often required by landlords as proof of steady income)
office	utility room (usually attached to kitchen)
parabólica	connected to satellite dish for TV
parqué/parquet	parquet flooring
piso	apartment or flat
planta	floor
plaza de garaje	garage parking spot
portero/a/conserje (físico)	concierge or caretaker, man or woman who takes care of the building
portero automático	automatic door
puerta blindada	reinforced/security door
razón portería/portero	contact the concierge/caretaker
reformado	renovated/'done up'
salón	living room
salón-comedor	living room–diner
semi amueblado	partially furnished
sin muebles	unfurnished
soleado	sunny, with lots of sunlight
sótano	basement apartment
suelo	floor
terraza (acristalada)	terrace (glazed/glassed over)
trastero	storage room
vacío	empty/unfurnished
vender/se vende	to sell/for sale
vistas	views

How Much to Pay?

In major cities like Madrid or Barcelona, you will not find anything with one or two bedrooms worth renting for less than €700 a month, and you could pay considerably more for something bigger or better. Expect to pay upwards of €1,200 for something big, nicely furnished, with three or four bedrooms and close to amenities. For a room in a shared flat, expect to pay a minimum of €300 a month. In cities such as Valencia, Seville or Málaga you will get a lot more for your money.

Once you have found suitable accommodation, you must enter into a contractual agreement with the landlord. Verbal contracts are still valid in Spain but are not advisable. The more that is stated in writing, the more chance you have of redress in case of dispute.

There are two basic types of **tenancy agreement** (*contrato de alquiler* or, in Catalan, *contracte de lloguer*) in Spain – *por temporada*, or seasonal, which covers all holiday lets, and *de vivienda* or long-term. A *por temporada* contract can have a maximum validity of one year, although most are for much less than that, with no automatic right of extension for the tenant. Most, but not all, properties let this way are furnished, and the contract should include a detailed inventory of contents. Contracts *de vivienda*, on the other hand, are initially valid for one year, often with an option to extend for further periods, by mutual agreement, after the first year. Leases for up to five years' duration are not unknown but you would need to be sure that you want to stay in the property for such a lengthy period. During this time the rent can only be raised in line with the official national inflation index.

The lease should be **registered** with the local housing authorities. If not, there is little chance of either the tenant's or the landlord's rights being guaranteed should there be any dispute. Some landlords prefer not to register leases, especially when renting to foreigners – not wanting to pay tax on the rental income. The tenant, in this case, cannot claim tax relief on rent paid. In resort areas, landlords often struggle hard not to give *de vivienda* contracts, even if you have been in residence for several months, in order to avoid conceding any permanent rights and so losing the option of getting you out for the summer and letting the property at higher rates in the peak holiday season. They may well prefer just to give successive *por temporada* contracts.

The agreement may state who is responsible for **repairs**. It is reasonable to insist on a clause making the landlord pay for structural repairs such as wiring and plumbing. On the other hand, the landlord can reasonably expect the tenant to pay for or replace damaged furnishings or fittings, though it is sometimes a fine line between what constitutes wear and tear and what is damage caused by carelessness or misuse. If the landlord refuses to pay for repairs of any kind, you may prefer to look elsewhere or protect yourself by taking out an insurance policy. However, make sure you know what the insurance company will pay for, otherwise you could be faced with expensive repairs only to find they are excluded by some clause buried in the small print.

Be certain from the outset whether or not the rent includes **utility expenses** and **community fees** (*gastos de comunidad*). This will depend on the landlord and the terms of the lease. Community fees usually cover the costs of the doorman, general maintenance of communal areas such as the entrance hall, stairwells and lifts, and services such as rubbish collection. One or more of the utilities may also be covered by the rent. But do not expect the landlord to pay your telephone bill! Heating, if you have to pay for it individually, can be quite expensive. With regard to the *comunidad de propietarios*, no matter how long you occupy a flat it is your landlord, not you, who is a member of the *comunidad* and gets officially informed of meetings. How much you are kept informed of decisions that might affect you in, say, an apartment block depends to a great extent on how good your relations are with your landlord and with your owner-occupier neighbours .

Another point to look out for in rental contracts are any clauses requiring the tenant to pay **local taxes**. Such clauses are illegal, and should be queried immediately: in law, any taxes paid by the tenant should be included in the rent, not added as an extra.

Rent in Spain is always **paid monthly**, and **in advance**, so you have to pay your first month's rent before you enter the property. Current tenancy law lays down the basic structure of rental contracts but it does not stipulate their every detail, which can vary a great deal. This is another area where you need to check things over with your lawyer and make sure you understand what you are agreeing to before you sign. One feature of all Spanish tenancies is that when you first sign the contract, in addition to the first month's rent you will be required to hand over a **deposit** (*depósito* or *fianza*), normally equivalent to one month's rent in unfurnished properties and two months' in furnished ones. This is meant to cover the landlord against any damage or breakages that occur during your stay and, unless you have caused serious problems, is returnable when you leave. By law you can now insist that this be held by an official body (there are different ones for each region and sometimes province), rather than passed directly to the landlord, although many landlords will resist this strongly.

Deposits are a long-standing bone of contention between landlords and tenants in Spain. There are countless stories of landlords finding spurious reasons for not paying back a deposit, while many tenants, who resent paying what is in effect an extra month's rent for nothing in the first place, simply refuse to pay the last month's rent when they decide to leave, rather than haggle over a refund. Yet most rental contracts state that the deposit may not be used to pay for the final month or two's rent. It is generally better to sort this out beforehand and to leave a rented property on good terms with the landlord. Non-return of deposits is far less of a problem, though, with short-term lets, although a landlord may deduct a small amount for breakages.

If either landlord or tenant wishes to **terminate** a rental contract before its full term, they have to do so in writing by notarised letter with good notice, usually at least two months. Read the lease very carefully. Do not sign it until every item is absolutely clear. If your language skills are weak, ask someone with good knowledge of the local language to help you. Leases are usually couched in 'legalese' and can be quite incomprehensible. If it includes an **inventory** of household items, make sure everything listed is really there. Check that all electrical appliances and utilities are actually working. Never accept a verbal guarantee that defective items will be fixed later. Get it written into the contract or make sure it is done before you sign.

In addition to the deposit, many landlords now ask for some **guarantee** of their prospective tenant's financial standing. Recent changes in the law have tended to protect tenants rather than the landlord, meaning that it is not unknown for individuals to rent a property, stop paying and then live rent-free for several months until an eviction order is finally issued. To protect themselves, many landlords ask for proof of a regular salary, by means of a wage/salary slip (nómina), and even a bank guarantee equivalent to a letter of credit (aval bancario) may be required. This can be difficult to obtain, especially if you are a foreigner (*see* Fiona Chapman's case study, p.159). For all questions concerning rental law, David Searl's *You and the Law in Spain*, published by Santana Books, is highly recommended. He is also good on property purchases, tax and other legal issues that affect foreigners.

Buying a House or Flat

The Spanish property market has enjoyed a remarkable boom, particularly in certain areas, with prices rising more than in any other country in the world over the past 25 years. This may seem strange when other statistics, such as high unemployment and low wages, are considered, but many middle-class Spanish families typically spend 30–50 per cent of their income on housing. Some predict that the bubble will burst and that prices will soon fall. A federation of savings banks has even predicted that negative equity might one day affect property in certain regions, such as Castilla-La Mancha, Extremadura and Galicia. However, it is unlikely that in prosperous regions like Madrid, Catalonia and the Mediterranean coast property values will drop to the levels of five or even two years ago. It is a more likely scenario that prices will level off over the next few years.

Meanwhile, building continues apace. Both in the Mediterranean coastal regions and in the major cities, cranes are as much a part of the skyline as church spires or the shining tower blocks of financial institutions.

Mortgage rates are at an all-time low (below five per cent) and are not predicted to go up too much in the foreseeable future. At the moment, the situation might be described as a buoyant sellers' market. A few years ago it was fairly simple to look around, see a few properties and then ponder which to buy. Today someone doing this could well find that the house they wanted to make an offer on had sold to someone else in the few days after they saw it.

Finding a place to buy is not unlike looking for somewhere to rent, in the sense that you can use print media, agents, online resources, word of mouth and other channels. The essential difference is that, when renting, a lease need only be for a limited time: you can start again if you are not happy with the accommodation. Buying property obviously entails more commitment.

Buying a property in Spain is as safe as buying a property in England. On reading this section – which must explain the potential pitfalls if it is to serve any useful purpose – it can seem a frightening or dangerous experience. But the same or similar dangers arise when buying a house in England, and you do not worry about those dangers because you are familiar with them and, more importantly, because you are shielded against contact with most of them by your solicitor. The same should be true when buying in Spain.

The system of buying and selling property in Spain is, not surprisingly, different from the system of buying property in England or Scotland. On balance, neither better nor worse – just different. Yet, it has many superficial similarities, which can lull you into a false sense of familiarity and overconfidence. The most important thing to remember is to take the right professional advice and precautions when doing so.

The sections that follow are necessarily, for reasons of space, just basic pointers to the house-buying maze and cannot in any way be considered a substitute for sound professional advice. There are plenty of books on the market dealing with house-buying in Spain. See in particular *Buying a Property: Spain* published by Cadogan. But even after that, talk to people who have been through the process and independent experts in areas of conveyancing, finance and tax. Take everything you are told by those trying to sell with more than a pinch of salt, and check and double check everything that you are unsure of.

Below is a list of some of the many Internet sites dedicated to purchasing property in Spain – by no means exhaustive, since there are hundreds of them. It is principally aimed at those looking to buy before moving to Spain.

- **www.4seasonsestates.com**. Apart from property searches, this site also has information on legal questions and more.

- **www.andalucia.com**. Property information and much more, focused, as the name suggests, on Andalucía.

- **www.apartmentspain.co.uk**. This site caters more for the cheaper end of the market.

- **www.buyaspanishhome.com**. Run in association with Fincas Corral, a Spanish estate agent so has access to lots of local agents.

- **www.countrylife.co.uk**. An offshoot of the well-known magazine which focuses on the upper end of the market.

- **www.expatfocus.com**. This site does not have property advertising but offers lots of advice for expats worldwide, including those living in Spain.

- **www.idealspain.com**. Legal and financial advice plus lots of links to property companies.

- **www.marbella-lawyers.com**. A very useful site covering all aspects of law affecting the foreign resident in Spain, from conveyancing to drinking and driving.

- **www.propertyfile.net**. Information about renting and buying in the Canary Islands, the Costa del Sol, the Costa Blanca and many links to other sites, including information on mortgages for those intending to buy in Spain, Portugal, France and Italy.

- **www.property-in-spain.com**. The website of Harringtons International, property consultants specialising in all the costas.

- **www.spain-info.com**. General tourist information and property links for most of Spain.

- **www.spanish-living.com**. Property and much, much more, including information about shopping, sport, children, schools and health and beauty.

- **www.spanishpropertyco.com**. Lots of useful information about many aspects of living in Spain.

- **www.vivendum.com**. A joint site of thousands of local estate agents, in Spanish.

Private Sales

It is far more common in Spain for property to be sold privately, 'person to person', than it is in the UK, especially in big cities and in the countryside. Depending on the area, private sales can amount to between 10 and 20 per cent of all property transactions. Provided you have the help and advice of your lawyer behind you, there is no reason to shy away from them. Cutting out agents and property companies will, of course, save a significant amount of money and, if you have found the property you want, don't want to look any further and have hit upon an amenable vendor, will also probably allow your deal to go ahead quite a bit faster.

There is a variety of ways to find out about properties available for private sale. First of all, wherever you go in Spain – in the entrance halls of city apartment blocks or at the ends of farm tracks – you will see a wide assortment of DIY for-sale signs (with the words *se vende* or *en venta*), nearly always with a contact phone number. To take advantage of property offered in this way you obviously have to be in the area, and will probably need to speak at least some Spanish. Even if you can't carry on much of a conversation in Spanish, though, it's still worth a trial phone call; if the person who answers does not speak English there may be a local English-speaker – perhaps in your hotel – who can make contact on your behalf. With rural properties you can often just walk up and knock on the door but, if a phone number is given, it's best to call first, and the chances of finding any English-speakers are wholly unpredictable. As a last resort you can phone your lawyer, who should be able to find out the necessary details for you and, if you wish, make arrangements to view. He will charge for this, but the saving on estate agents' fees will still work out to your advantage.

Local newspapers (which in Madrid and Barcelona include the local editions of national papers like *El País*, **www.elpais.es**) also carry lots of property ads in their classified sections, especially, in most cities, on Sundays. Most will have been placed by agencies, but there will be plenty from private sellers too. Another very good place to find private sales ads placed by Spanish owners is the free advertising magazine *Segundamano*, which has editions in many parts of the country, and a good website (**www.segundamano.es**). Again, you will have to phone to make contact. Local English-language papers also carry plenty of property ads, but beware of anyone advertising in this way who suggests a friendly Brit-to-Brit sale cutting out some of the Spanish formalities – there have been reports of property sharks working a variety of scams on other foreigners by this means, especially on the Costa del Sol. It is surprisingly common for people in the big expat clusters to think that they can agree property sales 'between themselves', ignoring most or all of the Spanish legal obligations, failing to register proper title and so on, and storing up big problems for themselves in the future. Even leaving aside the types who make a living out of exploiting this sort of naïve chumminess, this is absolutely to be avoided. Get a lawyer and do things by the book.

Buying at Auction

Property in Spain can be bought at auction, just as in the UK. Some auctions are voluntary, while others are run by court order following compulsory repossession. Low prices can make them very attractive – a few years ago, during Spain's last major recession, it was possible to find incredible bargains at auctions, with prices equivalent to only 30 per cent of normal market value. Today auctions no longer offer such spectacular discounts, but the prospect of getting large properties at prices well below the local norm still draws many buyers. Prices are so low primarily because, in judicial auctions in particular, the process is intended first and foremost to recover debts of various kinds, and once these and the costs have been covered there is little reason for auctioneers to press for a higher price.

Buying property at auction is not simple for non-locals, and if you are interested in trying it out it is vitally important that you have taken all the normal preparatory steps – including seeing a lawyer – before you embark on the process. Auctions are usually advertised six to eight weeks in advance: auctions ordered by the court will be officially announced in local papers and notices posted in the area, while non-judicial auctions will just be advertised in the press. Brief details of properties to be sold are published, but these are often very uninformative. To make any preliminary decisions you will need to inspect the property and decide whether it is of interest, a time-consuming and potentially costly process. An alternative to looking yourself is to get someone to do it for you: this is not as satisfactory, but a local estate agent will, for a fee, go to look at the property and give you a description of it, and can perhaps post or e-mail you some photographs. Buying blind at auctions, on the other hand, is really just for confirmed gamblers.

Another important preliminary, before the date of the auction, is to check out the legal situation of the property and, since many properties sold at auction are not in the best condition, get estimates of the likely cost of repairs or improvements, to make sure that the price you are going to bid plus these costs is not so high as to make the whole project non-viable. Finally, you should appoint a lawyer to act for you at the auction itself – only very brave or foolish foreigners take on these events without a lawyer to represent them or at least help them on the day. Your lawyer will explain precisely what needs to be done at each stage, while you will have to tell him the maximum price you want to offer and give him or her the bidding deposit – a refundable deposit levied by the auctioneer to allow you to enter a bid. You will also have to give the auctioneer various personal details, and a deposit amounting (usually) to ten per cent of the price you are offering, less the bidding deposit. This deposit must be paid over at the time your bid is accepted. You do not need to attend the auction in person, as your lawyer can do so for you, for which he or she will require power of attorney and the required funds.

Although auction prices are low, you should be aware that you will face additional costs over and above those you would have to pay in a normal house purchase, including the extra fees you will owe to your lawyer. These costs are likely to raise the overall transaction costs of the sale from the 10–11 per cent of the purchase price normal in Spain to around 13–15 per cent.

Estate Agents (*Agencias Inmobiliarias*)

Whether you buy through an estate agent or by private agreement with the seller, estate agents serve as a shop window for the housing market. Properties are displayed, complete with photo, description and price – so you can easily get an idea of what is available and for how much.

If you choose an estate agent, there are a few things you should know about them before committing yourself to using their services. Estate agents may be small, locally run outfits or large multinational companies with central offices in Zurich, London or Paris. Between these extremes are franchise establishments which may bear the same logo and colour scheme, but operate independently from each other. Some common names you see are Tecnocasa, Frimm, Don Piso and Remax. Others may be 'cowboy' outfits, though happily these are the minority these days. Bona fide estate agents belong to professional associations. There are two recognised professional bodies for estate agents in Spain, membership of which should ensure a professional service. One is the nationwide **Gestores Intermediarios en Promociones de Edificaciones** or **GIPE (www.gipe.es)**. This professional body is the only organisation with direct links to the Confédération Européenne de l'Immobilier (CEI, **www.webcei.com**), through whose website you can find a listing of GIPE members in Spain. The other association is the older and much larger **Agentes de la Propiedad Inmobiliaria** or **API**, of which there is a different *colegio oficial* for each province. This is the equivalent of the UK National Association of Estate Agents. Estate agents' membership details should be displayed on the premises, available on request and provided in all written documents.

There are estate agents who do not belong to either. There is nothing illegal about this, as recent legislation aimed at liberalising the housing market removed the obligation to belong to any officially recognised body. You may feel more confident, though, dealing with one that has such recognition. If an agent displays no professional sticker and cannot show proof of membership, you may prefer to look elsewhere.

In any case there are certain guarantees to look for before committing yourself to any agent. Check (for example) whether the agent has a **Bonded Clients' Account**, into which any deposits may be paid and made inaccessible to both seller and buyer until the sale has gone through. This means neither side can back out after an initial promissory contract has been signed, at least not without comeback.

In the Spanish property market, it is not always the seller who pays the estate agent's **commission**. This is the most common practice, but there are local variations in different towns and regions. In some places, paying the commission actually falls to the buyer; in others they might be expected to contribute half. Be clear when you are looking at property whether the price mentioned includes or excludes these fees. The API recommends that the estate agent's charge should be in the region of three per cent of the value of the property. In tourist areas, where many house sales are for second or holiday homes, the fee can range between 5 and 15 per cent. Make sure you know exactly how much you will be expected to pay before committing yourself. Cheaper properties generally carry a higher percentage commission than more expensive ones, and properties in main tourist areas tend to carry more commission than those in less sought-after areas. In some cases, in order to protect his commission, an agent may ask you to sign a document before he takes you to see a property. This does not necessarily mean that you will have to pay anything, but is a statement that it is he who has introduced you to the property, so avoiding later arguments about who should be paid the commission due.

One general tip: if you are going around properties on your own, and meeting up with agents *en route*, take a mobile phone. Rural *fincas* and modern developments can all be exasperatingly hard to find if you're unfamiliar with the territory and don't have very complete directions.

Lawyers

Always keep in mind that the estate agent is working on behalf of the seller. It is therefore in your interest to seek independent professional advice. You may go to a UK lawyer or solicitor specialising in Spanish property, as your normal English solicitor will know little or nothing of the issues of Spanish law. Or you may choose to go to a Spanish lawyer or *gestor* (*see* p.113). If you choose either of the last two, you may want an English-speaking one. British, American and Irish consulates can supply a list of English-speaking lawyers in your area. Inclusion on the list does not constitute endorsement of the lawyers in question. A lawyer's fee should generally come to about one per cent of the property's value but be certain it is clear (and agreed) from the outset.

It will save you a lot of time and trouble if you see your lawyer *before* you find a property. There are a number of preliminary issues that can best be discussed in the relative calm before you find the house of your dreams rather than once you are under pressure to sign some document to commit yourself to the purchase. These issues will include:

- **who should own the property, bearing in mind the Spanish and British tax consequences of ownership.**
- **whether or not to consider mortgage finance and if so in which country.**
- **what to do about buying the euros needed to pay for the property.**
- **how to structure your purchase to minimise taxes and cost.**
- **sorting out the tax and investment issues that will need to be dealt with *before your move* if you are to get the best out of both systems.**

The Spanish Notary

Some local agents will tell you that you do not need to use a lawyer – that the services of the local Notary Public (*notario*) will suffice. Ignore that advice. It is quite true that the average Spanish person would not use the services of an independent lawyer when buying a house unless there were something complex, unusual or contentious about the transaction or about their own circumstances. For a foreigner, however, this is generally not good enough. There are many issues on which you will need guidance that it is not part of the notary's duty to provide. Furthermore, your Spanish notary will almost certainly know nothing about British law and so will be unable to give you any help as far as such vital issues as who should own the property in order to make the most of UK *and* Spanish tax and inheritance rules.

The notary is a special type of lawyer. He or she is in part a public official but is also in business, making his or her living from the fees s/he charges for his or her services. Notaries also exist in England, but are seldom used in day-to-day transactions. Under Spanish law only deeds of sale (*escrituras de compraventa*) approved and witnessed by a notary can be registered at the land registry (*registro de la propiedad*). Although it is possible to transfer legal ownership of property such as a house or apartment by a private agreement not witnessed by the notary, and although that agreement will be fully binding on the people who made it, it will not be binding on third parties. Third parties – including people who want to make a claim against the property and banks wanting to lend money on the strength of the property – are entitled to rely upon the details of ownership recorded at the land registry. So if you are not registered as the owner of the property, you are at risk. Thus, practically speaking, all sales of real estate in Spain must be witnessed by a notary.

The notary also carries out certain checks on properties sold and has some duties as tax enforcer and validator of documents to be presented for registration. His or her basic fee is fixed by law. For an average property, however, it will be about 0.4 per cent of the price, though there can sometimes be 'extras'.

Price more than	Up to	Charge	Cumulative total fee
€0	€6,000	€90	€90
€6,000	€30,000	0.45%	€200
€30,000	€60,000	0.15%	€240
€60,000	€150,000	0.1%	€330
€150,000	€600,000	0.05%	€600
€600,000	No limit	0.03%	

The notary is, in theory, appointed by the buyer, but in many cases – particularly with new property – the seller will stipulate the notary to be used. The notary is strictly neutral. He or she is more a referee than someone fighting on your behalf. He or she is, in the usual case, someone who checks the papers to make sure that they comply with the strict rules as to content and so will be accepted by the land registry for registration.

Many Spanish notaries, particularly in rural areas, do not speak English – or, at least, not well enough to give advice on complex issues. Very few will know anything about English law and so will be unable to tell you about the tax and other consequences in the UK of your plans to buy a house in Spain. In any case, the buyer will seldom meet the notary before the signing ceremony and so there is little scope for seeking detailed advice. It is, in any case, rare for notaries to offer any comprehensive advice or explanation to the buyer.

Property Inspection

Whatever property you are thinking of buying, you should think about having it inspected before you commit yourself. It costs just as much to repair property in Spain as in the UK, so you don't want any surprises.

A new property will be covered by a short guarantee running from the date of handover and covering minor but not trivial defects in a new property. New properties also benefit from a guarantee in respect of major structural defects that will last for 10 years. As a subsequent purchaser you assume the benefit of these guarantees. After 10 years you are on your own. For property more than 10 years old (and, arguably, for younger property too) you should consider a survey.

If you decide on a survey there are several options available to you.

Do-it-yourself

There are several things that you can do yourself. These will help you decide when to instruct a surveyor to do a proper survey and help direct him to any specific points of interest. (*See* the checklist, pp.148–9).

Estate Agent's Valuation and 'Survey'

It may be possible to arrange for another local estate agent to give the property a quick 'once over' to comment on the price asked and any obvious problem areas. Check the cost of this survey with your estate agent.

Mortgage Lender's Survey

This is no substitute for a proper survey. Many lenders do not ask for one and, where they do, it is normally fairly peremptory, limited to a check on whether it is about to fall over and if it is worth the money the bank is lending you.

Spanish Builder

If you are going to do a virtual demolition and rebuild, then it might make more sense to get a builder to do a report on the property. A reputable and experienced builder will also be able to comment on whether or not the price is reasonable for the property in its existing state. Make sure you ask for a written quotation for any building work proposed. As in any country, it is as well to get several quotes, though this can be tricky; there is a lot of work for builders at the moment.

Spanish Surveyor

Your lawyer can put you in touch with the right people. In most rural areas there will be limited choice but if you prefer you can select 'blind' from a list of local members supplied by the surveyors' professional body. The cost of this survey is considerably higher than an estate agent's survey.

You will find that the report is different from the sort of report you would get from an English surveyor. Many people find it a little 'thin', with too much focus on issues that are not their primary concern. It will, hardly surprisingly, usually be in Spanish. You will need to have it translated unless you speak very good Spanish and have access to a technical dictionary. Translation costs amount to about £60–100 per thousand words, depending on where you are located and the complexity of the document. (Incidentally, always use an English person to translate documents from Spanish into English.) An alternative to translation of the full report would be to ask your lawyer to summarise the report in a letter to you and to have translated any areas of particular concern.

A few Spanish surveyors, mainly in the popular areas, have geared themselves to the non-Spanish market and will produce a report rather more like a British survey. They will, probably, also prepare it in bilingual form or at least supply a translation of the original Spanish document.

UK-qualified Surveyor Based in Spain

A number of UK surveyors have seen a gap in the market and have set themselves up in Spain to provide UK-style structural surveys. As in this country they usually offer the brief 'Homebuyers' Report' or the fuller 'Full Structural Survey'. This is not as simple as it would first appear. To do the job well they must learn about Spanish building techniques and regulations; without this knowledge the report will be of limited value. Prices are generally slightly more expensive than for a Spanish report, but it will be in English and so avoid the need for translation costs. Your UK lawyer should be able to recommend a surveyor; alternatively, look for advertisers in the main Spanish property magazines.

Check they have indemnity insurance covering the provision of reports in Spain. Check also on the person's qualifications and experience in providing reports on Spanish property, and get an estimate. The estimate will only be an estimate because they will not know for sure the scope of the task until they visit the property and because travelling time means that visits just to give estimates are not usually feasible.

Most surveys can be done in seven to ten days. Contracts 'subject to survey' are unusual in Spain. Legally there is nothing to stop a Spanish preliminary contract containing a get-out clause (*condicion resolutoria*) stating that the sale is conditional upon a satisfactory survey being obtained, yet it is unlikely to meet with the approval of the seller or their agent unless the transaction is unusual. In an ordinary case the seller is likely to tell you to do your survey and then sign a contract. Whichever report you opt for, its quality will depend in part on your input. Agree clearly and in writing the things you expect to be covered in the report. Checks you may ask your surveyor to do may include: electrical condition and continuity; septic tank; drains, including assessment of drains to the point where they join mains sewers or a septic tank; adequacy of foundations; rot; cement quality in property constructed out of cement; underfloor areas, where access cannot easily be obtained; heating and air-conditioning; pool and all pool-related equipment and heating; wood-boring insect; evidence of asbestos, etc.

If you do not speak Spanish (and the surveyor doesn't speak good English) you may have to ask someone to write on your behalf. Your UK lawyer would probably be the best bet. Some of the matters you may wish to think about are set out below. Some of these will involve you in additional cost. Ask what will be covered as part of the standard fee and get an estimate for the extras.

Checklist: Do-it-yourself Inspection of Property

• **Title:** Check that the property corresponds with its description: number of rooms and plot size.

• **Plot:** Identify the physical boundaries of the plot. Is there any dispute with anyone over these boundaries? Are there any obvious foreign elements on your plot such as pipes, cables, drainage ditches, water tanks, etc.? Are there any signs of anyone else having rights over the property – footpaths, access ways, cartridges from hunting, etc.?

• **Garden/Terrace:** Are any plants, ornaments, etc. on site not being sold with the property?

• **Pool:** Is there a pool? If so: What size is it? Is it clean and algae-free? Do the pumps work? How old is the machinery? Who maintains it? What is the annual cost of maintenance? Does it appear to be in good condition?

• **Walls:** Stand back from property and inspect from outside. Any signs of subsidence? Walls vertical? Any obvious cracks in walls? Are walls well pointed? Any damp patches? Any new repairs to walls or repointing?

• **Roof:** Inspect from outside. Does roof sag? Are there missing/slipped tiles? Do all faces of roof join squarely? Lead present and in good order?

• **Guttering and downpipes:** Inspect from outside property. All present? Fall of guttering constant? Securely attached? Any leaks? Any recent repairs?

• **Enter property:** Does it smell of damp? Does it smell musty? Does it smell of dry rot? Any other strange smells?

• **Doors:** Signs of rot? Close properly without catching? Seal? Locks work?

• **Windows:** Signs of rot? Close properly without catching? Provide proper seal? Locks work? Excessive condensation?

• **Floor:** Can you see it all? Does it appear in good condition? Any sign of cracked or rotten boards?

• **Under floor:** Can you get access under the floor? If so, is it ventilated? Is there any sign of rot? How close are joists? Are joist ends in good condition where they go into walls? What is maximum unsupported length of joist run? Is there any sign of damp or standing water?

• **Roof void:** Is it accessible? Is there sign of water entry? Can you see daylight through roof? Is there an underlining between the tiles and the void? Is there any sign of rot in timbers? Horizontal distance between roof timbers. Size of roof timbers (section). Maximum unsupported length of roof timbers. Is roof insulated – if so, what depth and type of insulation?

• **Woodwork:** Any sign of rot? Any sign of wood-boring insects? Is it dry?

• **Interior walls:** Any significant cracks? Any obvious damp problems? Any sign of recent repair/redecoration?

• **Electricity**: Check electricity meter: how old is it, what is its rated capacity? Check all visible wiring: what type is it, does it appear in good physical condition? Check all plugs: is there power to plug, does plug tester show good earth and show 'OK', are there enough plugs? Lighting: do all lights work, which light fittings are included in sale?

• **Water**: Do all hot and cold taps work? Is flow adequate? Do taps drip? Is there a security cut-off on all taps between mains and tap? Do they seem in good condition? Hot water: is hot water 'on'? If so, does it work at all taps, showers, etc.? What type of hot water system is fitted? Age?

• **Gas**: Is the property fitted with city (piped) gas? If so: age of meter, does installation appear in good order, is there smell of gas? Is the property fitted with bottled gas? If so, where are bottles stored? Is it ventilated to outside?

• **Central heating**: Is the property fitted with central heating? If so: is it on? Will it turn on? What type is it? Is there heat at all radiators/outlets? Do any thermostats appear to work? Are there any signs of leaks?

• **Fireplaces**: Is the property fitted with any solid fuel heaters? If so: any sign of blow-back from chimneys? Do chimneys (outside) show stains from leakage? Do chimneys seem in good order?

• **Air-conditioning**: Which rooms are air-conditioned? Are units included in the sale? Do the units work? What type of unit is it? How old?

• **Phone**: Does it work? Number?

• **Satellite TV**: Does it work? Is it included in the sale?

• **Drainage**: What type of drainage does property have? If septic tank, how old? Who maintains it? When was it last serviced? Any smell of drainage problems in bathrooms and toilets? Does water drain away rapidly from all sinks, showers and toilets? Is there any inspection access through which you can see drainage taking place? Is there any sign of plant ingress to drains? Do drains appear to be in good condition and well pointed?

• **Kitchen**: Do all cupboards open/close properly? Any sign of rot? Tiling secure and in good order? Enough plugs? What appliances are included in sale? Do they work? Age of appliances included?

• **Bathroom**: Security and condition of tiling? Ventilation?

• **Appliances**: What appliances are included in sale? What is not included?

• **Furniture**: What furniture is included in sale? What is not included in sale?

• **Defects**: Is seller aware of any defects in the property?

• **Repairs/improvements/additions**: What repairs have been carried out in last two years? What improvements have been carried out in last two years/ten years? What additions have been made to the property in last two years/ten years? Are there builders' receipts/guarantees? Is there building consent/planning permission for any additions or alterations?

General Enquiries and Special Enquiries

Certain enquiries are made routinely in the course of the purchase of a property. These include, in appropriate cases, a check on the planning situation of the property. This *informe urbanistico* will reveal the position of the property itself but it will not, at least directly, tell you about its neighbours, nor will it reveal general plans for the area. Checks on planning status (both current and future) need to be especially thorough for any non-development property in the Valencian region, including the Costa Blanca (*see* p.42).

If you want to know whether the authorities are going to put a prison in the village or run a new AVE line through your back garden (both, presumably, undesirable) or build a motorway access point or railway station 3km away (both, presumably, desirable) you will need to ask. There are various organisations you can approach but, just as in England, there is no single point of contact for such enquiries. If you are concerned about what might happen in the area, then you will need to discuss the position with your lawyers at an early stage. There may be a considerable amount of work (and cost) involved in making full enquiries, the results of which can never be guaranteed. Normal enquiries also include a check that the seller is the registered owner of the property and that it is sold (if this has been agreed) free of mortgages or other charges.

In order to advise you what special enquiries might be appropriate, your lawyer will need to be told your proposals for the property. Do you intend to let it? If so, on a commercial basis? Do you intend to use it for business purposes? Do you want to extend or modify the exterior of the property? Do you intend to make interior structural alterations? Agree in advance the additional enquiries you would like to make and get an estimate of the cost of those enquiries.

The Buying Process

The general procedure when buying a property in Spain seems, at first glance, similar to the purchase of a property in England: sign a contract; do some checks; sign a deed of title. This is deceptive. The procedure is very different and even the use of the familiar English vocabulary to describe the very different steps in Spain can produce an undesirable sense of familiarity with the procedure. This can lead to assumptions that things that have not been discussed will be the same as they would in England. This would be a wrong and dangerous assumption. Work on the basis that the system is totally different.

Initial Contracts

Most house sales in Spain begin with a **preliminary contract**, usually prepared by the estate agent, the signing of which implies a commitment to the transaction (and often the handing over of a sum of money). The type of contract will depend upon whether you are buying a finished or an unfinished property. Whichever type of contract you are asked to sign, always seek legal advice first.

Generally the preliminary contract is prepared by the estate agent – who is professionally qualified in Spain – or by the developer. Estate agents' contracts are often based on a pre-printed document in a standard format. Some contracts coming from estate agents are legally muddled and not properly thought through. They can blur or mix different types of contractual obligation, often referring to mutually exclusive concepts in the same document – for example, referring to it as a contract of sale and an option contract. Sometimes the contracts are extremely one-sided, giving their client – the seller – all of the rights and taking away all of the rights of the buyer. It is very important that these contracts are not just accepted as final. In many cases they will need to be modified, in some cases extensively.

If the buyer or seller drops out of the contract or otherwise breaks it, various arrangements may be made. A special **deposit** (*arras*) might be payable by the buyer. If he fails to complete, he will lose the deposit. If the seller fails to complete he will have to return double the deposit paid. Alternatively the contract may provide for a deposit to be paid as a simple part of the price of the property. The contract can provide for all or part of this deposit – and any other sums paid up to the relevant moment – to be lost if the buyer does not proceed.

If the parties fail to comply with their obligations there is the ultimate remedy of seeking a court order. As in any country, this is very much a last resort as it is costly, time-consuming and (as in any country) there is no guarantee of the outcome of a court case. If a court order is made in your favour, this order can be registered at the land registry.

If You Are Buying an Existing Property

You will be invited to sign one or more of three different documents. Each has different legal consequences. Each is appropriate in certain circumstances and inappropriate in others.

• **Offer to Buy**: This is, technically, not a contract at all. It is a formal written offer from the potential buyer to the potential seller. It will state that you wish to buy the stated property for a stated price and that you will complete the transaction within a stated period. The offer will normally be accompanied by the payment of a **deposit** to the estate agent or seller. The deposit is not fixed but will usually range from two to five per cent of the price offered.

This document binds you. It is not a mere enquiry as to whether the seller might be interested in selling. If he says that he accepts the offer then you (and he) become legally bound to proceed with the transaction. Generally we do not like written offers. We prefer the idea of making a verbal enquiry as to whether the seller would accept a certain price and, once he says yes, for a binding bilateral contract of sale (*contrato privado de compraventa*) to be signed.

• **Reservation/Option Contract**: This is a written document in which the seller agrees to take a stated property off the market for a fixed period and to sell it at a stated price to a stated person at any time within a stated period. The seller will usually require that any person taking up his offer pays him a deposit. Once he has received this deposit, the seller must reserve the property for you until the end of the period specified in the contract. This is similar to an English option contract. If you want to go ahead and buy the property, you can, but you are not obliged to do so. If you do not go ahead, however, you lose your deposit.

The contract could contain special 'get-out clauses' (*condiciones resolutorias*) stipulating the circumstances in which the buyer will be entitled to the refund of his deposit if he decides not to go ahead. The drafting of these clauses is of vital importance. See your lawyer. If you do want to go ahead you can exercise the option at any point up to the end of the agreed period. If the seller refuses to go ahead the buyer is entitled to claim compensation.

• **Full Preliminary Contract (*Contrato Privado de Compraventa*)**: This agreement commits both parties to the transaction, that is, the seller must sell to a stated person at a stated price within the terms of the contract and the buyer must buy. Given the compromising nature of this document, it is vital that you understand all the terms included. These will most likely be: the full names of seller and buyer; a description of the property and its property registry details; a date for signing of the deeds (*escritura*); the date when the buyer takes possession; the price; statement of deposit(s) paid and receipt thereof; guarantee of vacant possession; a statement that the property is free of any charges, debts or burdens and payment of outstanding debts before the signing of the *escritura*; a breakdown of who pays what associated costs; details of the agent and who pays the commission; steps to take in case one party breaks the agreement; the legal framework governing the contract.

If You Are Buying an Unfinished Property

Make sure the property has got planning permission/a building licence. You should be given a full specification for the property, a copy of the community rules and constitution if the property shares common facilities, and a copy of any agreements you have entered into regarding ongoing management or letting of the property. All are important documents. Pay particular attention to the specification. It is not unknown for the show flat to have marble floors and high quality wooden kitchens but for the specification to show concrete tiles and MDF.

• **Reservation Contract**: Usually in these cases there is a preliminary contract. This is the reservation contract (*see* above). This allows you to reserve a plot when you see it and allows you time to sign one of the other types of contract when you have made the necessary enquiries.

• **Full Contract**: There are three possible types of contract in this case.

  • **Contract for immediate sale of the land**: You sign a contract agreeing to sign the title deed in respect of the land – and anything the seller has so far built on it – now. This involves paying for the land and work so far undertaken in full at this stage. At the same time you enter into a contract to build your house on the land. As the building continues it automatically becomes the property of the buyer. The buyer, of course, has the obligation to pay the agreed price, usually by instalments dependent upon the progress of the building work. This has the great advantage of securing the money you pay to the builder. If the builder goes bust you own the land and everything built on it. It only really works for property built on its own plot rather than, say, apartments. It can be tax- and cost-inefficient.

• **Contract 'on plan'**: You agree to buy a property once it has been built and agree to make payments in stages as the construction progresses. Sometimes the payments are dependent upon the progress of the building works. On other occasions they are due on set dates. The latter are now the more common, though less attractive to the buyer.

Once the property has been built, you will sign the deed of sale and pay the balance of the price. It is only then that you become the owner of the property and register your title. Until then, if the builder goes bust you are simply one of many creditors.

Since 1968 the law has required that the contract must give details of a guarantee to secure completion of the construction in the event, for example, that the seller goes bust. In most parts of Spain these guarantees are furnished with no problems. In other places builders simply refuse to give the guarantee. 'I am your guarantee. I am a man of honour. I have been building for over 30 years!' This is part of the commonplace experience in Spain of the law saying one thing but people blatantly doing something entirely different. Why do they do it? They think that they save money (guarantees have to be paid for and the bank will probably not release all the money until the property is finished) and they think the law is a bureaucratic imposition. In Spain there is a saying (*refran*): 'Spain is a constitutional monarchy with 40 million kings'.

• **Contract to buy once the property has been built**: You agree to buy a plot of land and building. You agree to pay once it has been built. Simple! You take title and pay the money at the same time. This is really the same as buying a resale property. This type of contract is little used.

Checklist – Signing a Contract

• **Are you clear about what you are buying?**

• **Are there any 'extras' included in the sale?**

• **Have you taken advice about property ownership and inheritance issues?**

• **Are you clear about boundaries and access?**

• **Have you seen the seller's title and an up-to-date simple land registry extract?**

• In the case of an existing property: are you sure you can change the property as you want? Are you sure you can use the property for what you want? Is the property connected to water, electricity, gas, etc.? Have you had a survey done?

• Have you made all necessary checks or arranged for them to be made?

• Have you included 'get-out clauses' for all important checks not yet made?

• Is your mortgage finance arranged?

• Is the seller clearly described?

• If the seller is not signing in person, have you seen a power of attorney/mandate to authorise the sale?

• Are you fully described?

• Is the property fully described? Identification? Land registry details?

• Is the price correct?

• Are any possible circumstances in which it can be increased or extras described fully?

• In the case of an unfinished property: are the stage payments fully described? Are arrangements for stage payments satisfactory? Is the date for completion of the work agreed? Does the property have planning permission/licence to build?

• In the case of an existing property: does the contract say when possession will be given? Is there a receipt for the deposit paid? In what capacity is the deposit paid? Does the property have a habitation licence?

• Is the date for signing the *escritura* agreed?

• Does the contract provide for the sale to be free of charges and debts?

• Does the contract provide for vacant possession?

• Which notary is to act?

• Is the estate agent's commission dealt with?

• What happens if there is a breach of contract?

• Are there any financial guarantees of satisfactory completion?

• Are all the necessary special 'get-out' clauses included?

Signing the Deeds

Once all this has been concluded, you and the seller meet, as agreed, for the signing of the deeds. The date stated in the contract for signing the *escritura* could, most charitably, be described as flexible or aspirational. Often it will move, if only by a day or so. The signing of the deeds takes place before a notary who, after certain formalities (such as ascertaining both buyer's and seller's identities), checks the contents of the *escritura*, albeit superficially, and the signing takes place. Both parties' lawyers may be present, as may the notary's clerk, an interpreter, a representative of your mortgage lender, the estate agent and any sub-agent. Most are there to take their 'cut'!

If you do not speak Spanish, an interpreter should be present when you sign the *escritura*. The attitude of notaries when it comes to assessing when an interpreter is necessary varies enormously. A written translation is not provided as a matter of course.

After the *escritura* has been signed, the taxes must be paid. Once the taxes are paid, your title and any mortgage should be presented for registration at the land registry. This should be done as quickly as possible. He who registers first gets priority. After several months the land registry will issue a certificate to the effect that the title has been registered.

Checklist - Steps before Completion

• **Check what documents must be produced on signing the *escritura*.**

• **Confirm all outstanding issues have been complied with.**

• **Confirm all other important enquiries are clear.**

• **Confirm arrangements (date, time, place) for completion with your lender if you have a mortgage.**

• **Confirm arrangements (date, time, place) for completion with the notary.**

• **Send necessary funds to Spain if you don't have the funds in Spain.**

• **Receive rules of community.**

• **Insurance cover arranged?**

• **In the case of an unfinished property: sign off work or list defects.**

• **In the case of an existing property: proof of payment of community fees and other bills.**

The Price

This can be freely agreed between the parties. Depending on the economic climate there may be ample or very little room for negotiating a reduction in the asking price.

How Much Should be Declared in the Deed of Sale?

For many years there was a tradition in Spain (and other Latin countries) of under-declaring the price actually paid for a property when signing the deed of sale (*escritura*). This was because the taxes and notaries' fees due were calculated on the basis of the price declared. Lower price, less property transfer taxes for the buyer and less capital gains tax for the seller. The days of major under-declarations have now largely gone. In rural areas you can still sometimes come under pressure to under-declare to a significant extent, but it is now rare. In many areas the seller will still suggest some more modest form of under-declaration. Under-declaration is illegal and foolish. There are severe penalties. In the worst case the state can buy the property for the price declared. In the best case there are fines and penalties for late payment. In addition, unless when you sell your buyer under-declares, you create an entirely artificial capital gain – taxed at 35 per cent.

Where Must the Money be Paid?

The price, together with the taxes and fees payable, is usually paid by the buyer to the seller in front of the notary. This is the best and safest way. You can, in fact, agree to pay in whatever way and wherever you please. So, for example, in the case of a British seller and a British buyer the payment could be made in sterling by bank transfer. In the case of a seller who is not tax resident in Spain, the buyer is obliged to retain five per cent of the price and pay it to the taxman (*agencia tributaria*) on account of the seller's potential tax liabilities.

Avoid arrangements, usually part of an under-declaration, where part of the money is handed over in cash in brown-paper parcels. Apart from being illegal it is dangerous at a practical level. Buyers have lost the bundle – or been robbed on the way to the notary's office.

Your Civil State (*Estado Civil*) and Other Personal Details

When preparing documents in Spain, you will be asked to specify your civil state. This comprises a full set of information about you. They will not only ask for your full name and address but also, potentially, for your occupation, nationality, passport number, maiden name and sometimes the names of your parents, your date and place of birth, date and place of marriage and, most importantly, your **matrimonial regime** (*regimen matrimonial*). In Spain when you marry you specify the *regimen matrimonial* that will apply to your relationship. There are two main options for a Spanish person – a regime of common ownership of assets (*comunidad de bienes*) or a regime of separate ownership of assets (*separacion de bienes*). Under the first, all assets acquired after the marriage, even if put into just one party's name, belong to both. Under the second, each spouse is entitled to own assets in his or her own name, upon which the other spouse has no automatic claim. The effect of marriage under English law is generally closer to the second than the first. If possible the notary, when specifying your matrimonial regime, should state that you are married under English law and, in the absence of a marriage contract, do not have a regime but your situation is similar to a regime of *separacion de bienes*. This is no idle point. The declaration in your *escritura* is a public declaration. It will be hard in later years to go against what you have declared.

If appropriate you will declare that you are single, separated, divorced, widowed, etc. at this point. The authorities are entitled to ask for proof of all of these points by birth certificates, marriage certificates, etc. If the documents are required, the official translations into Spanish may be needed. Often the notary will take a slightly more relaxed view and ask you for only the key elements of your *estado civil*. It is worth checking in advance as to what is required, as it is embarrassing to turn up to sign the *escritura* only to find the ceremony cannot go ahead because you do not have one of the documents required. In the worst case that could put you in breach of contract and you could lose your deposit!

Tax Identification Number (NIE)

To own a property in Spain you need to obtain an NIE – foreigner's tax identification number (*see* **Red Tape**, p.116).

Purchasing Costs

There are fees and taxes payable by a buyer when acquiring a property in Spain. They are sometimes known as completion expenses or completion or closing costs. They are impossible to predict with total accuracy at the outset of a transaction. We can, however, give a general guide.

These costs are calculated on the basis of the price that you declared as the price paid for the property in the *escritura*. Overall, expect to add on in the region of 10 or 11 per cent to the sale price of a property to cover various intermediaries' costs and other fees. These may typically include:

- **Notary's fees:**These are fixed by law according to the value of the property so are not negotiable (*see* p.145). As a general guide, allow around 0.4 per cent. If you have asked the notary to do any additional work over and above the transfer of title or for any advice there will be additional charges.

- **VAT (*Impuesto sobre el Valor Añadido*):** Only applied to properties bought from companies, where the rate is 7 per cent. This is sometimes, but not always, included in the price of the property quoted to you. Check to see whether it is in your case. There is no IVA in the Canaries. Instead there is a local tax called IGIC which is charged at 5 per cent.

- **Property Transfer Tax (*Impuesto sobre Transmisiones Patrimoniales*):** An additional tax payable only on properties subject to VAT. In most areas it is 7 per cent.

- **Stamp duty (*Impuesto sobre Actos Jurídicos Documentados*):** Again only payable on properties subject to VAT. It is 1 per cent.

- **Land registration fees:** Approximately the same as the notary's fee.

- **Mortgage costs:** Typically around 4 or 5 per cent of the amount borrowed.

- **Estate agents' fees:** If payable by the buyer. If an estate agent has sold the property the seller usually pays his fees, but this can be varied by agreement. These fees will be subject to IVA.

- **Miscellaneous other charges:** Architect's fees, surveyor's fees, legal fees, first connection to water, electricity, etc. Most of these will be subject to Spanish IVA at varying rates.

Financing and Mortgages

Financing the purchase of a property depends very much on whether, having moved to Spain and decided to stay, you have a property to sell or remortgage at home, or whether you are starting from scratch. Naturally enough, it also depends on your earnings, any savings you might have and what your prospects are *vis-à-vis* continuing employment. Here it is assumed that you are living and working in Spain, so the following concerns financing a purchase 'from within'. Spanish mortgage rates are currently lower than UK ones, often less than 5 or even 4 per cent.

Applying for a Mortgage

A Spanish mortgage may be obtained from either a Spanish bank or a UK bank registered and trading in Spain. (You cannot take out a mortgage on your new Spanish property from your local branch of a UK building society or high street bank.) The basic concept of a mortgage to buy property is the same in Spain as it is in England or Scotland. It is a loan secured against the land or buildings that you purchase. If you cannot keep up with payments, your property will be repossessed by the bank.

Spanish mortgages are almost always created on a **repayment basis**. That is to say, the loan and the interest on it are both gradually repaid by equal instalments over the period of the mortgage. Endowment, PEP, pension and interest-only mortgages are not known in Spain. There are often restrictions or penalties on the ability to impose penalties for early payment of the loan.

Most Spanish mortgages are usually granted for **15 years**, not 25 as in England. In fact, the period can be anything from five to (in a few cases) 25 years. Normally the mortgage must have been repaid by your 70th (sometimes 65th) birthday. The maximum loan is generally 80 per cent of the value of the property, and 75 or 66 per cent is more common. As a planning guide, you should think of borrowing no more than two-thirds of the price you are paying.

Fixed-rate loans are common, and rates are currently low as there is stiff competition to lend money. Banks often have a minimum loan and are reluctant to lend for really cheap properties.

Banks as a rule will not lend you more than the amount of monthly payments that come to 30–33 per cent of your net income (after tax and other deductions). The starting point is your net monthly salary after deduction of tax and National Insurance but before deduction of voluntary payments such as to savings schemes. If there are two applicants, the two salaries are taken into account. If you have investment income or a pension, this will be taken into account. If you are buying a property with a track record of letting income, this *may* be taken into account. If you are over 65, your earnings will not usually be taken into account, but your pension and investment income will be. If your circumstances are at all unusual, seek advice, as approaching a different bank may produce a different result.

Case Study: Fiona Chapman

Fiona Chapman, 40, from East Sussex, went to Spain from Mexico to work as a primary teacher in a British school in Madrid. Still there 12 years later, she is now also joint owner of a Mexican restaurant.

How did you sort out accommodation when you first arrived?

At first I slept on a colleague's floor, whilst scouring *Segundamano*. It is getting harder for new arrivals to find rented accommodation. Things are over-priced and you have to move quickly as there are lots of people looking, particularly in September/October. I bought a house a year ago – a nerve-racking experience! I paid a deposit of two million pesetas (about £8,000) with a written agreement that I would sign for the property six weeks later. This is a normal anti-gazumping agreement. I would lose my money if I didn't go through with it and the owner would pay me double if she pulled out. Fine, off I went to get a mortgage. Only then did the banks all tell me I needed a guarantor (*aval*), who had to be a home-owner. Only a close relative would do something like that, and as this home-owner had to be a resident in Spain it is very difficult for a foreign buyer. Luckily I was saved by an *enchufe*, someone I knew who had high standing in a bank, and with six days to go the bank agreed to give me a mortgage!

How did you find your jobs?

I sorted out my job before coming, through an ad in the *Times Educational Supplement*. I would recommend this for any teachers planning on coming. Having said that, schools often need staff at short notice when someone walks out on them. Working in a British school here is a damn sight easier than working in a state school in London! Most schoolteachers here come from the English state system, though moving from state to private education can be a bit of a shock. One of the main differences is that schools are often owned and run by a single person, or a family, so decisions on spending, hiring and firing and salaries are also made by one person, not by a board. Profits aren't usually ploughed back into schools so facilities may be poor and salaries are low. Holidays, however, are fantastic! We get 10 weeks in the summer. My workload is manageable. The downside is the money. I earn what I earned in London 18 years ago as a newly qualified teacher. Back home I could double or triple my salary, but for what price? Giving up a life!

The formalities involved in making the application, signing the contract subject to a mortgage and completing the transaction are more complex and stricter than in the UK. The paperwork on completion of the mortgage is also different. There is often no separate **mortgage deed**. Instead the existence of the mortgage is mentioned in your purchase deed (*escritura de compraventa*). It is prepared by and signed in front of a notary public (*notario*).

A bank's willingness to grant a mortgage can depend on many factors, not least your employment situation. If you are self-employed they will want to see proof of earning power over a certain period of time – at least two years. Banks may also require a guarantor (*aval*) before granting a mortgage.

On making an application, you may get preliminary approval within a few days. Allow four weeks from the date of your application to receiving a written mortgage offer, as getting the information to them sometimes takes a while. It can take longer than four weeks. You will then have a further month to accept the offer, after which time it will lapse. Be careful of making any down-payments before you have secured a mortgage. Conversely, if you are made an offer, get moving on finding and/or buying a/the property.

The Cost of Taking Out a Mortgage

This will normally involve charges amounting to about 4 or 5 per cent of the sum borrowed.

You will also probably be required to take out **life insurance** for the amount of the loan, though you may be allowed to use a suitable existing policy. You may be required to have a medical. You will be required to **insure** the property and produce proof of insurance – but you would probably have done this anyway.

The offer may be subject to **early repayment penalties**. Early repayment penalties are of particular concern in the case of a fixed-rate mortgage.

New Properties and Properties Needing Restoration

In Spain, when buying a new property one normally makes payments as the development progresses and takes title at the end. This can pose problems for banks, as you do not own anything you can mortgage until you make the final payment and take title. In most cases the mortgage will therefore only be granted to cover the final payment. As this is often 60 or 70 per cent, this is seldom a problem. In some cases if the earlier payments are more substantial the banks will offer a credit facility to make the earlier payments. Once the property has been delivered to you (and thus the full loan has been taken), the normal monthly payments will begin.

Not all banks will finance properties needing restoration. If you have enough money to buy a property but need a mortgage to renovate it, you must apply for the mortgage before buying the property.

Getting Money from the UK to Spain

For EU nationals there is no longer any exchange control when taking money to or from Spain. There are some statistical records kept showing the flow of funds and the purposes of the transfers. When you sell your property in Spain you will be able to bring the money back to the UK if you wish to do so.

If you have funds in the UK that you want to use for the purchase, there are several ways of getting the money to Spain.

Electronic Transfer

The most practical is to have it sent electronically by SWIFT transfer from a UK bank directly to the recipient's bank in Spain. This costs about £10–35 depending on your bank. It is safer to allow two or three days for the money to arrive in a rural bank, despite everyone's protestations that it will be there the same day.

In 2005 Europe introduced unique account numbers for all bank accounts. These incorporate a code for the identity of the bank and branch involved as well as the account number of the individual customer. These are known as **IBAN** numbers. They should be quoted on all international currency transfers.

You can send the money from your own bank, via your lawyers or via a specialist currency dealer. For the sums you are likely to be sending you should receive an exchange rate much better than the 'tourist rate' you see in the press. There is no such thing as a fixed exchange rate in these transactions. The bank's official inter-bank rate changes by the second, and the job of the bank's currency dealers is to make a profit by selling to you at the lowest rate they can get away with! Thus if you do a lot of business with a bank and they know you are on the ball you are likely to be offered a better rate than a one-off customer.

Specialist currency dealers often give a better exchange rate than an ordinary bank. Sometimes the difference can be above 1 per cent. But be sure that your dealer is reputable; you could be at risk if they are not bonded or protected.

However you make the payment, ensure that you understand whether it is you or the recipient who is going to pick up the receiving bank's charges. If you need a clear amount in Spain you will have to make allowances for these, either by sending a bit extra or by asking your UK bank to pay all the charges. Make sure you have the details of the recipient bank, its customer's name, the account codes and the recipient's reference precisely right. Any error and the payment is likely to come back to you as undeliverable – and may involve you in bearing the cost of it being converted back into sterling. The bank in Spain will make a charge – which can be substantial – for receiving your money into your account.

Banker's Drafts

You can arrange for your UK bank to issue you with a banker's draft (bank certi-fied cheque), which you can take to Spain and pay into your bank account. Make sure that the bank knows that the draft is to be used overseas and so issues you with an international draft. Generally this is not a good way to transfer the money. It can take a considerable time – sometimes weeks – for the funds deposited to be made available for your use. The recipient bank's charges can be surprisingly high. The exchange rate offered may be uncompetitive.

Cash

This is not recommended. You will need to declare the money on departure from the UK and on arrival in Spain. You must by law do this if the sum involved is over €8,000. You are well advised to do so for smaller amounts. Even then, if you declare £200,000 or so they will think you are a terrorist or drug dealer! To add insult to injury, the exchange rate you will be offered for cash (whether you take sterling and convert there or buy the euros here) is usually very uncompetitive and the notary may well refuse to accept the money in his account.

Who Should Own the Property?

There are many ways of structuring the purchase of a home in Spain. The choice of the right structure will save you possibly many thousands of pounds in tax and expenses during your lifetime and on your death. Because, in Spain, you do not have the total freedom that we have in the UK to deal with your assets as you please on your death, the wrong choice of owner can also result in the wrong people being entitled to inherit from you when you die. This is a particular problem for people in second marriages and unmarried couples.

Sole Ownership

In some cases it could be sensible to put the property in the name of one person only. If your husband runs a high-risk business or if he is 90 and you are 22, this could make sense. It is seldom a good idea from the point of view of tax or inheritance planning.

Joint Ownership

If two people are buying together they will normally buy in both their names. Your half is yours and your fellow owner's is theirs. On your death your half will (subject to the requirement of your matrimonial regime, *see* p.156) be disposed of in accordance with Spanish law. A person who owns in this way, even if they own by virtue of inheritance, can usually insist on the sale of the property. So if your stepchildren inherit from your husband, they could insist on the sale of your home. If you decide to buy together then, in certain cases, it can make sense to split the ownership other than 50/50. If, for example, you have three children and your wife has two then to secure each of those children an equal share on your death you might think about buying 60 per cent in your name and 40 per cent in your wife's name.

Adding Your Children to the Title

If you give your children the money to buy part of the property and so put them on the title now, you may save quite a lot of inheritance tax. This only works sensibly if your children are over 18. Of course, there are drawbacks. For example, if the gift is not properly structured it could become subject to gift tax in Spain immediately. If the children fall out with you, they can insist on the sale of the property and receiving their share.

Putting the Property in the Name of Your Children Only

If you put the property only in the name of your children (possibly reserving for yourself a life interest – *see* below) then the property is theirs. On your death there will be little or no inheritance tax and there will be no need for them to incur the legal expenses involved in dealing with an inheritance. Remember, however, that you have lost control. It is no longer your property. If your children divorce, their husband/wife will be able to claim a share. If they die before you without children of their own, you will end up inheriting the property back from them and having to pay inheritance tax for the privilege of doing so.

A **life interest** (*usufructo*) is the right to use the property for a lifetime. So, on your death, your rights would be extinguished but your second wife or partner, who still has a life interest, would still be able to use the property. Only on their death would the property pass in full to the people to whom you gave it years earlier. This device can not only protect your right to use the property but also save large amounts of inheritance tax, particularly if you are young, the property is valuable and you survive for many years. As ever there are also drawbacks, not least being the fact that after the gift you no longer own the property. If you wish to sell, you need the agreement of the 'owners', who will be entitled to their share of the proceeds of sale and who would have to agree to buy you a new house. If you wish to do this, you must structure the gift carefully. Otherwise it could be taxable at once in Spain.

Limited Company

For some people, owning a property via a limited company can be a very attractive option. You own the shares in a company, not a house in Spain. There are various types of company.

• **Spanish commercial company:** Ownership via a company will mean that the income from letting the property is taxed in the way usual for companies – meaning you only pay tax on the profit made. This can reduce your tax bill. Ownership in the form of a company also gives rise to certain expenses – accountancy, filing tax returns, etc. Buying through a Spanish company gives rise to a host of potential problems as well as benefits.

• **Offshore (tax haven) company:** This has the added disincentive that you will have to pay a special tax of 3 per cent of the value of the property every year. This is to compensate the Spanish for all the inheritance and transfer taxes that they will not receive when the owners of these companies sell them or die. This tax treatment has more or less killed off ownership via such companies, yet they still have a limited role to play.

The Use of Trusts

As a vehicle for owning a property, trusts are of little direct use. Spanish law does not fully recognise trusts and so the trustees who are to be named on the title as the owners of the property would be treated as 'private individual' owners, having to pay all of the income, wealth and inheritance taxes applicable in their case. In a few cases this could still give some benefit but there are probably better ways of getting the same result.

Restoration and Remodelling

Depending on the condition of the property, or its layout, you may wish to carry out restoration work ranging from simply taking out a partition wall to a full-blown refurbishment. Older properties (needing lots of work) may seem attractive for their low price and 'charm factor' but you may find that restoration is extremely expensive – without adding substantially to the property's value. This is because Spanish buyers prefer modern, well-equipped apartments over renovated 'ruins' with character.

You might want a makeover (*una reforma*) of an apartment to get better use of the space or to suit your taste. Generally you will need permission from your town hall (*licencia de obra*). There are basically two types of licence, for **major refurbishment** (*obra mayor*), or **minor work** (*obra menor*). The former includes such things as gutting and repositioning internal walls, or installing a new bathroom and kitchen. The latter might cover taking out a partition wall or two to make two small rooms into one larger area. Many people undertaking minor work do not bother to apply for permission, but you are advised at least to check with the owners' community first. Retiling a bathroom, rewiring or having new plumbing fitted will probably not cause problems, but anything involving excessive noise or rubble (even a 'skip' left outside the property) needs permission, since the authorities can and do order unlicensed work to be stopped, as well as fining the owner. Any external work must be done with permission, while some older (protected) buildings may have restrictions.

Condominium/Community Fees (*Gastos de Comunidad*)

Since most people in Spain live in flats, effectively just a 'space in the air', they have exclusive use of that space (in a manner equivalent to commonhold in the UK) but they also share common parts of the building with other owners. These may include the entrance hall or lobby, stairwells, lift shaft, corridors, any garden space belonging to the building, parking areas and (most importantly) the communal roof and foundations.

The proprietors as a whole constitute an owners' community (*comunidad de propietarios*) which agrees collectively on what maintenance or repair work is needed in common areas. The costs are then shared out proportionately (according to the size of each individual's flat) among the members, by agreement, at regular or extraordinary meetings at which all members have a right to vote. Fees should include routine costs plus providing for a fund to be used in case of major work. If this fund is insufficient, the meeting may agree to raise extra by charging more over an agreed period of time. Some communities have collective heating, the cost of which is included in the monthly fee; others do not, in which case you can spend as much or as little to heat your home as you like. The community elects a president and a secretary for day-to-day affairs, both of whom must reside in the community, though management is usually delegated to an *administrador*, a solicitor or paralegal who need not be a member of the community.

Each community has a set of rules, mostly aimed at ensuring the well-being of the community as a whole. They could, for example, deal with concerns about noise (no radios by the pool), prohibit the use of the pool after 10pm, ban the hanging of washing on balconies, etc. More importantly, they could control pets or any commercial activity in the building. These *reglementos* are important documents. Every buyer of a property in a *comunidad* should insist on a copy of the rules. If you do not speak Spanish you should have them translated.

Property Taxes

The main property tax is the **IBI** (*impuesto sobre los bienes inmuebles*) which is payable to your local council by whoever occupied the property on January 1 of that year. The amount depends on the size of the property (calculated on the square metres that figure in the *escritura*), the location within the city, the quality of construction and the municipality itself. There are massive regional variations. In Barcelona, for example, a flat of approximately 100 sq m costs more than double a similar property in Valencia. Madrid, despite being the capital, comes out quite well in comparison. The local council (*ayuntamiento*) should send you the form that you use to pay. Actual payment is usually into one of several designated banks and, if you wish, you can ask your own bank to pay automatically during the collection period – usually from October through to early December. Late or non-payment can mean a fine or an automatic percentage charge on the amount due – up to 20 per cent.

You will also have to pay **refuse tax** (*basura*). Rubbish collection charges are, in some areas, raised separately. Town halls can also raise taxes for other projects and to cover shortfalls.

The combined level of these taxes is low, perhaps €150 for a small cottage up to €400 for a large house or swanky apartment.

Home Insurance

The general practice is for home-owners to take out a multi-risk household policy, covering the **building** (*continente*), the **contents** (*contenido*) and any **third-party liability** (*riesgo a terceros*). Look for a policy that covers damage caused by fire, smoke, storms, flooding, freezing, burglary, vandalism, terrorist acts and natural catastrophes. Parts of Spain suffer from severe weather – flash floods and forest fires in summer are common in dry regions. If you own a house, external buildings and fittings (satellite dishes, garden furniture, fences and garages) should also be covered. Have a thorough inspection carried out prior to purchase. You cannot later claim for damages that are demonstrably caused by structural faults or sub-standard construction. Contents should be insured against the same risks. Most policies pay for items such as bedding, furniture and clothing to be replaced. Contents insurance often also covers accidental damage to plumbing, damage caused during a burglary, new locks after burglary or loss of keys, alternative accommodation if your house is rendered unliveable-in – and property belonging to third persons that is in your home.

Make sure that the **level of cover** is adequate. Just as in the UK, if you under-insure the building and the worst happens the company will not pay out for the full extent of your loss. The amount for which you should be covered as far as civil liability is concerned should be a minimum of one million euros and preferably higher. Because the risk of a claim under this category is small, the premiums for this part of the insurance are low and so high levels of cover can be provided at low cost. The amount of cover you should have for the building itself should be the full cost of reconstruction of the building. If you own an apartment then the cost of the buildings insurance for the whole block of apartments should be included in your service charge. You will then only need to buy contents and public liability insurance.

As far as contents are concerned, you should make a detailed **estimate** of the value of your furnishings and possessions likely to be in the property at any time. Pay particular attention to the details of this policy and study the small print about what you have to specify when taking out the insurance and any limitations on claims that can be made against it. Notice in particular whether there is a requirement to stipulate items of high value. If you have any items of high value, it is worth having them photographed and, possibly, valued. The original receipts should be kept for making a claim.

The insurance company might specify **security measures** that must be in place in your home. If you do not use them, you may find that you are not covered. If your home is a villa or ground-floor apartment, the insurance company will usually insist on the installation of iron bars (*rejas*) over the windows, a reinforced door (*puerta blindada*), alarms and other security devices. Have new locks fitted when you move in, especially if the property itself is new or you have had work done before moving in. Some modern blocks include video cameras attached to the doorbell; others have CCTV surveillance. These are included in the community fees (*see* p.164). If you are going to spend long periods away from home, you are likely to find that one of the conditions of the policy is that cover will lapse if the property is empty for 30 or 60 days.

There are some Spanish companies that also have the facility for dealing with claims in English. This should not be underestimated as an advantage. Unless your Spanish is fluent, you would otherwise have to employ somebody to deal with the claim on your behalf or to translate what you have said into Spanish.

If you have to **make a claim**, note that there are usually time limits for doing so. If the claim involves theft or break-in, you will usually have to report the matter to the police. This should normally be done immediately after discovery of the incident and in any case within 24 hours. No claim is admitted without a copy of the police report or *denuncia*. The claim should be notified to the insurance company without delay. Check the maximum period allowed in your policy, which could be as little as 48 hours. As with all-important documents in Spain, the claim should be notified by recorded delivery post.

Your **premium** will be calculated according to the size, age, value and location of your property, any security measures in place, and the contents. Premiums are comparatively cheap in rural areas, more expensive in Madrid and the Costa del Sol.

General Insurance Companies

* **AXA, t** 902 212 123; **www.axa-seguros.es.**
* **Caser, t** 902 011 111; **www.caser.es.**
* **La Estrella, t** 902 333 433; **www.laestrella.es.** A subsidiary of Grupo Generali.
* **Pelayo, t** 902 352 235; **www.pelayo.com.**
* **Santa Lucía, t** 902 242 000; **www.santalucia.es.**

Home Utilities

Moving into rented or bought accommodation involves getting connected to utilities – otherwise life is impossible. There is no equivalent of the TV licence in Spain. Payment for electricity, gas, telephone and water can easily be arranged through your bank.

Since January 2003, Spain's energy market has been liberalised and, while you must still contract gas or electricity supplies from the company with the infrastructure in your area (the distributor), you can choose which company bills you for your electricity and piped gas, allowing you to shop around for the best deal. This will not necessarily mean lower tariffs, as industry chiefs claim that they were artificially depressed for years, owing to regulation. Indeed, tariffs are actually expected to rise by about 1.5 per cent a year for the next few years but will still be subject to maximum 2 per cent raises until 2010.

The main benefits to consumers will be better levels of service owing to competition. At present, the competing companies are all falling over themselves to design personalised supply and payment schemes to suit each customer, including incentive discounts to lure custom away from rival companies. They are offering other products, from the installation of air-conditioning and heating systems to home insurance and even communications. It will certainly pay from now on to look at each and see how you can benefit.

The 'big four' competitors for business are:

- **Endesa; www.endesaonline.com.**
- **Gas Natural; www.gasnatural.com.**
- **Iberdrola; www.iberdrola.es.**
- **Unión Fenosa; www.unionfenosa.es.**

Electricity (*Luz*)

Almost all property in Spain is now connected at 220 volts, in line with European standards; this current is entirely compatible with British 240v equipment. However, a few old properties in Spain are still wired for the 110-volt system that was used in many parts of the country until the 1970s. They can be converted, but at your expense, so this is something else that you should check for when buying a property of a certain age that has not been recently renovated. All Spanish plugs are of the standard European, two-round-pin type. If you are taking a lot of electrical appliances from the UK, with three-pin plugs, change the plugs or stock up on adaptors before you go, as they will be cheaper and much easier to find in the UK than in Spain.

Blackouts are surprisingly common, especially in rural areas, though things are improving. Much of the problem stems from lack of preparation for rain. Substations and junction boxes are often built in stream beds, so get flooded and short out. Cuts may last a split second or many hours. Get a UPS (uninterruptible power supply) to protect computers and other vital equipment and a surge protector to guard sensitive devices.

New properties must be connected to the electricity supply. If the property is rented, then the landlord should take care of this. If it is your property, contact the distributor and stipulate how much electricity you want. If you are not sure, consult an electrician or the company, stating the number of appliances you might want to use and how much wattage would cover the demand at peak usage times. Be careful not to underestimate the amount of power needed, especially during winter. If you contract too little, your supply will cut out at times of highest demand.

To contract supply, you will need to produce the usual documents (passport, NIE, bank details – if you wish to pay by direct debit). Being a resident is not, *a priori*, a requisite for getting supplied. Before moving in, ask the company to make a special meter reading to avoid paying the previous occupant's bill. If your house is in a remote rural area and is not already connected to the electricity supply, get a quotation for connection before committing yourself to the purchase. It may prove expensive.

If you are renting, there will usually be an existing electricity supply. It may be in the landlord's name, so he will either charge you or include it in the rent. Some landlords may insist that you have the contract put in your name,

The Language of Bills (Facturas)

darse de alta to sign up for supply
darse de baja to terminate a supply contract

Words and phrases frequently seen on bills:

General – Electricity/Gas/Water
alquiler equipos de medida meter rental
consumo consumption/use
consumo medio average daily consumption
domiciliar/domiciliación to order a direct debit/standing order
electricidad electricity
energía consumida energy consumed
facturación billing
forma de pago means of payment
historial de consumo record of consumption, usually a graph with last 12
   months' consumption
importe total (a pagar) amount payable
impuesto sobre electricidad tax on electricity
intereses de demora interests charged for late payment of previous bills
IVA VAT
lectura (actual/anterior) (current/previous) reading
potencia contratada wattage/power contracted
servicio clientes – customer service

Specific – Telephone
detalle de consumo/llamadas, etc. breakdown of consumption/calls etc.
línea básica basic line
llamadas (metropólitanas/provinciales/interprovinciales/internacionales/
   automáticas/a móviles) (local/provincial/interprovincial/international/
   automatic, i.e. not via the operator/to mobiles) calls made

depending always on the terms of the lease. Others may insist that you contract electricity from the outset, in which case you will have to contact the company yourself. The process is straightforward and involves a small fee. If you think the existing supply will not be sufficient, ask for it to be upgraded, again for a small fee. Make sure to terminate the contract with the company on leaving!

Bills are usually bi-monthly, generally in Castilian Spanish, though you can request them in Catalan or Galician and possibly Basque, but not in English. They come with the standing charge to be paid in advance, the consumption in arrears. They may be paid by direct debit (*domiciliación*) from your bank account. Otherwise you can pay at specified banks. Note that most banks have limited hours for payment of 'non-domiciled' bills, usually 8.30–10.30am.

Gas

Mains Gas

Mains gas is only widely available in larger cities, although the network is slowly extending to other areas. If your property is on the network, connection and payment arrangements are similar to those for electricity. As with electricity, different companies operate regional monopolies: for a new or renovated property that has not previously been connected up to the mains system, contact your local gas company and make a contract for supply.

Getting connected involves contacting the company – providing the necessary identification and your NIE, plus bank details if you plan to pay by direct debit. You will almost certainly be asked for a safety certificate from an authorised gas fitter (*fontanero de gas*) before supply can commence.

Bills are issued bi-monthly. Payment is best done by direct debit, though if you wish you can pay directly into one of the specified banks. As with electricity, you pay standing charges in advance and consumption in arrears.

Bottled Gas (*Butano*)

Many Spanish homes still use bottled butane gas. This form of energy is cheap: the standard 12.5kg bottle (*bombona*) costs around €10 when delivered, usually paid in cash to the man who brings it. It is slightly cheaper if you fetch bottles yourself.

Repsol Butano has a near monopoly on butane supply and you have to sign up with them to be supplied. Check in the telephone book for their local number. They usually order a safety check first, and older properties often need modifications (such as air vents) to meet safety standards. Some form of ID will be necessary, otherwise contracting is straightforward. If you are taking over a flat or house from a previous occupant it is simple to have the contact changed to your name.

On signing the contract, a **deposit** of around €20 per bottle is payable. Keep a spare to avoid running out when showering or cooking! Ask a neighbour to show you how to change gas bottles. The snap-on regulator valve, known as an *alcachofa* (artichoke), requires a certain knack to fit and, if incorrectly fitted, can be extremely dangerous.

Repsol also insist on five-yearly **inspections** and may send an authorised technician to carry them out, usually with advance warning. Be wary of 'cowboy' operators with a fake Repsol logo on their overalls who arrive unannounced, change tubing and *alcachofas* unnecessarily, charge the earth (on the spot) and then disappear without trace. The orange gas tubes that connect to your appliances have the date printed on them, are sold in hardware stores and can be changed easily without the help of a technician.

As you will soon notice, delivering *butano* is very hard work. It is standard to give the delivery man a tip.

Water

Water is scarce in many parts of Spain and is a precious resource. Average rainfall provides sufficient water overall but 'green Spain' gets too much, the rest not enough. To offset this problem, various expensive engineering projects have been set up: desalination plants in the Canaries, pumped water in the Balearics and recycled waste water for irrigation and watering golf courses on the Costa del Sol. A hugely controversial (and expensive) national hydrological plan, designed to canalise water from north to south, was scrapped by the socialist government soon after coming into office. Instead, the idea now is to invest in desalination plants along the Mediterranean coast. Despite this, in many tourist areas water is used with irresponsible abandon. Many towns barely hold their own, and supplies may be restricted. One solution is to install an independent water tank, a *depósito*, filled by a tanker. This system was used before piped water and is coming back into fashion as an emergency back-up.

Water supplies are generally **metered** in Spain. If your property does not have a meter, consider having one fitted; the water company will fit one for a small charge. If the house you propose to buy is not connected to the water supply, check how much connection costs before committing yourself to the purchase – you may find it prohibitively expensive. Strangely, water prices in Spain are still low, as little as a thirtieth of prices elsewhere in Europe, according to *The Economist*, and families only dedicate 1 per cent of their income to water bills. It is felt that prices will have to be increased dramatically to force people to use water more carefully.

All Spanish tap water is drinkable, unless marked otherwise.

Heating and Hot Water

In the north and centre of Spain it can be as cold and wet as Britain. Even in southern Spain you should consider installing a decent heating system.

In many modern Spanish buildings heating (usually gas-fired) is under-floor rather than through radiators, and in apartment blocks there may be a central system for which you pay in part through your community charge and in part according to your own consumption. In Spain there are more types of water heater on the market than in the UK. Install a heater that can cope when the property is fully occupied by people who shower a lot. Many 'standard equipment' heaters and hot water tanks in older properties are far too small.

Air-conditioning

Air-conditioning is not an expensive, unnecessary luxury in southern Spain; consider installing at least a minimal system. If the 2am temperature is 30°C (86°F) you will not regret the outlay. Portable air-conditioning units can be bought in hypermarkets and electrical stores, and installers of larger, built-in systems advertise frequently in the local expat press, or can be found in the *Yellow Pages* under *aire acondicionado*. Some systems combine a cooling and heating function, which is obviously more economical than having two separate systems. Individual air-conditioning units can be noisy, so always have them switched on and listen to them for a while before buying. Anyone with a record of asthma or any other respiratory problems should be doubly careful when buying any system, and get independent advice on its health effects.

There are, on the market, alternatives to installed air-conditioning, for keeping individual rooms cool. The *pingüino* (penguin) is basically a fan that blows out air which has been passed through a tank for water and/or ice which is then pulverised. This system avoids the problems endemic to installed air-conditioning systems.

Telephones and Communications

While you have to get your landline from the former state monopoly **Telefónica**, you are under no obligation to use it for calls. Several national and several regional landline providers operate in Spain, though Telefónica continues an 80.5 per cent market share; many customers stay with them out of inertia despite savings that can be made by switching to other providers.

To get the best rate, work out who you will be calling and how often, then shop around. Some providers offer **flat-rate charges** (*tarifas planas*), which are useful if you will be calling a lot, and some offer discounted indirect phone access via four-digit dialling prefixes (10XX). Dial the prefix before every call in order to get their rates. If you forget to dial it, you'll be billed at Telefónica rates. Some now offer automatic pre-dialling (*marcación automática*).

Most providers make offers for cheaper **international calls**, which may be special rates to a certain number or country, a certain amount of time for free, or cheaper weekend rates, etc. This is certainly an area where shopping around before contracting any provider's services is recommended.

Another option is to buy a prepaid **international calling card**. These offer huge reductions and can usually be used from any landline or mobile. The best thing is to try out several different cards over a period of time to see which is cheapest overall, as some include a connection charge, which can work out expensive if you make many, short calls. It is also worth checking how long the card remains 'alive', as most expire after 30, 60 or 90 days.

General Telefónica information is on the web (**www.telefonica.es**) but is presented in a very confusing, over-technical way and only a small (and not very useful) part is linked in English. More helpful is the company's general customer service and sales freephone number: **t** 1004. Operators sometimes speak English, or you can ask for one that does.

Main Providers

- **Auna; www.auna.es.**
- **BT Ignite; www.bt.es.**
- **Euskaltel,** information line **t** 1717; **www.euskaltel.es.**
- **Jazztel; www.jazztel.es.**
- **Iberdrola; www.iberdrola.es.**
- **Ruta 10; www.ruta10.com.**
- **Telefónica,** customer attention **t** 1004; **www.telefonica.es.**
- **Tele2; www.tele2.es.**
- **Orange; www.orange.es.**

Getting a Phone Line and Making Calls

If your new Spanish home has no previous phone connection, to get a line installed you need to go to the nearest local office (*oficina commercial*) of Telefónica to take out your first contract. This and other phone business can also be done at many of the company's high-street phone shops (*tiendas telefónicas*) and at independent shops that are authorised Telefónica agents, indicated by the company's blue and green logo. If you call **t** 1004, operators can tell you the location of the nearest one, or you can do some of the procedures over the phone. You will need to show your passport or residence card, proof of your new address, such as a recent utility bill, and a copy of the *escritura*, or property deed, to your new home. If you are a tenant rather than the owner of the property, you will need to show your rental contract rather than the *escritura*. In towns and resort areas, new lines are generally installed within about four days of the contract being signed.

If you are buying a property with an existing phone line, once the date of the sale is known, you or your lawyer should contact Telefónica to inform the company that the property is being sold on that date and instruct them to close the phone account, send a final bill to the previous owner and start your new account with the same number on the same day. Transferring a phone line to a new subscriber costs around €30 plus VAT plus the usual line rental. You will usually keep the number but, in Spain, when you move house, for a small fee you can take your number with you as long as it is within the same province, otherwise you may be given a new one.

Note that anyone over 65 is entitled to discounts on many Telefónica services.

Public Phones and Phone Centres

Most Telefónica **public phones** take coins and credit cards, but the most convenient way of using them is with a **phone card**, available to the value of €5, €10 and €15, from tobacconists and post offices, saving the need for fumbling

Operator and Emergency Numbers

The following information and emergency numbers are used throughout Spain. Phone directories (*guías telefónicas*) are published by province, except for the larger cities, which have their own. There are general directories and *Yellow Pages* (*Páginas Amarillas*). All have very useful opening sections with a wide variety of information – special numbers and addresses and so on – on many local services. Some cities – Barcelona and Madrid, especially, but also some smaller cities – operate an enormously useful citizens' information line, t 010, a great way of finding information that's otherwise hard to locate.

t 1002	breakdowns
t 1004	Telefónica customer service and sales
t 1005	international operator for most of the world
t 1008	international operator for Europe and North Africa
t 1009	operator for national calls
t 091	national police line
t 092	municipal and local police (for whichever area you are in)
t 093	speaking clock (high-rate calls)
t 096	wake-up call
t 112	general emergency numbers (fire, police, ambulance)
t 012	general citizens' information line

Directory enquiries have now been opened up to competition. Telefónica has replaced its old 1003 service with 11818 (straight directory enquiries) and 11822 (offering a wider range of information). 11825 is international directory enquiries. There is also a whole plethora of other 118xx information numbers belonging to the various competitors in this field.

with change. Most phones now in use have a digital display that lights up when you pick up the phone, and have a 'select language' (*selección de idioma*) button with which you can change the display into English. As you are speaking, the display will show how much time you have left for your coins or units left on your card. There are **coin-only phones** in most bars, but they are nearly always expensive, because the bar owner is entitled to charge extra for their use.

Still popular for international calls, and a bit cheaper, are **phone centres** (*locutorios*), offices where you are allotted a booth, make all your calls and then pay at the counter when you leave. They are often found at larger railway stations.

Mobile Phones

Mobile phones can be purchased in a variety of places including department stores, supermarkets, at service providers' own outlets, and shops specialising in mobile phones, such as the Phone House.

There are three principal mobile phone service providers: **MoviStar** (owned by Telefónica, **www.movistar.com**), **Vodafone** (**www.vodafone.es**) and **Orange** (**www.orange.es**). All three offer both contract and pre-paid service. To establish contract service, all three providers require personal information, including your residence or passport number. They also require bank details enabling them to withdraw your monthly charges directly from your bank account.

For contract and pre-paid service, most plans include a 12 per cent charge for establishing a call, and the contract services generally charge a fee to establish service. Time for pre-paid plans can be purchased (usually at a minimum of €5–10) at cashpoints, newspaper kiosks, tobacconists, supermarkets, department stores, through the mobile itself, over the Internet and elsewhere.

Mobiles from the main UK networks work perfectly well in Spain provided they have a roaming facility, allowing you to connect via a Spanish network affiliated to your home provider. This is expensive; while fine for holiday trips, if you are staying much longer it will be much cheaper to get a Spanish mobile, or, if you have a phone which is not locked to a UK network, buy a Spanish pay-as-you-go SIM pack and replace the card.

Mobile phone service providers frequently offer new plans and reduce rates often enough to making a summary of the basic plans futile. The plans offered by MoviStar (who have a 65 per cent market share) are given to provide benchmark figures. A good place to get an overview is at the Phone House (**www.phonehouse.es**) which compares operator tariffs on the back of its brochures and on the web (only in Castilian).

- **MoviStar; www.movistar.es.** The main pre-paid packages are:

  - *Activa 24 Horas*: 30 cents per minute 24/7

  - *Activa Total*: 21 cents per minute to MoviStar mobiles and landlines; other calls 48 cents per minute

  - *Activa Club*

MoviStar also offers several contract plans for national calls, starting from 15¢ calls and a monthly minimum of €30.

- **Vodafone; www.vodafone.es.**

- **Orange; www.orange.es.**

Internet

Getting online in Spain is relatively straightforward. Once you have a landline telephone, you only have to choose the type of connection that you want. The options available, depending on your needs, are dial-up, ISDN (less in demand than previously), ADSL (more in demand than before) and cable. Wi-Fi is also increasingly being used. For straightforward **dial-up** connections, CD-ROMs with installation software are often given away by newspapers and computing magazines. In addition, many newly bought computers actually come with a pre-installed installation package enabling you to configure a dial-up connection to an ISP (Internet service provider) by yourself in just a few easy steps. Most dial-up ISPs offer three types of access: a pay-as-you-go service; a flat rate service (*tarifa plana*) for which you pay a fixed amount per month for unlimited access (starting from €20 a month or even less) or a combination of the two, which usually means a flat fee during off-peak hours and a charge per minute the rest of the time. If your needs are limited to checking and sending e-mail for an hour or so a day, one of these deals will suit you.

If your Internet traffic is heavy, for example if you listen to radio over the Internet, or make and receive telephone calls via a VOIP provider like Skype (**www.skype.com**), then you should try to get a **broadband** connection. ADSL broadband is available throughout most parts of Spain but in some smaller villages the necessary cabling has yet to be laid. A basic ADSL line with a package including calls can cost as little as €30 a month, but prices are coming down all the time.

If you already have any form of dial-up connection you can contract your broadband service online. Allow between 10 and 20 days – minimum – between the time you agree to contract a service and having it up and running. It might take longer. High-speed access is usually contracted for a minimum of one year, and if you terminate the contract early you may face stiff penalties or a lawsuit, so be sure to read the small print before you sign up.

It is usually possible to find a deal which includes free installation and a free router, allowing more than one computer to use the connection at the same time. You might also be interested in one of the many packages that give you an ADSL connection plus cheap rate or flat rate telephone calls (local and national), all for one price.

For occasional access to the net, most towns will have Internet cafés and work centres, which allow you to drop in and pay for anything from 15 minutes' connection upwards.

Some Internet Providers

- **www.terra.es**
- **www.jazztel.com**
- **www.ya.com**
- **www.tiscali.es**
- **www.telefonica.es**

Faxes

If you require a fax machine at home or at work, then simply plug the machine into your phone socket. Telefónica offer deals on a second line, either business or domestic, and you should expect to pay an additional standing charge of around €30. In theory a UK fax machine will work on the Spanish telephone system. The phone-jack socket is different, however, which, together with the need for a different mains plug, will be sufficient to invalidate any guarantee. Fax machines have in any case dropped massively in price in recent years owing to the growth in e-mail use, so you can pick up a decent model cheaply.

If you have only occasional need to send or receive a fax, some photocopy shops, stationers and *estancos* may offer fax services.

Postal Services

The Spanish postal system remains in state ownership and for the most part is as efficient as any modern European country.

There are main **post offices** (*oficinas de correos* or, more commonly, just *correos*) in all cities and large towns, and smaller offices in town districts, all towns, many villages, larger railway stations and airports. They are identified by yellow signs with a logo like an old-fashioned post horn. In larger post offices there are separate counters for all the different services, such as parcel post, fax, *poste restante* (*lista de correos* in Spanish) and so on. You can rent your own post office box (*apartado de correos*) in any post office. Main post offices are usually open from 8 or 9am to 9pm Mon–Sat, and some also open 9am–2pm on Sundays; local offices, though, generally open Mon–Sat (or sometimes just to Friday) only, 9am–2pm. If all you want are **stamps** for a letter, you do not need to find a post office but can buy them from your local tobacconist, or *estanco*, identified by a brown and yellow sign with the word *tabacos*. As well as standard post you can also send letters and cards *urgente*, for an extra charge.

Normal **post boxes** are yellow, with two red stripes around them, and usually have two letter boxes, one for local mail and one for everywhere else. There are also a few red boxes specially for urgent mail, usually only found outside city post offices, in railway stations and in a few other prominent locations, collections from which are made every one or two hours. If you only want to buy stamps, you can go to the local tobacconists' shop, the *estanco*.

Businesses make great use of private **courier services** (*mensajeros*) when sending anything valuable or requiring guaranteed delivery. SEUR is the biggest Spanish courier company and has the largest network of depots throughout the country but, for international parcels, the big international players such as DHL or UPS will be quicker, if more expensive. All will be in the provincial *Yellow Pages* under *mensajeros* or *transportes*.

Well worth knowing about is the **Postal Exprés** mail service, the equivalent of Parcel Force in the UK (but actually better) which, although run by the Post Office, is reliable. Parcels sent within Spain are guaranteed for delivery within 24 hours, to most EU countries within 48 hours. Postal Exprés is available at all post offices. It's naturally more expensive than standard post, but still a lot cheaper than private courier companies. Other information about mail services can be found at the official post office website (**www.correos.es**).

Television

Spanish **terrestrial television** consists of five main channels in most areas of Spain. TVE 1 and TVE 2 are the state channels, while Antena 3 and Tele5 are private national channels (*see* p.69). Each region also has its local channel, which in the case of Catalonia and the Basque Country broadcasts in the regional language. You may also come across some minority channels which are broadcast on single transmitters with a limited range. All Spanish terrestrial TV carries advertising and there is no TV licence. However, if you live in an apartment building you may need to seek permission before putting up an aerial or satellite dish. Most multi-dwelling buildings already have a communal aerial.

Spanish **satellite TV** offers a considerable improvement on terrestrial channels. Digital +, formed from the merger of Canal + Digital and Via Digital, provides the usual mix of news, film and sports channels. This is of course the same company as the French Canal Plus, but Spanish operations seem to have been unaffected by the recent crisis in the parent group Vivendi. English Premier League football is available on Digital + and subscription starts from €40 a month. For most films on Digital + you can choose between the dubbed Spanish version or the original language version.

The Canal + single channel is also still available, through the rather old-fashioned set-top decoder, which has the benefit of reduced advertising content. However, many British people resident in Spain, subscribe to Sky's satellite services, which has the added benefit of carrying British terrestrial channels as part of the package together with major national radio channels. Strictly speaking Sky is not offered in Spain, and consequently you need to subscribe from a British address to get your Sky card. While this may not be entirely legal, thousands of people have been doing it for years with no repercussions. In areas popular with UK nationals, agencies sometimes obviate the need for a British address to receive Sky, providing and installing the necessary hardware. Check the directory sections of the English language papers and magazines.

Apart from in a few *urbanizaciónes*, **cable TV** is pretty much unheard of in Spain. In large apartment buildings however, the *comunidad*, may contract satellite TV (probably not Sky!) which is then cabled to all the building.

Money and Banking

Slow and inefficient bank employees (along with state functionaries) can be one of the downsides of life in Spain. In fact, the industry has undergone a transformation in recent years. A series of mergers and the application of IT have made banking more modern, efficient and pleasant, though the level of service still very much depends on the person sitting behind the counter. Good, bad or indifferent, banks are an essential aspect of life anywhere, and everybody who goes to Spain to live and/or work needs an account.

Types of Banks and Choosing an Account

Spanish banks fall into two broad categories: **clearing banks** (*bancos*) and **savings banks** (*cajas de ahorros*, or *caixes d'estalvis* in Catalonia, *caixas d'aforros* in Galicia and *aurrezki kutxa* in the Basque country). Nowadays there is little to distinguish one category from another, certainly in terms of the range of services they offer. Clearing banks usually offer accounts with cheque books (*talonarios*; a cheque is a *talón*). **Cheques** may be used to pay for certain services or for settling accounts between private individuals, but it is almost completely unheard of to use them in supermarkets or department stores. Note that if one of your cheques should bounce, however unwittingly on your part, you have technically committed a criminal offence.

Savings banks usually provide a **savings book** (*libreta de ahorros*) which is updated every time you make a deposit or withdrawal.

Most banks or *cajas* will offer the possibility – if not from the very outset, certainly once you have held an account for a short period of time – of a **cash card** to use in the extensive network of ATMs or cashpoints (*cajeros automáticos*). ATMs operated by *cajas* also have a slot for entering your savings book and using it for transactions. Many offer the possibility of choosing the language displayed on the screen.

Banking Advice

Some important things to know are:

• **When writing a cheque in Spain you first state the amount in figures, and then in letters; the date is always written in full, in letters. Learn to do this in Spanish**, and in figures use the continental 'crossed' 7 rather than the English 7.

• **In Spain, numbers are punctuated differently from in Britain: €5,500.00 is written €5.500,00.**

• **Keep a close eye on your bank statements, and check them against the payments you have had sent to Spain and the items you paid out in Spain.**

• **Make sure you never write a cheque when there are insufficient funds in the account to cover it.**

• **Set up direct debits and standing orders from your Spanish account to cover all the regular payments needed to keep your house going – phone bills, utility bills, community charges – and make sure there is always enough in the account to cover these bills.**

For most day-to-day purposes a **current account** (*cuenta corriente*) should cover your needs. If you have a job, your salary will usually be paid into this account. If you wish, utilities bills can all be 'domiciled' (*domiciliada*), meaning you issue instructions to have the money paid by **direct debit** out of your account every time bills come in. Do not expect to gain much interest on a current account. If you want to save money and earn interest you are advised to also open a deposit or **savings account** (*cuenta de ahorro*).

Bank branches are usually open 8.30 or 9am to 2 or 2.30pm. Some open from 9am until 1pm on Saturdays while others, *cajas* especially, extend their hours into the late afternoon/evening one day a week. During the summer months – often meaning from 1 May to 30 September – opening hours may be cut by about 30 minutes either end of the working day.

Opening an Account (*Abrir un Cuenta*)

The type of account will depend on your particular needs. Anyone aged over 18 may open an account, usually on production of some valid form of ID, address, possibly your marital status (*estado civil*) and your NIE tax code.

There are two types of account available for foreigners: resident and non-resident accounts (*cuenta extranjera*, a foreigner's account). **Residents** may open bank accounts under exactly the same conditions as nationals. **Non-resident accounts** are subject to different rules, barely perceptible on a day-to-day basis, except perhaps that the bank may be more reluctant to issue a credit card or provide overdraft facilities. For non-resident accounts you may be asked for a non-residence certificate (*certificado de no residencia*) which may be applied for at the foreigners' police station, though many banks waive this technicality nowadays. Until recently, residents had to produce their *tarjeta de residencia* when opening an account. However, EU citizens who are working, self-employed or running a business no longer need to apply for this card (*see* **Red Tape**, pp.112–17). A passport should suffice.

If you aim to move money on a regular basis from a UK or Irish account, make sure that you have an understanding with your branch back home and that they can make transfers on request. International transfers can, in any case, take some time – from a few days to more than a week – despite the lack of restrictions on movements of money within the EU and the application of electronic technology. You will also be charged for the transaction.

Taxation

All tax systems are complicated, and the Spanish system is no exception. It is helpful to have some sort of understanding about the way in which the system works and the taxes that you might face. You also need to be particularly careful about words and concepts that seem familiar to you but which have a fundamentally different meaning in Spain from in the UK. Of course, just to confuse you, the rules change every year.

Books (and lengthy ones at that) have been written about the subject of Spanish taxation. This general introduction does little more than scratch the surface of an immensely complex subject. It is intended to allow you to have a sensible discussion with your professional advisers and, perhaps, to help you work out the questions that you need to be asking them. It is not intended as a substitute for proper professional advice.

Your situation when you have a foot in two countries – and, in particular, when you are moving permanently from one country to another – involves the consideration of the tax systems in both countries with a view to minimising your tax obligations in both. It is not just a question of paying the lowest amount of tax in, say, Spain. The best choice in Spain could be very damaging to your position in the UK. Similarly, the most tax-efficient way of dealing with your affairs in the UK could be problematic in Spain.

Just as different clients have different requirements, so different advisers have differing views as to the function of the adviser when dealing with a client's tax affairs. One of your first tasks when speaking to your financial adviser should be to discuss your basic philosophy concerning the payment of tax and management of your affairs, to make sure that you are both operating with the same objective in mind and that you are comfortable with the adviser's approach to solving your problem.

A Short Summary

The Spanish **tax year** follows the calendar (i.e. runs January to December). Most people file tax returns (*declaración de la renta*) annually during the first six months of the following year. Self-employed people must file quarterly returns and keep copies of all invoices sent to clients as well as receipts for anything that may be tax-deductible.

Technically, once resident in Spain you are obliged to declare your worldwide income there. If you only earn a salary in Spain this is no problem, as you will receive a certificate of tax deducted on your personal income (*certificado de retenciones*). Add it into the calculations and file your return.

Basic income tax is known as **IRPF** (*impuesto sobre la renta de las personas físicas*). The rate starts at 15 per cent and rises to 45 per cent for incomes above €45,900. If your taxes are being withheld (i.e. you are employed) and you earn less than €8,000, you need not file a return.

Freelancers with clients in other countries face greater complications, as not all countries' tax systems (or types of work carried out) oblige you to charge clients VAT, or not at the same rate. Squaring things up with the Spanish tax office (**Agencia Tributaria, www.agenciatributaria.es**, also known as **Hacienda**) can therefore be complex. You must declare the income without deductions (*sin retenciones*) and will then pay 20 per cent IRPF on it. For more information on freelancers' tax questions, and some useful websites giving general tax information, *see* Working in Spain, 'Freelancing or Part-time Work', pp.245–8.

Are You Resident or Non-resident for Tax Purposes?

The biggest single factor in determining how you will be treated by the tax authorities in any country is whether you are resident in that country for tax purposes. This concept of tax residence causes a great deal of confusion. Tax residence can have different meanings in different countries. In Spain tax residence is known as *domicilio fiscal*.

Let us first look at what it does not mean. It is nothing to do with whether you have registered as resident in a country or with whether you have obtained a residence permit or residence card (though a person who has a card will usually be tax resident). Nor does it have anything to do with whether you simply have a home (residence) in that country – although a person who is tax resident will normally have a home there. Nor is it much to do with your intentions. Tax residence is a question of fact. The law lays down certain tests that will be used to decide whether you are tax resident or not. If you fall into the categories stipulated in the tests, then you will be considered tax resident whether you want to be or not and whether it was your intention to be tax resident or not. The decision as to whether you fall into the category of resident is, in the first instance, made by the tax office. If you disagree you can appeal through the courts.

Because people normally change their tax residence when they move from one country to another, the basis upon which decisions are made tends to be regulated by international law.

The Rules that Determine Residence

You will have to consider two different questions concerning tax residence. The first is whether you will be treated as tax resident in the UK and the second is whether you will be treated as tax resident in Spain.

United Kingdom

In the UK there are two tests that will help determine where you pay tax. These assess your domicile and your residence.

> • **Domicile:** Your domicile is the place that is your real home. It is the place where you have your roots. For most people it is the place where they were born. You can change your domicile but it is often not easy to do so. Changes in domicile can have far-reaching tax consequences and can be a useful tax reduction tool.

• **Residence:** Residence falls into two categories. Under UK law there is a test of simple residence – actually living here other than on a purely temporary basis – and of ordinary residence.

A person will generally be treated as **resident** in the UK if he or she spends 183 or more days per year in the UK. A visitor will also be treated as resident if he or she comes to the UK regularly and spends significant time here. If he or she spends, on average over a period of four or more years, 91 or more days here, he or she will be treated as tax resident. A person can continue to be **ordinarily resident** in the UK even after he or she has stopped actually being resident here. A person is ordinarily resident in the UK if his or her presence is a little more settled. The residence is an important part of his or her life. It will normally have gone on for some time.

The most important thing to understand is that, once you have been ordinarily resident in this country, the simple fact of going overseas will not automatically bring that residence to an end. If you leave this country in order to take up permanent residence elsewhere then, by concession, the Inland Revenue will treat you as ceasing to the resident on the day following your departure. But they will not treat you as ceasing to be ordinarily resident if, after leaving, you spend an average of 91 or more days per year in this country over any four-year period. In other words, they don't want you to escape too easily!

Spain

Tax residence in Spain – *domicilio fiscal* – is tested by a number of rules, the main ones of which are as follows:

• **If you spend more than 183 days in Spain in any tax year, you are tax resident in Spain. This time can be in one block or in bits and pieces through the year. The Spanish tax year runs from 1 January to 31 December.**

• **If you spend less than 184 days in Spain but do not have a home elsewhere or your principal residence is in Spain, you will be treated as tax resident in Spain.**

• **If your centre of economic interests is in Spain, you are tax resident in Spain. Your centre of economic interests is where you have your main investments or business or other sources of income and, usually, where you spend much of your money.**

• **If you work in Spain, except where that work is ancillary to work elsewhere, you will be tax resident in Spain.**

• **If your family is resident in Spain, you will be assumed to be resident in Spain unless you show the contrary. If you satisfy the taxman that you are not resident in Spain, then you will pay tax on your income and assets as a non-resident but your husband/wife will pay taxes on their income and assets as a resident.** *See* **below for details.**

Tax Residence in More than One Country

Remember that you can be tax resident in more than one country under the respective rules of those countries. For example, you might spend 230 days in the year in Spain and 135 days in the UK. In this case you could end up, under the rules of each country, being responsible for paying the same tax in two or more countries. This would be unfair, so many countries have signed reciprocal 'Double Taxation Treaties'. The UK and Spain have such a treaty. It contains 'tie breakers' and other provisions to decide, where there is the possibility of being required to pay tax twice, in which country any particular category of tax should be paid. *See* 'Double Taxation Treaty', p.189 and p.247.

Decisions You Must Make

The most basic decision that you will have to make when planning your tax affairs is whether to cease to be resident in the UK, whether to cease to be ordinarily resident in this country and whether to change your domicile to another country. Each of these has many consequences, many of which are not obvious.

The second consideration is when in the tax year to make these changes. Once again, that decision has many consequences. It is vital that you seek proper professional advice before making these decisions. You will need advice from specialist lawyers, accountants or financial advisers.

Taxes Payable in the UK

The significance of these residence rules is that you will continue to be liable for some British taxes for as long as you are either ordinarily resident or domiciled in the UK. Put far too simply, once you have left the UK to live in Spain:

- **You will continue to have to pay tax in the UK on any capital gains you make anywhere in the world for as long as you are ordinarily resident and domiciled in the UK.**

- **You will continue to be liable for UK inheritance tax on all of your assets located anywhere in the world for as long as you remain domiciled in the UK. This will be subject to double taxation relief. Other, more complex rules also apply in certain circumstances.**

- **You will always pay UK income tax (Schedule A) on income arising from land and buildings in the UK – wherever your domicile, residence or ordinary residence.**

- **You will pay UK income tax (Schedule D) on the following basis:**

  - **Income from 'self-employed' trade or profession carried out in the UK (Cases I and II) – normally taxed in the UK if income arises in the UK.**

  - **Income from interest, annuities or other annual payments from the UK (Case III) – normally taxed in the UK if income arises in the UK and you are ordinarily resident in the UK.**

• Income from investments and businesses outside the UK (Cases IV and V) – normally only taxed in the UK if you are UK domiciled and resident or ordinarily resident in the UK.

• Income from government pensions (fire, police, army, civil servant, etc.) – in all cases taxed in the UK.

• Sundry profits not otherwise taxable arising out of land or building in the UK – always taxed in the UK.

• You will pay income tax on any income earned from salaried employment in the UK (Schedule E) only on any earnings from duties performed in the UK unless you are resident and ordinarily resident in the UK – in which case you will usually pay tax in the UK on your worldwide earnings.

Paying Tax in Spain

Under Spanish law it is your responsibility to fill in a tax return in each year when you have any taxable income. The tax office is generally known as Hacienda, though its proper name is now **Agencia Estatal de Administración Tributaria (t** 901 33 55 33; **www.agenciatributaria.es**). It is organised by province.

The tax office provides a lot of help and advice – including tax forms and guidance notes – over the Internet. It is, not surprisingly, almost all in Spanish. If you doubt their advice, go to a private *gestor* (*see* p.113).

Spain is (taken overall, not just in relation to income tax) a high tax society.

Taxes on Income – *Impuesto sobre la Rent a de las Personas Fisicas* (IRPF)

The Spanish tax system is very complex. What follows can only be a very brief summary of the position. The detail is immensely complicated and is made worse because it is so different from what you are used to.

Tax Threshold – Gross Income

If your income is less than €8,000 per year, you need not file a tax return unless you are running a business or are self-employed. If you are over these limits you are best consulting a tax adviser, at least for the first couple of years. It is not usually expensive to do so.

Types of Income Tax

Income is divided, as in the UK, into various categories. Each category of income is subject to different rules and allowances. For a married couple, income tax is generally assessed by reference to the income of your household, rather than on your sole income. Unmarried couples are assessed as two households – which is, generally, a disadvantage. When assessing the income of the household, the income of any dependent children is included.

As a tax resident you will generally pay tax in Spain on your worldwide income.

Deductions from Taxable Income

From your gross income you can deduct:

- **any payments made to the Spanish social security scheme.**
- **your (or your family's) personal allowances.**
- **75 per cent of any *plus valia* tax paid in the year.**

The personal allowances are a scale of allowances for the first two children, which are different if they are under 3 or aged 3–16; then for 'extra' children under 3 or aged 3–16; extra allowances for handicapped children; allowances for you and your spouse if you are below retirement age, and if you are over retirement age. There are other deductions too. See your adviser.

Tax Rates

The tax payable is calculated using the table below. The tax is calculated in tranches; that is, you calculate the tax payable on each complete slice and then the tax at the highest applicable rate on any excess. Taxes are paid partly to the national government and partly to the regional government. The table shows the combined total.

Tax Credits

Various tax credits are available. These are deducted from the tax otherwise payable as calculated above. The rules are complex. They include credits for:

- **mortgage interest and other housing costs in certain cases – usually 15 per cent of applicable amounts.**
- **tax paid abroad (or part of it) on income also taxable in Spain.**

Income Tax Rates – 2005 (payable 2006)

Income from (€)	Up to (€)	National Income Tax Rate (%)	State Tax Rate (%)	Total Rate (%)	Total Tax Payable at Top of Band (€)
Nil	4,080	9.06	5.94	15	612.00
4,080	14,076	15.84	8.16	24	3,011.04
14,076	26,316	18.68	9.32	28	6,438.24
26,316	45,900	24.71	12.29	37	13,684.32
over 45,900		29.16	15.84	45	

The state tax varies in the Basque Country, Navarra and in certain others.

Personal Allowances

Single person	€3,400 (under 65)
Married couple	€6,800

Payment of Tax Due

You must complete your tax form 210 and submit it between 1 May and 30 June each year. Late submission incurs a penalty.

Notional Income Tax

This is a purely notional or theoretical income tax based on 2 per cent of the *valor catastral* of any property you own in Spain. This rate drops to 1.1 per cent of the official value (*valor catastral*) if this has been revised since 1994. This tax no longer applies in the case of your first residence in Spain, but will still apply to any other properties owned. The tax is paid by adding it to your other income and calculating the tax accordingly.

Corporation Tax

These taxes are not considered further here.

Taxes on Wealth – *Patrimonio*

As a resident you will be taxed on your worldwide wealth. That includes any sums hidden in tax havens. Wealth includes:

- **real estate (land and buildings).**
- **cars, boats and other personal property in Spain.**
- **shares in Spanish companies.**
- **debts due to you in Spain.**
- **cash, gold, jewels, etc.**
- **any shares in a non-Spanish company owning mainly real estate in Spain.**

You can deduct from your taxable assets any debts you owe in Spain or that are secured against the asset. The primary purpose of wealth tax, when it was introduced in 1978, was to force people to disclose their assets so that they could be taxed effectively on those assets when they died or sold them. It was not to raise money. Remember that no one ever told the tax man anything! The

Wealth Tax Rates – 2005 (Payable 2006)

Assets from (€)	Up to (€)	Rate (%)	Total Tax Payable at Top of Band (€)
Nil	167,129	0.2	334
167,129	334,253	0.3	836
334,253	668,500	0.5	2,507
668,500	1,337,000	0.9	8,523
1,337,000	2,673,999	1.3	25,904
2,673,999	5,347,998	1.7	71,362
5,347,998	10,695,996	2.1	183,670
Over 10,695,996		2.5	

rates of tax are therefore, for most people, quite low. Tax is applied on your wealth, after any deductions, at the rates shown in the table below. An individual resident in Spain can also have €108,182 of otherwise taxable wealth without paying tax. A couple will each have the benefit of the allowance. Most people who are tax resident in Spain in fact – because of the deductions and allowances – pay no wealth tax. The autonomous regions (the Canaries, Andalucía, etc.) have been given the right to fix wealth tax rates for their area, so the rates could in the future vary from one part of Spain to another. Your tax return must be filed (if you are British) by 16 July. Tax must accompany the declaration. Assets are valued as at 1 January.

Taxes on Capital Gains

You will pay tax on your worldwide gains. Gains are generally only taxed when the gain is crystallised – e.g. on the sale of the asset. Gains are taxed as part of your income, subject to a maximum of 15 per cent. If a resident sells his main residence and then uses the money to buy another then the gain will not be taxed. People over 65 who sell their residence will pay no capital gains tax whether they reinvest or not.

Taxes on Death

Inheritance tax is paid in Spain on the value of worldwide assets as at the date of death, subject to the provison of double taxation treaties. The tax is an inheritance tax rather than, as in the UK, an estate tax. That is, the tax is calculated by reference to each individual's inheritance rather than on the basis of the estate as a whole. Thus two people each inheriting part of the estate will each pay their own tax. Even if they each inherit the same amount, the amount of tax they pay may be different, depending on their personal circumstances.

The overall value of the part of the estate you inherit is calculated in accordance with guidelines laid down by the tax authorities. Real estate, for example, is valued at market value, *valor catastral* or the tax office's estimated value – whichever is the greatest. Furnishings and personal effects are valued – unless you choose to the contrary – at three per cent of the value of the real estate. Other assets such as shares and bank accounts are generally valued as at the date of the death. This is declared by the person who inherits but is subject to challenge by the tax authorities. Any debts (including mortgage or overdraft) are deducted from the asset value as are medical bills and funeral costs. Some gifts on inheritance are partly tax exempt.

But this is not the end of the matter. The percentage rates of tax payable depend on the relationship between the deceased and the person inheriting *and* on their pre-existing wealth in Spain. In other words, if you leave money to someone only distantly related to you, or not related at all, and they happen already to be very wealthy, they will have to pay up to 2.4 times the inheritance tax percentage as a spouse or child inheriting the same amount who is not well off. A very large gift to someone to whom you are not related and who is worth over €4,000,000 could attract tax at over 80 per cent!

Residents in Spain who leave their real estate to their husband/wife or children will find the tax on that asset reduced by 95 per cent for the first €120,000. If it is worth more than that, then tax will be paid as normal on the balance. The person who inherits must keep it for 10 years or pay the tax. There are also reliefs in respect of businesses left to wives or children.

See also 'Inheritance and Wills', pp.212–13.

VAT and Other Taxes

VAT is a major generator of tax for the Spanish; see 'Shopping', p.194. There is a miscellany of other taxes and levies on various aspects of life in Spain. Some are national and others local. See p.165, and **Working in Spain**, pp.245–7.

New Residents

New residents will be liable to tax on their worldwide income and gains from the date they arrive in Spain. Until that day they will only have to pay Spanish tax on their income if it is derived from assets in Spain. The most important thing to understand about taking up residence in Spain (and abandoning UK tax residence) is that it gives you superb opportunities for tax planning and, in particular, for restructuring your affairs to minimise what can otherwise be penal rates of taxation in Spain.

Double Taxation Treaty

See p.247. The detailed effect of double taxation treaties depends on the two countries involved. Whilst treaties may be similar in concept they can differ in detail. Only the effect of the Spain/UK treaty is considered here. The main points of relevance to residents are:

- **Any income from letting property in the UK will normally be outside the scope of Spanish taxation and, instead, will be taxed in the UK.**

- **Pensions received from the UK – except for government pensions – will be taxed in Spain but not in the UK.**

- **Government pensions will continue to be taxed in the UK but are neither taxed in Spain, nor do they count when assessing the level of your income and calculating the rate of tax payable on your income.**

- **You will normally not be required to pay UK capital gains tax on gains made after you settle in Spain except in relation to real estate located in the UK.**

- If you are taxed on a gift made outside Spain, then the tax paid will usually be offset against the gift tax due in Spain.
- If you pay tax on an inheritance outside Spain, the same will apply.

Double tax treaties are detailed and need to be read in the light of your personal circumstances.

Shopping

The 1980s boom totally changed Spanish shopping. Before that, apart from in Madrid and Barcelona, shopping was a low-key, almost parochial affair. Designer boutiques were rare, large fashion chains were still in their infancy, most people did their food shopping on a daily basis either in small, local shops or at most in medium-sized supermarkets. By the 1990s the out-of-town shopping mall (*centro comercial*) had imposed itself and doing a weekly or fortnightly shop at a hypermarket had become a habit for many Spaniards. Several large fashion chains, with stores in every sizeable town, had become household names, and designer labels were becoming commonplace.

Types of Shop

Food

Hypermarkets (*hipermercados*) have had a massive impact on the shopping habits of urban Spaniards in the last 15 years. The name is no exaggeration, Spanish hypermarkets are truly 'hyper' – massive places the size of a hangar (the definition is a commercial space of over 2,500 sq m) which sell just about everything under one roof: clothes, toys, sports goods, electrical appliances, books, CDs and videos as well as all the groceries and fresh produce you could possibly need. They usually have bakeries and cafeterias incorporated into the main shopping space.

You will get used to seeing Carrefour, Hipercor (a subsidiary of the Corte Inglés), and Alcampo (translated from its French name – Auchan). The Caprabo chain is a newer arrival, together with the German chain Lidl. As a rule stores are to be found on the highways around major (and minor) towns and cities, and parking is rarely a problem.

For outright convenience hypermarkets are hard to beat, with the widest possible range of products. If you want to buy the cheapest, then most chains have their own-label (*etiqueta blanca*) products that are often 20 per cent less than named brands. There is nearly always a good number of products on offer (*en oferta*), usually of the 'three-for-the-price-of-two' variety, and most chains have customer cards which allow you to accumulate points with every purchase until you qualify for a discount or prize.

Real Shops

While it is possible to do practically all of your shopping in super- and hyper-markets, if you do not like the bland, sterile atmosphere of *las grandes superficies* and also want to practise the language, visit your local shops where service is friendlier, produce often better and prices sometimes quite competitive. Here are the main ones.

Carnicería: Butcher where you can get the cuts of meat you want.

Colmado: General grocery store, stocking most types of food and drink; sometimes they display a sign saying *Alimentos, Alimentación* or *Ultramarinos*.

Droguería: Not a drugstore but a shop selling cleaning products, shower gel and shampoo, and paint, turpentine and other decorating materials.

Farmacia: Pharmacy or dispensing chemist's, usually indicated by a flashing green cross. Pharmacies, it should be noted, may often sort out your minor ills with an over-the-counter product once you've explained the problem, thus avoiding the need to go to the doctor.

Ferretería: Ironmonger and hardware store, often good for pots and pans.

Frutería: The best shops for fresh fruit and vegetables.

Panadería: Bakery. You will sometimes see the words '*horno*' or '*forn*' (oven in Castilian and Catalan respectively), or '*tahona*'. Open daily in most places, baker's shops offer an ever-better range of fresh bread including the standard *barra* (like a thick French stick), the *pistola* (like a baguette) and the Italian-style ciabatta.

Papelería: Stationer's, which often sells books also.

Pastelería: Cake shop, sometimes combined with the *panadería*, always open on Sundays. It is customary, when being invited to a meal with a Spanish family, to take a selection of small cakes as a gift.

Pescadería: Fishmonger. Fresh fish is usually cheaper and fresher here than in the hypermarkets. Usually they also sell seafood (*mariscos*).

Librería: Bookshop.

Tabacos: Known to everybody as the *estanco*, the tobacconist; apart from smoking materials also sells stamps, local transport tickets, phone cards, sweets, postcards and a range of official forms such as tax declarations.

The downside of hypermarkets is that fresh fruit and vegetables may not be as good – or as fresh – as in the local market or frutería and often come pre-packed. As well as this, some recent studies blame the hypermarkets (and their high profit margins) for a huge increase in fruit and vegetable prices. Spanish-produced tomatoes or green beans, for example, cost more in a Madrid hypermarket than in Berlin!

An alternative to the hypermarkets is the '**large supermarket**' (around 1,000–2,500 square metres) which are often located within cities and towns and offer many of the same advantages but better prices on fresh produce.

Many are 'in-town' versions of the hypermarkets and, in fact belong to the same chains. Sabeco, for example, is another outlet for Auchan's products; Champion belongs to Carrefour, and there are numerous smaller branches of Lidl. Mercadona is another very well-stocked and reasonably priced chain. The cheapest end of the market is represented by the 'no-frills' Día chain where you often have to rip open packaging to get at products. There are also many smaller, private supermarkets that can often be surprisingly competitive.

Despite the rise of the hypermarket, the **small-shop economy** is still much more a feature of Spanish life than it is in the UK, although it represents less than 30 per cent of the overall market (down from 50 per cent in the 1980s). Nevertheless, small family-run shops are still one of the main access points to the local community. The range of products and quality of goods can vary, and few can compete in price with the supermarkets or hypermarkets.

If there are three or four bakeries, butchers, fishmongers or greengrocers in your neighbourhood you will find yourself patronising the one that gives best value for money or offers the best service. It can be a pleasurable experience buying meat and fish from an expert local butcher or fishmonger, rather than pre-cut on a Styrofoam tray and wrapped in clingfilm! Much depends on where you live. Most districts of larger towns and cities (particularly Madrid and Barcelona) as well as most provincial capitals have a full range of small shops and services. You can therefore choose never to set foot in a hypermarket.

Clothes (*Ropa*)

Over the past 20 years Spain has seen a revolution in clothes shopping. There is now a range of **fashion chains** catering to all ages offering stylish, trendy or casual wear at highly competitive prices. One of the pioneers was Zara, now an international chain, but still found in just about every Spanish town or city. This chain established itself by running up 'lookalikes' of designer fashions and getting their own versions into the shops within a couple of days. Zara is now part of Inditex, a group of companies that dominates the Spanish clothing market. Other members of the group include: Pull & Bear (clubwear aimed at 14–28-year-old urbanites); Often (for cosmopolitan men between 20 and 45); Massimo Dutti (formal and sportswear for young professionals); Oysho (sexy, designer-like lingerie). For good underwear look also for the Women's Secret and Gianco Bassani chains.

The fashion business also includes other big **Spanish chains** such as Mango. For trendy party-girls there is the Blanco chain, as well as **international stores** such as United Colours of Benetton, C&A and even Topshop. Many expats still regret the closure of Marks and Spencer's outlets in Europe; if you cannot live without them, go to Gibraltar!

For those with plenty to spend, Madrid, Barcelona and the other major cities have a range of **designer shops** with international names such as Armani and

Versace, alongside Spanish designers such as Adolfo Domínguez, Armand Basi, Antonio Miró, Amaya Arzuaga, Purificación García and Sybilla.

When all else fails, Spaniards will resort to **El Corte Inglés**. Though pricier than most, 'El Corte' does offer excellent customer service, money-back guarantees and end-of-season sales with incredible bargains.

Furniture and Household Items (*Muebles y Menaje*)

If you are setting up home in Spain, it may be easier to sell your furniture back home and buy locally, since differences in price will very likely be offset by savings on transportation costs. For household goods and furnishings there is now a range of companies offering good-looking, hard-wearing, quality products all over Spain. IKEA is now firmly established, with shops in Madrid, Barcelona, Seville and the Canary Islands. For stylish household goods there is also the Spanish-owned franchise chain La Oca, with some 40 outlets throughout the country including Mallorca.

Hypermarkets are sometimes excellent sources of good household items at very competitive prices. As with fashion goods, you will find small designer shops in the major cities specialising in furniture and household goods. Barcelona, particularly, has many great shops of this kind.

Electrical Appliances (*Electrodomésticos*)

Large electrical appliances are generally more expensive in Spain than in the UK, but prices are falling. As with furniture, it may be as well to buy these items locally, not only to save on haulage costs but because it is so much simpler to get locally manufactured goods serviced and repaired. Small electrical appliances made in Spain (vacuum cleaners, hairdryers, etc.) are also relatively inexpensive and generally of good quality. Again, hypermarkets can be good places to buy these items but in Madrid, Avilés (Asturias), Badajoz, Córdoba, Jerez and San Fernando there are branches of the Menaje del Hogar chain.

Shopping Hours

Shopping hours vary hugely throughout Spain, as the laws governing them are at the discretion of each Autonomous Community. Throughout most of Spain, you can expect to find small shops open between about 9am and 8 or 8.30pm, often closing between 2 and 5pm for lunch and a siesta. However, this is beginning to change and many shops now stay open during the midday hours. Larger businesses such as super- and hypermarkets, department stores and fashion outlets are usually open between 9, 9.30 or 10am and 8 or 9pm.

Sunday opening is generally restricted in most areas to protect the small businesses although in tourist areas, especially during high season, rules are a lot more relaxed than elsewhere. In most areas, shops selling bread and newspapers (and other food items) are allowed to open for a certain number of hours on Sundays, and in some communities those selling 'cultural goods' (CDs, DVDs, books, etc.) are allowed to open. Depending on the community, there is also an allotted number of Sundays per year when all shops can open. Typically these are the first Sunday of each month, those corresponding to bank holiday weekends and most Sundays during the December pre-Christmas rush.

Queueing and Basic Etiquette

Preconceptions that Spaniards have no regard for queueing are based on an ill-informed assumption that to queue you necessarily have to stand in line. Actually, at small shops and market stalls a very precise queueing system operates. A group of ladies may not be standing in a row, but they will know exactly when their turn comes around, and anyone who bustles in can expect a sharp retort. When you arrive in a shop or at a stall, ask *¿quién es el último/la última?* ('who's last?', for men/women) or *¿quién da la vez?* ('whose turn is it?'); look to see who nods back at you, and go after them. Remember to nod or say *yo* ('me') to the next person who asks the same question.

Another feature of shopping in Spain, large- or small-scale, is that you don't just walk up to an assistant and ask for what you want, or just plonk it on the counter, without any previous courtesies, as many would in British cities. When you enter a shop, say *buenos días* (or *bon dia* if you really want to get on in Catalan-speaking areas) and the shop person will say the same back to you. Polite formalities completed, you can begin your transaction.

Paying

Except in small family-run establishments, market stalls and shops in remoter villages, credit and debit cards are now more or less universally accepted in Spain. Cards issued by Spanish banks raise fewer eyebrows but any major card from abroad (Visa, American Express or MasterCard) will be accepted. Note that you may well be asked for some form of ID when paying by card. When shopping in smaller establishments, try to make sure you have small-denomination euro notes. Many shopkeepers may not have change for €50 notes or above.

VAT

Spain has differential rates of VAT, called IVA (*impuesto sobre el valor añadido*). For basic foodstuffs, some other essential items and cultural goods like books, the rate is just four per cent; for most other foods and hotel and restaurant bills it is seven per cent. For most clothing, car hire, luxury-grade hotels (five-star) and restaurants and many other things it is 16 per cent. In the Canaries, because of the islands' non-EU tax status, VAT does not apply. Instead there is a flat-rate local sales tax, the IGIC, at 4 per cent. This is why larger items, like cars, in the Canaries are so cheap.

Life in Cafés, Bars and Restaurants

From tiny villages to major cities, Spanish bars, cafés and restaurants are the hub of social life. Just about all sections of Spanish society (and all ages) go to bars and cafés, and, although drinking habits vary from region to region, such places are generally your best chance of meeting local people and being

The Grand Style

Spain's golden age of café society lies in the past. Although *tertulias* – regular gatherings in which politics, art or philosophy were discussed at length by leading intellectuals – may continue, they are usually more genteel nowadays. Nevertheless, the cafés themselves, at least in the major cities, still exist, offering a reminder of days gone by.

Typical of the faded grandeur of Spain's great cafes is the **Café Comercial** in Madrid. Situated on the Glorieta de Bilbao, on the edge of the city's nightlife district, the Comercial opened its doors back in 1887 and during its life has been a favourite with Madrid's 'great and good'. Ernest Hemingway famously enjoyed the hospitality at this imposing establishment – though it would be fair to say that he spread his custom far and wide during his stay in the capital.

In the 21st century you still enter the Café Comercial through a heavy revolving door, the tables are marble and the waiters dress in their traditional white jackets. It's just that everything feels a little worn. Café Comercial is still a great place to stop for a snack, a *bocadillo* or a *pincho de tortilla*, after a hard day – working or shopping. It is also good for meeting friends before moving on to the more brash *locales*. Upstairs there are smaller rooms which house *tertulias* and other group meetings, but there is also an Internet café, showing how the Comercial has evolved over the years.

In Barcelona the **Café de l'Opéra**, on the Rambla dels Caputxins, offers much the same by way of historical ambience. The ornate 1920s décor invites you to linger over a cup of coffee and one of the inviting cakes on display. It is divided into two separate sections; the area at the front feels more like a café-restaurant, while at the back you will find lively bar area. As with the Café Comercial, and many other similar establishments in cities throughout Spain, the food and drink offered is only part of the reason for stepping through the door. Essentially, they provide a glimpse of a more genteel era – evocative and nostalgic. Here, for the price of a cup of coffee, you can indulge your sense of romance, while outside the modern world goes on its way.

accepted by them. Distinctions exist between types of establishment and the people who frequent them. The following is intended as a general guide.

Bars and Cafés

The local bar is the least pretentious. Often family-run, it is not unusual to find bars which are open before the working day until past midnight – although some may close for a couple of hours after lunch. People will usually drink wine or beer, perhaps a dry sherry in the south, although good quality coffee is usually available and it is not unusual to see blue overall-clad workers ordering a generous *copa* of brandy with their morning caffeine. Some small bars have no chairs, others have tables, where there is usually a supplement charged, or perhaps a *terraza* in the summer, again with a supplement.

Some bars have a set-price menu (*menú del día*) at lunchtime, usually in a dining room (*comedor*) at the back of the establishment, and most will offer some form of *tapas*, ranging from a simple dish of a few olives to the highest quality ham. Whether or not you receive free *tapas* with a drink varies from region to region but it is not uncommon to be able to fill up quite nicely on free food if you have a few glasses of wine.

The floor in your local bar might well be covered in discarded paper napkins and cigarette ends but this should not be taken as any negative indicator of the standards of hygiene, as the floor will be swept as soon as trade dies down.

The difference between bars and cafés is often purely nominal, but you find grander cafés with marble tables and waistcoated waiters, which may be considerably more expensive than your street corner bar, though prices (especially for wine) are still generally much lower than in the UK. Cafés also usually serve a very reasonably priced *menú del día*. In all bars and cafés you pay for your drinks and any food you have ordered as you are about to leave. It is normal to leave the few small coins you may receive in change, but tipping as such is rare.

Bares de Copas and Disco Pubs

A *bar de copas*, like a *pub* (in the Spanish sense of the word, and pronounced '*paff*') is aimed at a younger clientele. These are usually only open in the evening, perhaps not opening their doors until as late as 10pm. The lighting is dimmer, the drinks more expensive and there is generally no food available. It is quite common to find a DJ playing music in a *pub* or *bar de copas*; some may specialise in particular styles of music and there may be a small dance floor. It is also customary to drink spirits (generically called a *cubata*, whatever the mix), and while a gin and tonic may be as much as €5 the measures are considerably more generous than you would get in Britain.

As the night wears on, such places can become extremely busy and you will then probably be asked to pay for your drinks as you order them. A typical

Smoking Ban, Spanish-style

Since the start of 2006, Spain became one of the most unlikely European countries to ban smoking in many public places, incensing its many red-eyed and gravel-voiced smokers. Almost a third of Spaniards smoke, making Spain the EU's second biggest tobacco market and smoking its biggest killer, with 50,000 deaths a year. But now puffing away is banned in offices, shops, schools, hospitals, public transport and theatres. Bars and restaurants larger than 100 square metres have had to install separate smoking areas with ventilation systems. But Spanish law has always been liberal compared to other European countries – usually with as many loopholes as laws – and the smoking ban is no exception. Since the thousands of Spanish bars under 100 square metres in size can choose to allow smoking, and 90 per cent do, the days of a guaranteed smoke-free *cafe cortado* or *cerveza* are still a long way off.

Spanish night out involves visiting various bars, perhaps only stopping for one drink in each.

Spain's big cities and resort areas also have more than their fair share of *ersatz* Irish-style pubs. For most expats the chief attraction of the Irish pub is that most have a television showing British sports and Guinness on tap but, although generally very expensive, they are also popular with young Spanish people.

Restaurants

Although many bars and cafés offer a *menú del día* at lunchtime, and there are also cheap eateries (*restaurantes económicos*) in every neighbourhood, a proper restaurant is usually taken to mean somewhere that that offers food *a la carta*, both at midday and in the evening. All are obliged by law to provide the midday *menú*, which can cost as little as €7.50 or about €15 for somewhere quite smart. Eating out in Spain is therefore a popular pastime, particularly at the weekend when whole families of three (sometimes four) generations will go to a restaurant for lunch. Children are not only tolerated but positively fawned over in most Spanish restaurants and, though the concept of a 'children's menu' has still not taken hold in Spain, the kitchen is usually happy to alter dishes to suit particular preferences.

The Spanish are usually demonstrative and demanding diners and make it plain if they think the food is not up to scratch – happily sending back food that they feel is underdone, overdone or not quite what they fancied after all. As a result, it is not difficult to find excellent but very reasonably priced restaurants!

Spain is primarily a land of meat-eaters, and it is unusual to find a vegetarian option on the menu outside specialist restaurants. If you are a vegetarian it is

> ### Tipping
> Service is rarely included in restaurant bills (if it is, it will say *servicio incluído*) but, even so, Spaniards are not big tippers. There is no obligation to tip, and no set percentage to calculate, but waiters always appreciate it (and often expect tips more from foreigners than locals). It's reasonable to leave five to ten per cent, and to give more if service has been especially good rather than just apply a flat rate. No matter how many people have eaten, a tip of over €10 would be considered magnanimous by your grateful waiter. Many locals also leave a bit of the change behind after paying in bars, even if they have not sat at a table.

probably wise to think of a few dishes which you will be able to request when faced with a menu designed entirely for carnivores. If you eat fish there will be no problem. If you are a vegan...good luck.

Typical times to eat are 2–4pm for lunch and after 9pm for dinner. Dinner servings usually finish at around midnight although at the weekend it is possible to find a restaurant open later. Prices per head vary considerably but throughout Spain it should be possible to eat very well, *a la carta*, for €30 a head or less (including wine).

Transport

Public Transport

Trains

The Spanish rail network is operated by the state-owned Red Nacional de los Ferrocarriles Españoles (RENFE) which provides local, regional, intercity and international services. Around major urban conurbations, Madrid, Barcelona, Valencia, Málaga, Seville and Bilbao among them, RENFE provides a system of *cercanías* trains which serve the surrounding villages and dormitory towns. *Cercanías* trains usually run at frequent intervals and it is possible to buy a season ticket (*abono de transporte*) which will also cover the use of the metropolitan buses and metro (where applicable). The trains are clean, apart from the inevitable graffiti, efficient, and run to time.

As the name suggests, *regionales* trains operate on longer routes than the *cercanías* but still not from one end of the country to the other. While usually punctual and comparatively cheap, *regionales* trains are much less frequent and can be quite slow, stopping at every station en route. For example, the train between Valencia and Tarragona costs less than €20 but runs once a day and takes four hours to complete its journey.

The *grandes líneas* run over longer distances between major cities and cover a slightly bewildering group of sub-classifications. Intercity, Talgo, Alaris and

Euromed trains all fall under the *grandes líneas* umbrella. Some of these names refer to the type of train and some to specific routes: Trenhotel and Tren Estrella are night-time sleeper trains. There can be price differences for different types of train running on the same route but fares are generally very reasonable. There is a relatively small supplement, about 30 per cent, for first class travel. The *grandes líneas* trains are generally well appointed but again can be slow – to travel from Barcelona to Seville takes 10–12 hours.

The jewel in the Spanish railway crown is the AVE (Tren de Alta Velocidad Española), a high-speed train very much on the French TGV model. The AVE runs between Madrid and Seville, with a journey time of 2hrs 30mins, and a route is under construction from Madrid to Barcelona with service now in operation between the capital and Lleida. Some people claim that the newer Talgo trains would actually be faster than the AVE, if they were allowed to run on the same lines. The Madrid–Málaga Talgo 200 takes a reasonable 4hrs.

All of this can be confusing but RENFE operate an excellent website (**www.renfe.es**) with all the information you need available in English and with online booking facilities for the *grandes líneas* and the AVE.

See p.109 for a map showing Spain's major rail network.

Internal Air Travel

With train travel still relatively slow over many routes, people often choose to fly within Spain. A comprehensive range of domestic flights enables those in a hurry to travel between most major towns and cities.

The major Spanish airline is still the flag carrier Iberia, for which there remains a residual loyalty amongst Spanish travellers despite a series of industrial disputes which have often disrupted passengers. As yet Spain does not have a 'no-frills' airline (similar to easyJet) but Spanair and Air Europa are smaller airlines which fly on domestic routes.

The busiest route is between Madrid and Barcelona where a *puente áereo* (air bridge) operates at half-hourly intervals at peak times. The flight between Spain's two main cities takes 1hr 10mins, compared to 7hrs by train.

As always, prices vary depending on the time of the year and the day of the week. A typical return fare between Seville and Palma de Mallorca might be around €80 if you are booking in advance but could rise to as much as €350 for a last-minute booking in the summer months.

For detailed flight information you can go to a travel agent but for up-to-date schedules and online booking the airline websites are your best bet.

• **Air Europa**, Spain t 902 401 501; **www.air-europa.com**. Flights between **Madrid and Barcelona and all Spain's main cities, the three main Balearic islands and the Canaries. It usually has the best fare offers, and Air Europa tickets can be bought at any branch of Halcón Viajes, Spain's largest chain travel agency.**

- **Binter Canarias,** Gran Canaria **t** 928 579 601, Tenerife **t** 922 635 644; **www. bintercanarias.es**. Internal flights in the Canaries, with frequent services between all the islands, centred on Gran Canaria and Tenerife.

- **Iberia,** Spain **t** 902 400 500; **www.iberia.com**. The most comprehensive flight network within Spain, with routes to every part of the country including the islands, mostly centred on Madrid (many journeys involve changing there) but also focused on regional hubs like Barcelona, Valencia and Seville. Many flights to and from the Balearics are by **Air Nostrum**, Spain **t** 902 400 500, **www.airnostrum.es**, a wholly owned subsidiary.

- **Spanair,** Spain **t** 902 131 415; **www.spanair.com**. A slightly smaller operation than Air Europa that also has flights to most parts of Spain and the islands, centred on Madrid. Again, very competitive fare offers..

Coaches

Various coach companies operate long-distance *autocar* services within Spain. While coach travel is not for everyone, the prices are extremely reasonable and journey times often faster than the trains. The Madrid to Granada coach shaves an hour off the usual train time. The main drawback with coach travel is that routes are operated by different companies, so it can be hard to find comprehensive travel information. The main companies are **ALSA, www. alsa.es**, and **Continental, www.continental-auto.es**. The local bus station will usually provide timetables and sell tickets for all coach companies operating from there.

Transport in Towns and Cities

In any large town or city you should find an excellent public bus service. Fares are usually charged at a flat rate for journeys within the central zone, and it is possible to buy either a monthly *abono* or a 10-journey ticket (*billete de diez*). In Madrid, Barcelona, Bilbao and Valencia there are underground metro railways. In these cities a monthly *abono* will cover use of both buses and metro. Prices for all types of tickets are very reasonable.

Both metro and buses are usually clean and safe. On most metro stations there are security guards and the stations are well lit and spacious. However, despite being recently built or extended, Spain's metro systems are not at all friendly to people with disabilities. Only a few stations have lifts, and wheelchair ramps are virtually non-existent. Some of the most modern buses have the facility to 'kneel', allowing disabled passengers to board more easily.

Taxis

Taxi services exist in every town or city. Taxis are usually white and have a green light on the roof to show when they are available. Most taxis also have a flip-over notice on the windscreen which will say *LIBRE* to indicate their availability. Taxi fares are very reasonable in comparison to the UK, but you should be aware of the system of supplements for being picked up at an airport, station or bus terminal or for having large quantities of luggage. Supplements vary from town to town but should be displayed within the taxi. If you feel that the fare is not correct you can always ask for a receipt (*recibo*), which the driver is obliged to give you and which may be presented to the local authorities.

All taxis in Spain are licensed by the local governments, and while there are some private hire cars there is no equivalent of mini-cabs in the country.

Private Transport

Although Spanish public transport will get you most everywhere, you will probably want to have the use of a car, particularly if you are living outside a large town. Whether you bring a car from the UK or buy one in Spain, it is important that you are familiar with regulations concerning car ownership.

See p.107 for a map of Spain's main road network.

Cars

Importing a Car

If you are resident in Spain for no more than six months a year you can bring your UK car with you and use it while you are there without the need to import it officially. However, if you use a UK-registered car for longer than the specified six months in any one year, the police have the power to impound your vehicle. If you decide to import your UK car officially, it must be re-registered as a Spanish vehicle. This will involve having the car tested for its *Inspección Técnica de Vehículos* (ITV) certificate – the equivalent of the MOT. After the test the paperwork can become quite complicated, and if you do choose to import your car you would be well advised to get a *gestor* to deal with the bureaucracy.

In fact there are many arguments against importing a right-hand drive car from Britain. They are comparatively difficult to sell at a later date – even other expats are unlikely to want a second-hand UK car. You should also consider the safety aspects of driving a right-hand drive car on Spanish roads, particularly on twisting country and mountain roads.

Buying a Car in Spain

With the complications of bringing your car from home, you may choose to buy, new or second-hand, when you arrive in Spain. One advantage is that new cars in Spain are generally cheaper than the same model in the UK. If you buy new or second-hand from a car dealer, they will normally register the vehicle for you, saving a lot of trouble.

However, if you have recently arrived in Spain it may be difficult to get credit to buy a new car. Lenders are reluctant to agree loans or hire purchase agreements for anyone who does not have a permanent work contract or who is not a property-owner. Buying a second-hand car privately is an option, although apart from any linguistic hurdles in discussing terms you will also have to handle the legal transfer of the car's ownership.

If you buy a second-hand car from a private individual, you will need to apply to register the car yourself within 10 days of its purchase. Application forms are obtained from the Jefatura Provincial de Tráfico, at the *vehículos* counter. Ask for a *notificación de transferencia de vehículos*. Once you have completed this form, you will also need to present the following:

- registration document (*permiso de circulación*). This is proof of the transfer of ownership, which should be stated on the back of the form, along with the seller's signature.

- vehicle tax receipt, which must be up to date.

- test certificate from an authorised ITV mechanic if the car is over four years old. This must be accompanied by a *ficha técnica*, or detailed breakdown of the tests carried out.

- a receipt showing that the transfer tax has been paid.

- your residence card if you have one (it is no longer essential), or a photocopy of your property deeds (the *escritura*) if you are a non-resident home-owner. If you are living in rented accommodation, you should present a copy of your rental agreement.

- a receipt showing that the registration fee has been paid.

- a stamped, self-addressed envelope so that the traffic authorities can send you the new registration document.

Vehicle taxes are mostly paid at different counters in the same building. Hence, overall, it's much easier to use a *gestor*.

Second-hand prices can seem quite inflated in Spain, but remember that the mostly dry climate and lack of salt on the roads in the winter means that cars are much less prone to rust.

Regulations, Fuel and Documents

The legal limit for a driver's blood-alcohol level, 0.05, is now lower than that in Britain. The frequently abused official **speed limits** are 120kph (75mph) on *autopistas* and *autovías*, 100 or 90kph (62 or 56mph) on most N and country roads, and 50kph (30mph), or sometimes less, in towns. Note that these limits are reduced for vehicles towing caravans or trailers.

The same EU-recognised **fuel** grades are on sale: unleaded is *sin plomo* (or *sense plom* in Catalan), regular, lead-replacement petrol is *super*, and diesel is *gas-oil*. Petrol prices in Spain are considerably cheaper than in the UK, with a litre of unleaded petrol costing around 89 *centimos* in January 2006. Diesel cars are extremely popular and diesel fuel is available at all service stations for around 83 *centimos* a litre. Four star, or *super*, is still widely available and is usually a couple of *centimos* more expensive than unleaded.

Whether you have imported your car or bought one in Spain, you should carry the following **documents** when you are driving:

- *Periso de Circulación*: **this is the registration document which shows the car to be registered in your name.**

- **ITV: if your car is over four years old, you must have a current ITV (*Inspección Técnica de Vehículos*) certificate, the equivalent of the MOT, showing that your car is roadworthy. This should be accompanied by the *ficha técnica* which details the tests carried out for your car's ITV.**

- **in addition you must pay your annual vehicle tax at your local town hall, (*ayuntamiento*). This tax is usually due at the end of March.**

- **driving licence.**

- **insurance documents including a bank receipt to show the insurance is paid and up to date.**

Insuring Your Car

As in the UK, Spanish law requires that your car be insured at least for **third party liability** (*terceros*). Above and beyond the minimum insurance coverage there are also **third party, fire and theft** (*terceros, incendio y robo*) and **fully comprehensive** (*todo riesgo*) policies available. Insurance premiums are calculated in the usual way, with age, sex, vehicle type and your address taken into account. One factor you should bear in mind is that even *todo riesgo* policies may not cover you as the driver or passengers in your own car for injury or death.

- **Linea Directa, t 902 123 335 (English-speaking); www.lineadirecta.com:** Spanish wing of Direct Line which allows you to insure your car on the phone or on the Internet.

- **Fénix Directo, t 91 325 55 44; www.fenixdirecto.com:** one of the cheaper Spanish insurance companies which again allows you to get a policy online.

Also try the general insurance companies listed on p.167.

Licences

European Union law states that a UK driving is valid for use in Spain for both residents and visitors and that there is no obligation to swap it for a Spanish licence. In practice, if you are in Spain for the long term then it makes sense to swap your UK licence for a Spanish one at the Jefatura de Tráfico of your province. Insurance companies will usually want a copy of your licence before issuing your policy and the police will probably ask to see it sooner or later – a Spanish document makes things that much easier. In any case, if you are resident in Spain but do not obtain a Spanish driving licence you are still legally obliged to present your UK licence to the Jefatura Provincial de Tráfico for your details to be entered into their computer system.

Motorbikes

The law governing the use of motorbikes over 50cc is almost identical to that applying to cars. Again you have the right to exchange your UK motorbike licence, although it is not strictly necessary. The need for registration and insurance of 50cc plus bikes is also the same as for cars.

Small mopeds of 49cc or under can be driven on a standard driving licence or, if you do not have a driving licence, it is comparatively simple to get a licence which applies to these small bikes. Talk to a *gestor* or a local driving school. Children as young as 14 are allowed to ride mopeds and buying one is also much simpler, as it is not necessary to produce any official documentation.

Though frequently ignored (particularly by teenagers), it is a legal requirement to wear a helmet on all types of motorbike, no matter what the engine capacity.

Bicycles

Cycling in Spain is regarded more as a leisure activity or sport than a mode of transport. There are few dedicated cycle lanes in cities and drivers often pay scant regard to cyclists. It is certainly advisable to wear a helmet even in the heat of a Spanish summer.

Crime and the Police

Like most European countries, Spain has a growing crime problem. Large cities and tourist areas attract their fair share of thieves and other shady characters and it is likely that, as a foreigner in Spain, you will be seen as a potential target. Most crime remains property-based (rather than physical violence) and with sensible precautions you can reduce the chance of becoming a victim. Nevertheless, violent crime is on the increase, especially in the larger cities, often involving rival gangs of drug-traffickers settling scores. Sadly, innocent bystanders sometimes get caught in the crossfire.

Street Crime

The most common sort of criminal activity is someone trying to make off with your bag, wallet or camera. This is usually attempted by stealth rather than outright confrontation – mugging as such is less common in Spain than in Britain or North America, and street theft is more likely to occur in crowded areas than on deserted streets. Typical ploys involve someone asking you directions while their partner rifles through your belongings or 'accidentally' spilling a drink or ice-cream over you and then brushing you down while slipping a hand into your pocket. Know where your bags are at all times, try to carry them slung over your front rather than your back, and keep your wallet in an inside pocket.

Car Crime

Theft of and from cars is quite common, especially in cities and resort areas. Never leave anything of value, or important documents, unattended in your car. A simple crook-lock may be enough to deter a potential thief.

It is not unheard of for people to break into cars in order to sleep. There is almost nothing you can do to prevent this apart from parking on busy streets. If you should find someone in your car it is best to go to the police and avoid confrontation. It is also a fact of life that cars with foreign number plates are more likely to be broken into.

Spanish Police

If you are unfortunate enough to fall victim to a crime you will find yourself dealing with one or other of the Spanish police forces. Below is a summary of the responsibilities of the main forces and how to recognise them.

• *Policía Municipal* (may also be called *Policía Local* or *Guardia Urbana*): This force is responsible for traffic and parking violations in the area of their jurisdiction and may also deal with minor crimes. They usually wear dark blue uniforms with either white or light blue shirts. t 092.

• *Policía Nacional*: The *Policía Nacional* deals with serious crime and it is usually this force that you contact if you are the victim of a crime. In the case of theft it is necessary to make a statement (*denuncia*) at your nearest Policía Nacional station in order to claim on your insurance. The *Policía Nacional*, with dark blue uniforms, also deal with residency issues. t 091.

• *Guardia Civil*: Although their *tricorne* hats are now only worn for ceremonial occasions, the *Guardia Civil*, in their green uniforms remain the most identifiable police force. The *Guardia* is responsible for Spanish customs and excise, policing the main highways and rural areas where there is no *Policía Municipal*. They can also be seen guarding state buildings. t 062.

• In Catalonia and the Basque country there are also regional police forces called, respectively, the *Mossos d'Escuadra* and *Ertxaintxa*. At the moment their duties still overlap to some extent with the roles of the *Policía Nacional* and *Guardia Civil*.

Taking Your Pet

Until recently, taking a dog or cat to Spain involved some soul-searching on the part of the owner. Britain's quarantine laws entailed a level of expense for the owner and distress for the animal which discouraged anyone who thought they might later wish to re-enter the UK. Thankfully the introduction of the Pets Travel Scheme (**PETS**), more commonly referred to as the **Pet Passport**, has made the prospect of moving your animal between Britain and Spain much less stressful – but not necessarily simple. There are definite (non-negotiable) steps which you must go through to get your animal permission to travel.

First your dog or cat must be microchipped and then vaccinated against rabies. A vet must then take a blood sample which will be sent to a government-approved laboratory for testing. Six months must elapse between the date of your animal's blood test and the issuing of a valid PETS certificate. Between 24 and 48 hours before your animal is due to travel, a vet must administer a treatment for ticks and tapeworms and issue a certificate confirming the treatment. Finally, on the day of travel you must sign a declaration of residency (form PETS 3) confirming that your animal has not been in any country *not* covered by the PETS scheme during the previous six months. The PETS certificate is valid for a limited time depending on the date of your animal's rabies vaccination, but can be renewed when a booster injection is administered.

It should be stressed that these steps are necessary to enter the UK rather than Spain, but it is highly recommended that you get your animal a PETS certificate on leaving the UK, even if you have no intention of returning. If unforeseen circumstances mean that you have to bring your dog or cat back into Britain, then it is better to have the paperwork already in order.

If you acquire a pet while in Spain – and with so many dogs and cats abandoned it can be be hard to resist – all the above steps can be performed in the country. However, there is currently only one Spanish laboratory, in Granada, that carries out the requisite blood tests, and results can be very slow in arriving. Stories of the lab subjecting the blood to the wrong tests abound.

If you are in a major city or near one of the main expat communities there will probably be an English-speaking vet or animal organisation that can guide you through the process. The PETS scheme only applies to dogs and cats and on certain approved routes, either air or sea. Visit the **DEFRA** website (**www.defra. gov.uk**) for up-to-date details.

It should also be remembered that there are regulations inside Spain which govern pet ownership, particularly with regard to dogs. These can vary from region to region but in most cases it is a legal requirement to have your animal microchipped and vaccinated against rabies. Consult a local vet for advice. In certain areas, regular treatment for particular parasites, such as heart worm, may be advisable or even mandatory.

Health and Emergencies

Public Healthcare

All Spanish citizens, and resident working foreigners, have a legal right to the healthcare provided by the **Insalud** (Instituto Nacional de la Salud), and around

90 per cent of the population actually use the system. Under this system, patients are seen first by a GP (*médico de cabecera*), usually in their local health centre (*ambulatorio* or *centro de salud*) and, if necessary, referred to a specialist (*especialista*). Generally speaking, if you need to see a doctor you can get an appointment within a couple of days of calling. If it is more urgent, go to *urgencias*, which may be available in your local health centre (depending on its size and staffing levels) or in the district hospital corresponding to your local district. You cannot usually get to see a specialist without first seeing the GP unless you go via the emergency system.

Waiting lists can be long for specialists, especially for non-emergency cases. This varies considerably from one Comunidad Autónoma to another, as do healthcare and other services in general. The system does not usually cover dental or eye treatment, but most prescription medicines are free or cost just a fraction of their price.

If you are working in Spain, your employer should make contributions to the **social security system** (*seguridad social*) on your behalf, which are partially deducted from your wages and partially an expense assumed by the employer. If you are self-employed, you must make these contributions yourself. Payment entitles you and your family to free or subsidised healthcare under exactly the same conditions as Spanish citizens. It is your employer's responsibility to register you with social security. If you work for yourself, then you must do the paperwork yourself. Once registered, after a few weeks you will receive a registration card (a cardboard *cartilla de la seguridad social* or a plastic smartcard (*tarjeta sanitaria*); the latter is more frequent nowadays. This card must be presented when you go to the health centre, where you must also register on taking up residency or moving to a new neighbourhood. In the case of married couples with only one partner working, the non-working partner, and any dependants, are covered by the same card. If you are both working you can each have your own card. In the case of common-law marriages, the law is still quite vague; some Comunidades Autónomas recognise this status, others do not. Check this; it may be advisable for each partner to have their own card.

If you are not a resident and remain officially a UK resident, you are still entitled to free basic care, on production of a European Health Insurance Card (EHIC) – which replaced the E111 form in 2005. The EHIC needs to be applied for in your home country; either online at **www.dh.gov.uk/travellers**; by phone via **t** 0845 606 2030; or by post, with forms available at post offices.

Private Healthcare

The private sector has grown recently, assuming greater importance, with an estimated 15 per cent of the population having private cover. Not everybody uses it all the time; for some it is a supplement, rather than an alternative, to the state system. Many use it to get around the waiting lists for specialists, having had a preliminary diagnosis from their state GP. Private companies have their own parallel network of hospitals, clinics and laboratories, though they are not always necessarily as well equipped as the better state hospitals where the latest equipment may be found. Medicines prescribed by a private doctor are not subsidised, less still free.

Prices for private coverage depend very much on the company, the amount of cover you are prepared to pay for and other factors such as the age, sex and state of health of the applicant. In general, premiums are higher for women. A policy may cost €35–55 per month.

Spanish Health Insurance Companies

- **Adeslas, t** 902 200 200, **www.adeslas.es.**
- **Asisa, t** 901 10 10 10, **www.asisa.es.**
- **Sanitas, t** 902 102 400, **www.sanitas.es.** Large-scale Spanish specialist health insurance provider associated with BUPA.

UK Health Insurers

- **BUPA International, t** (01273) 208181, **www.bupa-intl.com.** Offers a range of health plans designed specifically for expatriates.
- **Exeter Friendly Society, t** 08080 55 65 75, **www.exeterfriendly.co.uk.** Has health plans specifically for residents in Spain and Portugal.
- **PPP Healthcare, t** 0800 33 55 55/**t** (01892) 612 080, **www.ppphealthcare. com.** Special health plans for expatriates, valid worldwide.

Emergencies

Whatever your insurance status, in an emergency it is more important to save a life than to worry about who is later going to foot the bill, so get to the emergency department (*urgencias*) at your nearest hospital quickly. Spanish health services, both public or private, are obliged to provide treatment in an emergency. However, do not abuse this, as anybody seeking treatment for a problem that can reasonably be considered as not constituting an emergency – the decision rests with the doctor or nurse on call – may then have to pay the hospital if they are uninsured or not covered by social security.

To call an **ambulance**, dial the emergency number **t** 112.

If you want to find a doctor who can speak to you in your own language, ask at your embassy or consulate. In any case many doctors do speak English.

Pharmacies (*Farmacias*)

Pharmacies or chemists are easily spotted from a distance by their flashing green cross. They have the same opening hours as shops, and at night and on

Typical Purchases in a Pharmacy/Chemist

As in English, many popular brand names become synonymous with the product itself.

aspirina aspirin
bronceador (factor 15/20 etc.) (factor 15/20 etc. sun cream)
compresas (Evax) sanitary towels (Evax is a popular brand)
crema de labios lipsalve
laxante laxative
pastillas pills
preservativos condoms
receta prescription
somníferos sleeping pills
tiritas sticking plasters/Band-aids
vendas bandages

public holidays work a rotation system. Those open are known as *farmacias de guardia*. To find the nearest one, check the local section of any daily newspaper or look at the list displayed in the window. In the larger cities there are now some 24-hour pharmacies that supplement the *farmacias de guardia*.

Many people go to pharmacies instead of the doctor with minor ailments such as a cold or 'flu. Pharmacists are well trained (virtually paramedics) and are therefore able to recommend treatment on the spot. They may also sell you medicines over the counter that in other countries would only be available on prescription. If your problem is more serious you really should see a doctor.

Social Services and Welfare Benefits

If you are resident and working in Spain and paying (*cotizando*) into the social security system, either as an employee or a self-employed worker, you become entitled to a series of benefits that Spanish workers themselves enjoy, with no discrimination. The system covers healthcare (including sickness and maternity leave), workplace accidents, unemployment, old age, invalidity and death (survivor's pensions). Entitlement to the full range of benefits is not immediate as you have to have accumulated contributions (*cotizaciones*) over a certain period of time. For example, entitlement to 120 days of unemployment benefit requires 360 days' *cotizados*, and entitlement to an old-age pension requires a minimum of 15 years of working and *cotizando* prior to retirement.

For more information on unemployment benefit, sick leave and maternity leave, *see* **Working in Spain**, 'Being Employed', pp.238–42. Excellent information on a whole series of welfare questions in Spain is available on the EURES website (**http://ec.europa.eu/eures/home.jsp?lang=en**).

Previous contributions made into any other EU country's system (and that of other countries with which Spain has reciprocal agreements) usually count towards benefit entitlement in Spain, but this is a complicated issue since it involves liaison between the social security systems of two (or more) countries. The general underlying principle is that if there is a single market with free movement of labour, then benefits accumulated as a result of that labour and the entitlement thereto must be transferable within the common European space. In practice, it is not so simple and the bureaucracy involved can be slow. There are, though, many cases of EU citizens who, having worked for many years in their own country and then in Spain, have become eligible for Spanish unemployment benefit for the maximum duration permitted, and others who have finished their working life in Spain and become entitled to a full pension based partially on their previous contributions. The system does work!

For information on your contributions record from work performed in the UK, contact the Inland Revenue, National Insurance Contributions Office, Benton Park View, Newcastle upon Tyne NE98 1ZZ.

Retirement, Pensions and Investments

Workers in Spain retire and qualify for state pensions on reaching 60 (women) and 65 (men). The amount payable depends on the number of years' contributions made by the worker and his employer(s), from a minimum of 15, and earnings during the eight years prior to retiring. Contributions made previously in other EU countries also count towards entitlement in Spain and will be added to later contributions made on working in Spain. Like much of the developed world, Spain has a pensions crisis looming owing to its ageing population. Nobody should therefore be surprised if the retirement age is raised, as it is being in the UK.

Roughly three-quarters of all expats living in Spain are retired. There are many good reasons for choosing to retire to Spain, including relatively low living costs, affordable properties and the weather. The healthier Mediterranean diet also adds to the quality of life for retirees. Living costs are, however, subject to change, and Spain is no longer as cheap as it once was. The pound has also declined in value against the euro. While this position may change, it is worth remembering that UK pensions used for living in Spain can be vulnerable to currency fluctuations.

Pensions

UK (and other EU) state pensions can be paid into a Spanish bank account. The same applies to most company pensions, unless there are any stipulations to the contrary. If this is the case you can make arrangements for the money to be transferred from the receiving bank at home. Even as a non-EU citizen you can receive your pension in Spain; receiving funds from abroad, in fact, opens the door to obtaining residency. With sufficient means you can live – and spend your money – in the local economy, but will not compete with locals in the job market, and so you are welcomed.

If you receive a pension from abroad, look carefully into payment arrangements. Banks sometimes charge for transferring abroad and the receiving bank may also apply a commission (which is against EU regulations) so shop around. Monthly payments may be subject to proportionally higher transfer charges than quarterly ones so the latter option is often better, as long as you can spin the money out over a longer period. You may choose to make an annual arrangement with a currency dealer whereby they send you the money at an exchange rate that will apply for the whole year. This provides assured income, but you may lose out because of exchange rate fluctuations. It could, of course, work the other way too.

Anybody residing for more than 183 days per year in Spain becomes liable to taxation there, on their worldwide income. Your UK state pension is no longer taxable in the UK but in Spain it is, because it is regarded as income. If you receive a UK government pension, however, you will be taxed in the UK. In order not to pay tax again in Spain, or to get it reimbursed if you do, contact: Inland Revenue, Inspector of Funds, Lynwood Road, Thames Ditton, Surrey, KT7 0DP, England. You can obtain forms from this office, in English and Spanish, to claim exemption from UK tax. Take (or get your *gestor* to take) both forms to the Agencia Tributaria (Spanish Inland Revenue) where one will be stamped for return to the Inland Revenue in the UK, showing that tax has been paid in Spain.

Since not everyone receives income solely from pensions, the problem of double taxation will arise anyway, especially during your first year's residency in Spain. To become exempt from paying tax in the UK you have to be absent for a full year, and there is an overlap period between the UK tax year (5 April–4 April) and the Spanish tax year, which coincides with the calendar year. Your income may be taxable – and taxed – in both countries. A double taxation treaty (*see* p.189 and p.247) means one of the countries will give you credit for taxes paid in the other. This problem is best solved by taking expert advice.

If you have not yet retired and you move to Spain, whether you intend to work or not, your UK pension entitlement is frozen. Depending on the number of years' contributions made, you may or may not become eligible for a UK pension on reaching the age of retirement. To make sure that you are entitled you can make additional payments from Spain. The decision as to whether to continue to make UK payments is an important one: information and advice is obtainable from: Inland Revenue, National Insurance Contributions Office, Benton Park View, Newcastle upon Tyne, NE98 1ZZ (**www.hmrc.gov.uk/nic/offices.htm**). Also see **www. dwp.gov.uk** and **www.thepensionservice.gov.uk**.

Inheritance and Wills (*Herencia y Testamentos*)

A person who dies without a will dies intestate. This gets complicated. Will the UK rules as to what happens in this event apply (because you are British) or will it be the Spanish rules? This gives rise to many happy hours of argument by lawyers and tax officials. It is much cheaper to make a will.

You have to think very seriously, and take expert advice, before making a will, as there are numerous aspects concerning inheritance that should be considered. It is far too complex an issue to deal with fully, and there are differences from one Autonomous Community to another. Keep in mind the following important points:

• **A Spanish will for your Spanish assets** will avoid costly delays for your heirs. Another will for that part of your estate held outside Spain is recommended. It is always best to make a Spanish will. If you do not, your English will should be treated as valid in Spain and will be used to distribute your estate. This is a false economy, as the cost of implementing the UK will is much higher than the cost of implementing a Spanish will and the disposal of your estate set out in your UK will is often a tax disaster in Spain.

If you are not a resident in Spain, your Spanish will should state that it only applies to immovable property in Spain. The rest of your property – including movable property in Spain – will be disposed of in accordance with English law and the provisions of your UK will. If you are domiciled (*see* pp.182–4) in Spain you should make a Spanish will disposing of your worldwide assets. If you make a Spanish will covering only immovable property in Spain, you should modify your UK will so as to exclude any immovable property in Spain.

• **Always use a lawyer** to advise as to the contents of your will and to draft it. Lawyers love people who make home-made wills. They make a fortune from dealing with their estates because the wills are often inadequately drafted and produce lots of expensive problems.

• The Spanish cannot do just as they please with their property when they die. **Inheritance rules apply.** These rules for Spaniards are much more restrictive than the rules under English law. Certain groups of people have (almost) automatic rights to inherit a part of your property. Fortunately, if you are not Spanish you can dispose of your property in whatever way your national law allows. For British people this is, basically, as they please. Spanish citizens are obliged to leave two-thirds of their estate to their offspring; as a foreign resident you are permitted to leave your estate to whomever you want, not necessarily your children, though non-relatives may be liable for larger amounts of inheritance tax.

• **Inheritance tax** (*ley de sucesiones*) is largely unavoidable. Loopholes are difficult to find. Some Autonomous Communities are considering reducing or scrapping inheritance laws at some time in the future, a subject of much debate at present.

• **Foreign residents** are eligible for exemption on 95 per cent of the value of their property, for inheritance tax calculation purposes, up to the first €120,000.

Different types of will exist. All have their pros and cons:

• **Open will** (*testamento abierto*): Its contents are known to the notary (who draws it up) and three witnesses, all of whom must sign it. Copies are then filed at the registry of wills. The notary keeps the original. This is the most common and most suitable type of will.

• **Closed will** (*testamento cerrado*): Drawn up by a Spanish lawyer, signed by a notary, sealed and filed to be opened on the death of the testator.

• **Holographic will** (*testamento ológrafo*): Made in the testator's own handwriting without the need for witnesses, may be registered though this is voluntary. On the testator's death it must be authenticated before a judge. This is useful for small estates.

• **Verbal will** (*testamento verbal*): Made before five witnesses who then convey the testator's wish to the notary. The notary then draws up and certifies a written version.

You are strongly recommended to seek the advice of a Spanish lawyer before making any will, as well as a lawyer in any country where you also have assets.

Investments

If you are moving to live overseas you must review your investments. Your current arrangements are likely to be financially disastrous.

In financial terms, you may be worth more than you think. When you come to move abroad and have to think about these things it can come as a shock. Take a piece of paper and list your actual and potential assets. Check that you have included the following current assets: main home, holiday home, contents of main home, contents of holiday home, car, boat, bank accounts, other cash-type investments, bonds, stocks and shares, PEPs, Tessas, ISAs, SIPS, value of your business, etc. Also include future assets such as the value of share options, likely lump sum from personal/company pension, potential inheritances or other accretions, value of endowment mortgages on maturity, etc. This will give you an idea as to the amount you are worth now and, just as importantly, what you are likely to be worth in the future. Your investment plans should take into account both figures.

You may already have an investment adviser. You may be very happy with their quality and the service you have received. They are unlikely to be able to help you once you have gone to live in Spain. They will know about neither the Spanish investment that might be of interest to you nor, probably, many of the 'offshore' products that might be of interest to someone no longer resident in the UK. Even if they have some knowledge of these things they are likely to be thousands of miles from where you will be living. Nor is it a simple question of selecting a new local (Spanish) adviser once you have moved. They will usually know little about the UK aspects of your case or about the UK tax and inheritance rules that could still have some importance for you.

For British people the big issue is whether they should keep their **sterling investments**. Most British people will have investments that are sterling-based. Even if they are, for example, a Far Eastern fund they will probably be denominated in sterling and they will pay out dividends, etc. in sterling. But you will be spending euros. As the value of the euro fluctuates against sterling, the value of your investments will go up and down. That, of itself, isn't too important, because the value won't crystallise unless you sell. What does matter is that the revenue you generate from those investments (rent, interest, dividends, etc.) will fluctuate in value. You can experience a huge difference in your standard of living based solely on exchange rate variations. This is unacceptable, particularly as you will inevitably have to accept this problem in so far as your pension is concerned. In general terms, therefore, investments paying out in euros are preferable if you live in a euro country.

Trusts can be an important weapon in the hands of the person going to live in Spain. Trusts offer the potential benefits of:

- **allowing you to put part of your assets in the hands of trustees so that they no longer belong to you for wealth tax or inheritance tax purposes.**
- **allowing you to receive only the income you need (rather than all the income generated by those assets) so keeping the extra income out of sight for income tax purposes.**
- **allowing a very flexible vehicle for investment purposes.**

So how do these little wonders work? After leaving the UK (and before moving to Spain) you reorganise your affairs by giving a large part of your assets to 'trustees'. These are normally a professional trust company located in a low tax regime. The choice of a reliable trustee is critical. Those trustees hold the asset not for their own benefit but 'in trust' for whatever purposes you established when you made the gift. It could, for example, be to benefit a local hospital or school or it could be to benefit you and your family. If the trust is set up properly in the light of the requirements of Spanish law then those assets will no longer be treated as yours for tax purposes. On your death the assets are not yours to leave to your children (or whoever), and so do not (subject to any local anti-avoidance legislation) carry inheritance tax. Similarly the income from those assets is not your income. If some of it is given to you it may be taxed as your income, but the income that is not given to you will not be taxed in Spain and, because the trust will be located in a nil/low tax regime, it will not be taxed elsewhere either.

The detail of the arrangements is vitally important. They must be set up precisely to comply with Spanish tax law. If you do not do this they will not work as intended. Trustees can manage your investments in (virtually) whatever way you stipulate when you set up the trust. You can give the trustees full discretion to do as they please or you can specify precisely how your money is to be used. There are particular types of trusts and special types of investments that trusts can make that can be especially beneficial in Spain.

Living with Children

Moving to Spain with a family and children, rather than going as a single person or as a childless couple, involves totally different considerations and will influence many of the choices you make, especially where you decide to live.

Spain is an attractive place to bring up children. Many British families cite this as a prime reason for moving there in the first place. Generally speaking, Spaniards love children, even if they themselves are having fewer of them these days. Children in Spain are viewed as being very much part of society and are allowed to participate in many activities along with adults. For this reason, dedicated children's facilities (separate children's rooms) may seem somewhat thin on the ground. On the other hand there are increasing numbers of theme parks and play areas to satisfy children's needs. In many ways, Spanish life is more sympathetic to children than some other cultures. While dreadful things do happen and child-related crimes are committed, few parents would feel that their children were being raised in a climate of fear.

Small children often provide a guaranteed passport into local life. Visit a local shop a couple of times with your children and they will be recognised, and the shopkeeper will look out for them. In fact, you are more likely to become known at first as an adjunct to your child, rather than for yourself! With a child, making use of schools and other local amenities provides the opportunity to meet other parents and families with children of the same age.

Education

English-speaking parents face some tough decisions when it comes to educating their children in Spain. It really comes down to two or three choices which depend on your income level and/or expectations. First there is the state, or public, system, which is basically free apart from school books, lunches, possibly uniforms and extra-curricular activities. In the state system, your child will be taught in Castilian and/or in one of the other co-official languages in areas where these are spoken. Then there are private schools, generally quite expensive, whose principal language of instruction is English. There are also many other private schools where the education is in Castilian. In between there are the *concertados*, which are basically private but which receive some state funding. These are roughly equivalent to grant-assisted schools in the UK. Alternatively, you could send your children abroad to a boarding school.

The Spanish state system was until recently run according to the terms of the Law on the General Organisation of the Educational System (*Ley Orgánica de Ordenación General del Sistema Educativo* – LOGSE) passed in 1990 and in operation since 1991–2. This law overhauled state education, introduced compulsory secondary education (ESO), raised the leaving age from 14 to 16, substantially modified and modernised the curriculum and provided for more vocational training. But in the last decade educational reform has proceeded apace, and has particularly focused on measures to enable more autonomous governance of the system while at the same time ensuring national standards. Among the reforms were a 2002 Law on the Quality of Education (*Ley Orgánica de Calidad de Educación* – LOCE) which aimed to: 'reduce school failure, raise standards of education and promote a culture of effort'. In it were highly controversial proposals to put compulsory religious education back on the school curriculum and introduce selective streaming in the lower secondary education, at the risk of condemning under-performers or late developers to a lifetime of stacking supermarket shelves or manual trades.

However, in May 2004, the newly elected government indefinitely postponed the implementation of both these LOCE reforms. Instead it began a national debate that laid the groundwork for a reform programme which would have the support of most interested parties. The consultation resulted in the the 2006 Organic Education Law (*Ley Organica de Educación* – LOE). Concrete measures resulting from the act are beginning to be phased in the 2007 and include free daycare for children between 3 and 6 years; foreign language teaching in primary schools; new tests for 9 and 11 year olds; the upgrading of school libraries; and greater autonomy for schools, with increased regulation of admissions to provide more parental choice.

A brief summary of the state system follows, but more detail can be found at **http://europa.eu.int/ploteus**.

The State School System

Infant Education (3–6 Years)
Pre-school (*pre-escolar* or *educación infantile*) is universally available. Pre-school education aims to encourage the child's physical and personal development, promote independence and personal hygiene and create awareness of self and others.

Primary Education (6–12 Years)
Educación primaria is compulsory. Over three two-year cycles, it aims to further the child's socialisation and independence. The broad subject areas are: the natural, social and cultural environment; art and music; PE; Castilian (or the

co-official language where appropriate); mathematics and, from age 8, a foreign language, usually English (Castilian in Catalonia!). Evaluation is continuous and under-achievers sometimes repeat a year. Support teachers help integrate children with learning problems and disabilities. Classes have a maximum of 25 pupils. The school year runs from mid-September to late June, with two weeks' holiday at Christmas, just over a week at Easter, several public holidays throughout the year and some local holidays.

Secondary Education (12–16 Years)

Compulsory secondary education (*educación secundaria obligatoria*, ESO), comprises two two-year cycles and prepares students either for baccalaureate (*bachillerato*) or vocational training (*formación profesional*). Students cover a comprehensive range of subjects from the humanities, the natural and social sciences and the arts, and can choose from several optional subjects according to their talents and interests. Evaluation is similar to that in primary education, and insufficient progress can again mean repeating a year. The school year is basically the same as that in primary education but the day is shorter, usually from 8 or 8.30am until 2.15 or 2.30pm.

After Secondary Education (17–18 Years)

Those who do not pass ESO can either leave school or proceed to *formación profesional*. Those who pass receive their secondary school graduation certificate (*graduado en educación secundaria*) and may go on to either specific vocational training or the more academic *bachillerato* programme. This two-year course prepares them for university entrance exams (*selectividad*), although they can enter specific vocational training at this point. The university entrance exam may be abolished in the future.

University

Recently expanded, university education takes place in over 30 state universities and a growing range of private ones. Entrance requirements depend on qualifications gained during *bachillerato* and *selectividad* (*see* above). While a high percentage of secondary students go on to university, not all can do their chosen subjects owing to courses being over-subscribed or inadequate grades. Drop-out rates are quite high. Most degree courses are of five or six years' duration, for academic subjects, leading to *licenciatura* (equivalent to a bachelor's degree). Other, more vocational courses average three years in length and lead to a diploma (*diplomatura*). The language of instruction is mainly Castilian, though, in those communities where co-official languages are spoken, all or some courses may be done in that language.

Enrolment in Spanish State Schools

Enrolment in a Spanish school may require an interview and possibly an examination, although this is rare for foreign children. Schools have annual

Case Study: A Liver Bird in Andalucía

Denise Jones, 48, from Liverpool, a graduate in Spanish and Portuguese, moved to Madrid in 1979 as a private, live-in English teacher to a Spanish family. Three years ago, after 25 years working in language academies and then doing freelance business English tutoring, she, her Spanish husband and their two children moved to Cádiz to be closer to his family.

How do you find working here?

Since Spain joined the EU it is easier to work legally for yourself. Getting away from the traditional language academies was a must...the hours were impossible (sometimes I missed lunchtime), and the pay was awful – it still is!

What are the pros and cons of working and living here?

Higher quality of life, the climate. I enjoy the culture, Spanish people work to live. In some places, being a foreigner has meant always being treated like one or like an eternal tourist!

How easy did you find mixing with Spanish people? And do you have any expat friends?

Generally easy, although sometimes people see you as something exotic, maybe to show off to their friends. Spanish women of my age aren't easy to connect with (particularly in Cádiz) but younger women are more open and good company. The Spanish – even the most open-minded – generally don't like any creative criticism of their country from a foreigner. You either love or hate Spain, but can only integrate if you enjoy the country and its culture. I do mix with some other expats but most of them are, like me, 'lifers', who are integrated. In big cities you can meet English people and see original-language movies so you don't have to lose contact but can achieve a balance between your own culture and your adopted one.

How do you find bringing up children bilingually? What have you done about schooling?

Parents should speak to the children in their respective languages from birth – they associate each language with Mum or Dad. If both parents are English, they should speak English at home; kids pick up Spanish from nursery, school, their mates, TV. I'm not convinced by bilingual schools; some are money-making outfits and can isolate children from the country and customs of where they are living.

How do you find prices, especially with children?

Astronomical, since the euro was introduced! House prices have always been over the top, particularly in Madrid and Barcelona. You also have to pay for kids' school books and materials. VAT is on all books, and kids' clothes, so they are expensive.

quotas and places are allocated on a first-come, first-served basis. Enrolment is usually during the spring term prior to the year the child is to enter school, but may vary from one region to another. Check exact dates with any school in your area. If you hear good things about a particular school and want your child to attend, consider buying or renting in that area. You need:

- **the child's birth certificate or passport, plus a photocopy, and the parents' passports, also photocopied.**
- **your child's immunisation records.**
- **some proof of your residence.**
- **two passport-size photographs.**

For children who are of an age to enter the ESO third grade, at about 14 or 15, you need to produce your child's birth certificate, school record book and/or examination results. Contact the **Ministerio de Educación**, Cultura y Deportes, Calle Alcalá, 36, 28014 Madrid, **t** 902 218 500; **www.mec.es/educa**. Alternatively, contact the Education and Science Office of the Spanish Embassy at 20 Peel Street, London W8 7PD, **t** (020) 7727 2462. All necessary forms may be obtained and presented there. Try to complete the process before arrival in Spain. Theoretically a child will not be admitted until the official papers have been received and stamped by the Department of Education. Allow three to six months for this process.

Private Schools

Parents face a choice as to how and where to educate their children. The state education system (*see* above) has improved greatly, but as everywhere else has its drawbacks. For instance, you may not want to throw your child directly in at the 'deep end', since this could prove traumatic. Having to learn another language and use it for school work is only one aspect of the problem; there is also the impact of a totally different culture – something frequently underestimated by parents.

Integration is generally easier with younger children. Adolescents may find it more difficult. Children *are* adaptable, but do not expect too much of them too quickly. If you choose to put your child into the state system, then you are well advised to find them a private language tutor to get them to a reasonable level before they start school. You should also learn the language yourself, as quickly as possible, to allow communication with teachers (vital) and enable you to help your children with homework.

You may decide on a year's private English-speaking or bilingual school to get around these problems before going into the Spanish state system. Much depends on your income, since private schooling does not come cheaply. Some 40 schools are listed on the website of the **National Association of British**

Schools in Spain (www.nabss.org). They are found mainly in the major cities, the Mediterranean coastal areas and in the islands, both the Balearics and the Canaries. Annual fees vary but you should expect to pay upwards of €3,500, and closer to €4,000 per child for primary schools and €5,000–6,000 for secondary level. On top of this you may have to pay for uniforms, transport, school lunches, extra-curricular activities and school trips (often somewhere more expensive than the local museum).

Most of these schools take children aged from 3 to 18 and follow the national curriculum leading to GCSE and A-Levels, their American equivalents or the International Baccalaureate. They may also prepare students for Spanish ESO and *bachillerato* exams too. They provide a good, across-the-board education both academic and extracurricular. Facilities vary but often include sports halls, playing fields, swimming pools, music rooms, auditoria and even stables. Membership of clubs and societies and the pursuit of hobbies are often important features in these schools, as are trips to skiing resorts and even abroad.

Staff tend to be from Britain and other Anglophone countries along with some Spanish teachers. Students may be a mixture of Spanish with a sprinkling of other nationalities but foreigners are sometimes the majority. Students usually leave completely fluent in English and Castilian Spanish and perhaps another language or two. Academic results can be excellent – a very high percentage go on to university after leaving.

Sending your child to such a school may, however, isolate them from the local culture and reduce their chances of making friends locally, which could mean a social life dependent on children of other expats. You could easily find yourself driving miles to birthday parties and other social gatherings, which could just as well have been held in your own neighbourhood.

Studying in Spain

Just as the labour market is now open to EU citizens, so too is the 'educational market'. In principle, any EU national may enrol in a Spanish, state-run or private university under the same criteria as those applied to Spanish students: meeting the entrance requirements with the additional obligation of being sufficiently fluent in the language to be able follow a programme of study. For that matter, possibilities exist for students from just about anywhere else in the world under the same criteria.

In order to meet the requirements for university entrance, whether to follow an undergraduate or a postgraduate programme, foreign students must apply to have their previous educational qualifications (in the case of British students, GCSEs, A-levels, bachelor's degree, etc.) recognised and validated by the Ministerio de Educación, Cultura y Deportes (Education Ministry, known as the MEC). Recognition (*homologación* in Castilian Spanish) is understood to mean the following:'the recognition of a foreign qualification's equivalence to a determined official Spanish qualification which is valid throughout the national territory. It implies the recognition of the academic level in question and carries with it the recognition of the professional effects inherent in the Spanish qualification referred to.' A-levels are normally recognised as sufficient qualifications to enrol on an undergraduate programme, but American high school diplomas are not usually accepted. Holders of such diplomas are advised to complete the first two years at college in order to be deemed ready for entrance to a Spanish university. All foreigners are obliged to pass the same entrance exam (*selectividad*) as Spanish students.

If you hope to get a degree recognised in order to practise your profession, or study at postgraduate level, there may be problems if you have followed a previously broad-based degree programme that has only touched on some disciplines while majoring in others. There may be no officially sanctioned Spanish university degree course that follows such a structure. In these cases you may get partial recognition of your degree and be required to study certain courses in order to make up the difference. Spanish degree programmes have traditionally been notoriously rigid, but some universities are now offering broader-based multidisciplinary programmes.

For information on recognition, contact the MEC, Calle Alcalá 36, 28014 Madrid, **t** 902 218 500. In the UK, the ministry's representation is at 20 Peel Street, London W8 7PD, **t** (020) 7727 2462. In the Republic of Ireland, contact the Spanish Embassy (**www.mae.es/embajadas/dublin**). *See* also p.247.

If you have a vocational qualification (as opposed to an academic one) and want to know whether it is recognised in Spain or not, a useful contact is the Centro Nacional de Recursos para la Orientación Profesional en España (National Resource Centre for Vocational Guidance in Spain, **mjose.arias@educ. mec.es**; **www.mec.es/educa/cnrop/index.html**. This is also the contact for finding out about doing vocational courses in Spain.

Many EU students are able to study for terms or full academic years in other member states under the aegis of the **Socrates-Erasmus Programme**. This programme was set up as Erasmus in 1987 by the European Commission's Educational Programme for Higher Education Students, Teachers and Institutions, with the aim of increasing student mobility within the then European Community. In 1995 it was reorganised into the new Socrates Programme which covers education from school to university to lifelong learning. The Socrates-Erasmus Programme is administered in the UK by the UK Socrates-Erasmus Council, **erasmus@ukc.ac.uk**; **www.erasmus.ac.uk**. In the Republic of Ireland, contact the Erasmus National Agency, **mkerr@hea.ie**; **www. hea.ie**. In Spain, the organisation is the Agencia Nacional Sócrates, **a.socrates@ educ.mec.es**. Further information on studying throughout Europe is found at **http://ec.europa.eu/education/programmes/socrates/erasmus/what_en.html** and **http://europa.eu.int/ploteus**.

Paying for Your Studies

Spanish universities charge their students matriculation fees (*tasas de matrícula*) when enrolling for courses. As universities are autonomous entities, not responsible to the MEC, they set their fees in conjunction with the Autonomous Communities in which they are situated. Depending on the course you aim to study, you may expect to pay between €250 and €450.

Spain has never had an all-embracing system of **grants** (*becas*) like that which used to exist in Britain. Full grants, covering both fees and living expenses, are few and far between, and as a result the majority of Spanish students live at home with their parents. The chances of a foreign student getting a full grant from the Spanish government are minimal, unless perhaps it is awarded as part of a co-operation programme with developing countries. If you are resident in Spain, you may, however, be eligible; contact the MEC or look at **becas.mec.es/2003/univ.html**. Grants are often means-tested and therefore usually available only to persons with very limited resources. On the other hand, depending on where you come from and your grant eligibility there, you may be able to get financing from home. Many Socrates-Erasmus students do study abroad with a grant which, if awarded in the home country, is usually is often extensible to study abroad. Contact your own country's Socrates-Erasmus representative for information.

If you do not have access to a full grant, you may have to find work to support your studies. This is not easy (*see* **Working in Spain**) and probably the best way is to look for English-teaching and/or translation work, or any other type of employment that can be done at different times and therefore fitted around your study schedule.

If working and studying proves incompatible, there is always the option of distance learning. The Spanish equivalent of the Open University is the Universidad Nacional de Educación a Distancia (UNED) in Madrid (**www.uned.es**). Its purpose is to enable people who, for whatever reason, cannot enrol in a university or attend classes physically to follow courses which will eventually lead to a degree. There are faculties covering all subject areas and there is also a foundation course for students aged over 25.

Recreational Courses

In most Spanish towns and cities you will find a wide range of recreational courses. Whether you want to do pottery, photography, wine-tasting, cooking, creative writing, origami, theatre, tai-chi, or learn to play a musical instrument or to dance the tango, you are sure to find something in your area. If you want to pursue the activity in your own language, options will be limited except perhaps in the major cities or areas such as the Costas del Sol and Blanca, the

Balearics or the Canaries, where there are large concentrations of expats. If you feel confident enough in the local language, then more options will be available. Either way, you are likely to learn something, deriving pleasure and a sense of achievement, while also getting to know people (expats or locals), widening your circle of friends and expanding your horizons. And if you do a course in the local language, your understanding of it will also improve immensely.

Exactly what may be on offer varies greatly depending on where you are. Most borough councils (*juntas municipales*) in larger cities run local cultural centres (*centros culturales*) where day and evening courses are organised. Smaller municipalities also run such centres. Some local councils are more proactive in the provision of courses, whereas others make use of the space available, renting it out to teachers and organisations who then take responsibility for setting up, running and charging for courses.

Since the process of becoming a resident means having to register (*empadronarse*, see **Red Tape**, pp.112–13) with the local authorities, you can at the same time enquire about the location of the nearest cultural centre and call in to see what is available. Do not overlook the cultural services offered by the Autonomous Community where you live. As explained elsewhere, education has been devolved to the *autonomías* and some of them have huge budgets for cultural activities that include many subsidised courses, both vocational and recreational, often aimed at specific groups such as young people, the elderly, women or immigrants.

Apart from what may be offered by institutions, there are any number of privately run organisations, clubs and schools that run courses in just about anything you care to imagine. The problem is how to find them. The local cultural centre itself may well be able to provide a list of courses organised independently, or will at least have a noticeboard. Listings magazines are useful, such as *Guía del Ocio*, published in Madrid and Marbella, which has a section entitled 'A Saber', including contact information for recreational organisations and courses on offer. The Madrid edition publishes a pull-out supplement coinciding with the beginning of the academic year, in late September or early October, with pages of information on courses. The online edition (**www.guiadelocio.com**) also offers extensive information. Most major cities also have their own listings magazines. University and bookshop noticeboards can also be an invaluable source of information, with ads for courses from individuals and organisations.

If you are principally interested in doing a course in English or joining an English-language club, there are various options for finding information. The nearest British, American or Irish consulate (*see* **Red Tape**, pp.123–4) will usually provide a list of clubs and associations in their area. The British Embassy website (**www.ukinspain.com/English**) also has a list, principally of Madrid-based organisations. Wherever expats tend to congregate, there is likely to a

British or American club, possibly a newcomers' club, an expat wives' club or a church group. Apart from providing an immediate source of new contacts, these groups are often themselves involved in the setting up of clubs, societies and courses, or can at least point you in the right direction.

There are also the English-language newspapers and magazines: see **Spain Today**, 'Major Media', pp.68–9. Barcelona's *Metropolitan*, for example, has in its 'useful contacts' section the local English-language theatre group, an expat football league, a Claddagh Ring dancing group and a Gaelic football club. Similar information is to be found in *The Broadsheet* and the various other expat-orientated publications.

Useful websites include **www.spainexpat.com/ #Living** for a list of some 20 expat clubs throughout Spain; over 60 clubs are listed for the Costa del Sol alone on **www.andalucia.com/entertainment/ clubs/home.htm**. Finally, check out English-language bookshops; you may well find what you are looking for on their noticeboards.

Sports and Recreation

The Spanish are big on sport. You only have to take a look at the many sports newspapers available on any news-stand or the vast amount of televised sport to realise that. Sport in Spain was given a tremendous boost by Barcelona's staging of the 1992 Olympic Games, and EU development funds have helped build many excellent sports centres (*polideportivos*) in towns and cities all over the country.

As a rule, larger towns and cities (as well as tourist areas) are generally well equipped. Most local authorities offer inexpensive facilities ranging from the most basic to near-Olympic standard. There is also a plethora of private gymnasiums and sports centres offering the whole gamut of activities, such as tennis, golf, riding, swimming, squash and more, as well as privately owned and run facilities. If you join a club to play any competitive sport, you must get the corresponding player's licence from the provincial or regional federation, usually obtained via the club or team you join, which covers you for accidents. Wherever there are large concentrations of expats you will find football, rugby and cricket teams. In Barcelona there is even a Gaelic football club, see 'Recreational Courses', above.

Spain's climate and geography also encourages a wide variety of outdoor activities, such as fishing, hunting, hiking, trekking and rock-climbing, as well as more radical sports such as bungee-jumping, paragliding and hang-gliding. Cycling is a great favourite too – mountain-bikers in particular find plenty of challenging, rugged terrain. Then, of course, there are water sports. The long coastline is a paradise for windsurfers, sailors and water-skiers. At the simplest level, a jog along the beach in the sunshine followed by a dip in the sea is available to all, practically year-round, for the price of a pair of trainers and a bathing suit!

Armchair sports fans are also well catered for. Televised sport is everywhere. Football, basketball, handball, motor and water sports all get good coverage (*see* **Spain Today,** pp.78–80), and if you have access to Sky then your sports-watching options are multiplied. In addition, fans attend a considerable range of live competitions at all levels.

Information about municipal and private sports facilities, clubs and regional federations is generally found in the telephone directory or the Yellow Pages. Alternatively, ask at your local council for a list of sports centres and organisations. Here are some key sporting activities and contact points. Most are the national federations, and there will always be a corresponding body in the Autonomous Community in which you live.

- **General information**: The **Spanish Sports Council,** Consejo Superior de Deportes, is at Avenida de Martín Fierro s/n, 28040 Madrid (**t** 915 896 700; **www.csd.mec.es/csd**). A full list of all national sports federations is available on a web link. National federations can supply a list of their regional counterparts. Other websites with information about sports in Spain are **www.spanish-living.com** (click on 'sports' and then on the relevant region on the map) and **www.aboutspain.net/spain/sports.asp**. Highly useful for Costa del Sol dwellers is **www.andalucia.com**, with sports and general information.

- **Golf**: The **Spanish Golf Federation** is at Capitán Haya 9, 5°, 28020 Madrid (**t** 915 552 682; **www.golfspainfederacion.com**). Information in English about golf courses, clubs, green fees and much more can be found at **www.golfspain.com**.

- **Cricket**: Cricketers will find clubs on the Costa del Sol, the Costa Blanca, Mallorca and Ibiza. If you are on the Costa del Sol, try **www.andalucia.com**.

- **Cycling**: Cyclists looking for a club should contact the Spanish federation, **Real Federación Española de Ciclismo**, at Calle Ferraz 16, 5°, 28008 Madrid (**t** 915 400 841; **www.rfec.com**).

- **Tennis**: Tennis courts and clubs are everywhere. The **Spanish Tennis Federation** is based in Barcelona, Avinguda Diagonal, 08021 Barcelona (**t** 932 005 355; **www.rfet.es**). Alternatively, look at **www.playtennisspain. com** for independent information.

- **Sailing**: Sailors and yachters can contact the Real Federación de Vela at Calle Luis de Salazar 9, 28002 Madrid (**t** 91 5 195 008; **www.rfev.es**). Some 19 Spanish sailing clubs are listed, with links, on **www.sailing.org/sailing clubs/esp.asp**.

- **Windsurfing**: Windsurfers can find information and news, in Spanish, about all aspects of the sport at **www.windtarifa.com**.

- **Water-skiing**: Information about water-skiing is easily found in any resort town. The **Federación Española de Esquí Náutico** is at Plaça Universitat 4, 2°-1°, 08007, Barcelona (**t** 934 520 895; **www.feen.es**).

- **Winter sports**: Real Federación de Deportes de Invierno, Calle Arroyofresno 3A, 28035, Madrid (**t** 913 769 930; **www.rfedi.es**).

- **Riding**: Horse-riding is a joy in Spain, and there are many clubs. Contact the **Real Federación de Hípica Española** at Plaza Marqués de Salamanca 2, 28006 Madrid (**t** 914 364 200; **www.rfhe.com**).

Working in Spain

Many people are relocating to Spain to work and live. This trend, far from slowing down, is actually gathering pace. Most who have settled agree that the reasons they stay are down to the more relaxed Mediterranean lifestyle, helped by the climate, plus the feeling that in Spain you can have a better and healthier lifestyle with less money.

But nobody should be under any illusion that it is easy, and everybody should be aware that, despite the advantages that go with EU membership – free movement of labour, etc. – finding satisfying and/or well-paid work is actually quite difficult. In general, anybody planning to go to Spain to live and work should expect to earn less than they might be used to at home, and may find that there are fewer opportunities to make a 'real' career. On the other hand, some find that the way of life compensates for a less dynamic working life. Unemployment is a factor that contributes to the difficulties, although there are areas in which expats may enjoy better opportunities than locals. Anyone who is dynamic and resourceful need not starve or be poor; those who would be high-flyers at home can, and do, get ahead.

Business Etiquette

Handshakes are a standard part of Spanish business protocol. First-time introductions with Spaniards should be formal. Women sometimes touch cheeks while lightly kissing the air. While in social situations men and women also do this, business situations demand a handshake. In addition, male colleagues commonly hug or pat each other on the back. During conversations, Spaniards stand closer, make more physical contact and maintain eye contact for longer than you might be used to.

If you walk down Madrid's Paseo de la Castellana at lunchtime, one thing that is sure to catch your attention is that, despite temperatures of 100°F (almost 38°C) in the shade, Spanish businessmen will still be dressed in long-sleeved shirts, jackets and ties. This shows how important formal dress is for Spaniards. Jackets are never removed during a restaurant lunch, and at meetings only on the suggestion of someone senior. Suits are generally conservative grey or blue, though ties, with co-ordinated shirts, may vary in colour. Elegance in style (i.e. monogrammed shirts and cufflinks) is also the norm. For women, suits or business dresses made of high-quality fabrics are the norm, trouser suits are commonly worn, and in summer formality eases up, making skirts and lighter tops acceptable.

Though Spaniards are aware that other cultures place less importance on dress, they still find overly casual dress to be unbusinesslike. One Spanish businessman commented following a meeting with a Dutch counterpart, 'He was wearing a polo shirt, the legs of his trousers were two inches above his shoes

Case Study: Rob Gill, Working in a Spanish Company

Yorkshire-born Rob Gill, 44, graduated in Latin and French from the University of Manchester and moved to Madrid eight years ago with his partner, Sarah. Previously in charge of government relations at a UK electricity company, he was seconded to work with Unión Fenosa, an electricity supply company. New career challenges and the experience of living in a new culture were very attractive to them. When his secondment ended, he made the decision to stay on in Madrid, and works as a freelance translator and communications consultant.

How did you find your first job?

It was easy because I came to Spain as part of a secondment arrangement. Subsequently, work has not been so easy to find, and this has meant that I have had to become self-employed, relying on selling my own knowledge and experience.

How do you find working here compares with working at home?

The extended Spanish working day comes as a surprise to newcomers. I soon got used to meetings scheduled for 5pm (usually starting late) and emerging four hours later to find my office floor still two-thirds full. At first, though, my major preoccupation was whether I would survive until lunchtime! Overall, I found that the work relationships in Spanish companies were more formal and hierarchical and that other internal processes, such as procurement, worked more slowly than in the UK.

Do you live mainly in the expat community or have you integrated? Or is your life a bit of both?

I think there are several different expat communities rather than just one: for example, there are English-speaking executives working for multinational companies but also long-term residents working in schools and in business. Although we have Spanish friends, it's been harder to integrate than I imagined. However, the Spaniards are so naturally friendly and sociable that we get a good welcome in our local shops, cafés and bars, and there's always someone willing to strike up a conversation.

How did you learn the language?

My languages degree was certainly a help but I also had lessons in my company three times a week for the first six months or so. Since then it's been more a question of osmosis, but working full-time in the language is a great help. I've also continued to study and to pass exams.

and the sleeves of his jacket were rolled up! The deal went through smoothly, but we were all left wondering what was wrong with him.'

Similarly, although the formal 'usted' form of address is used less these days in conversation except when talking to elderly people, being replaced in most social situations by the informal '*tú*', in business culture '*usted*' is much more common. This is partly due to the respect older senior managers demand in a still hierarchical business environment. Recently, however – owing to the proliferation of business degrees and MBAs – more young people are found in senior management. Many will still take offence at being initially addressed as '*tú*', as they feel that you are not taking them seriously. The rule-of-thumb is: use '*usted*' until an invitation is made to use '*tú*' (which is usually forthcoming).

Businesses are generally open Monday to Friday 9am to 2 or 2.30pm and again from 3.30 or 4pm to 6.30 or 7pm. Many companies have half-day Fridays. However, people are often in their offices by 8 or 8.30am and may still be there at 8, 9 or even 10pm. It is also considered unwise to leave before the boss. Many companies adopt a summer timetable in July and August, when most people take their vacations; this *horario intensivo* is usually 8am to about 3pm. Long working days are partially a result of the Spanish work environment, as things take longer to accomplish. They are also explained by a business culture that encourages socialising. Chatting at the water cooler is considered important for establishing and maintaining good relations between colleagues. A person who spends all day in front of the computer is considered anti-social and, worse, overly ambitious (*ambicioso* in Castilian often has negative connotations). For appointments, although you should be punctual yourself, don't be surprised if you are kept waiting.

Lunch breaks have in contrast, become much shorter. Previously, they lasted up to three hours. Over the years, however, workers in the larger cities who cannot get home for lunch have pushed for a shorter lunch break with a correspondingly earlier finishing time. Be careful, though – most workers nowadays take 60–90 minutes for lunch, and still leave no earlier! Long lunches are still common, but usually have some business aspect connected to them.

Safe topics of conversation are your home country, travel and sports – especially football. Avoid bullfighting, religion and politics, and beware of making personal enquiries, especially during first introductions. Be sensitive to regional differences; making misinformed comments about a Spaniard's region of origin would be offensive (i.e. mistaking a Catalan for a Basque).

If you receive a gift, open it immediately, in front of the giver. Gifts you give should be of high quality and should advertise your company name only if it is a fine pen or a tasteful desk accessory. Local crafts, coffee-table books and CDs related to your home region will be appreciated.

The Labour Market

One aspect of working in Spain is that **EU citizens enjoy the same rights and obligations as Spaniards**. Anyone from another EU country who arrives in Spain to take up a job, finds one after arrival or sets up as a freelancer or in business is no longer obliged even to apply for a residence permit. Once an NIE (*see* **Red Tape**, p.116) has been obtained, EU workers are free to enter the labour market in free and fair competition with locals. This means that the EU worker cannot be discriminated against in selection processes and theoretically is chosen for a job on merit, qualifications and performance at interview.

This does not apply to **non-EU citizens**. Any company wishing to employ a non-EU worker has to prove that the person offered the post can do it better than any Spaniard or other EU worker currently available.

That is the theory. But in practice foreigners, even those of EU origin, are at a disadvantage in the labour market. The need to speak the local language(s) to a fairly high level marginalises the recent arrival who is not yet fluent. Those with no knowledge of the language are effectively excluded from large areas of the labour market. This is not to say that you cannot find work in areas where your native language is a plus; *see* 'Job Ideas', below.

Otherwise, the labour market is a cut-throat place, for several reasons. Unemployment in Spain is fairly moderate, currently about 7.6 per cent nationally, yet the problem is acute in certain areas and studies show that the 'best' places to look for work (i.e. the most prosperous areas, where most jobs are generated) are Catalonia, Madrid and Navarra, although the existence of the expat community in the *costas* and offshore Spain (where unemployment levels might be quite high for locals) does mean that English-speakers may be better placed for finding work there.

Hiring and firing laws have relaxed a lot in recent years but attempts by central government to loosen up the labour market further have met with stiff opposition from the unions. Even still, most jobs generated in recent years have been temporary and under what is known as *contratos basura* ('garbage contracts'), precarious and renewable only on the whim of the employer. Currently, nine out of ten work contracts issued are temporary. And the average duration of all these contracts is...10 days!

Another issue is that natives know the local market and conditions much better than the recent arrival. Finding work often does not depend so much on your 'marketability' as on whom you know. The Spanish have an expressive word, *enchufe*, literally 'plug' but which actually means 'knowing people in the right places'. Being *enchufado* ('plugged in') signifies access to job opportunities. Locals are in a stronger position than outsiders in this respect, at least until the newcomer gets to know people and can take advantage of it. *See* the case study of Salma Rashid in **First Steps**, p.93.

Job Ideas

Your ideal image of Spain may involve long lazy afternoons by the sea or on the *terraza* of your local bar, but unless you have already retired or have an independent income you will probably have to work while you are in the country. The good news is that, despite high unemployment figures, it is relatively easy to find certain kinds of job even if your knowledge of the local language is rudimentary. For a large percentage of British residents in Spain, work means teaching English either privately or in a language school, but this is far from being the only option.

If you are living in one of the coastal resort areas, and to a lesser extent in a major city, you will find a thriving micro-economy based around the English-speaking communities. English bars and cafés are always in need of waiters, bar staff and chefs. Irish pubs are every bit as ubiquitous in Spain as in the rest of Europe, and generally have a high turnover of staff. Similarly, travel firms will need extra staff in the high season, although the larger holiday companies will recruit in the UK rather than on the ground. In areas where there is an English language newspaper or magazine, it will be your primary resource in the hunt for a job. There will also be advertisements for office staff in the various estate agents, lawyers, and moving consultants who service the expat lifestyle. The magazines themselves are often looking for advertising sales staff to work on commission. If you have always wanted to work as journalist, this might be your perfect chance to get some poorly paid experience. In truth, none of the above jobs is likely to be *well* paid and, especially in bars and restaurants, hours are likely to be long.

If, however, you are an experienced plumber, electrician or builder then you are unlikely ever to lack reasonably paid work. Such is the shortage of skilled trades people in Spain that it is not unusual to find a good British electrician working for many Spanish customers.

You may have another skill which you wish to capitalise on in Spain. There are British dentists, gardeners, aromatherapists and interior decorators all making a living across the country. If you have ever fancied being self-employed then Spain may well be the place to do it; in the expat community there is a captive market which has more leisure time and more disposable income than equivalent social groupings in the UK.

If the idea of living entirely within an English-speaking ghetto does not appeal, then you will be looking for work with a Spanish employer. It goes without saying that if you are going to work with Spanish people you are going to need some knowledge of Spanish, or indeed Catalan, Galician or Basque where applicable. The level of language skill you need will depend on the type of job you are looking for. In a practical or manual work environment you may get away with a beginner's level, but to work in a Spanish office you will need to be fluent, at least in the spoken language. See **Getting to Know Spain**, pp.21–8, and **Living in Spain**, pp.126–31.

Some industries are more open to employing foreigners than others. Media and communications and the IT sectors often have to use English in trade documents and are aware of the advantages of having a native speaker on-board. An increasingly global economy means that the financial sector needs experienced candidates from abroad. Similarly, for shipping or travel companies your nationality might prove to be a plus rather than a negative point. Many Spanish employers stress the importance of spoken English for their staff. Often this is merely a device to reduce the number of candidates for a job, but in any industry where there is a real and obvious need for bilingual staff you should stand a reasonable chance of success.

There are many skills which are in demand in Spain, and others where there is a positive glut. Unemployment among doctors and nurses is surprisingly high; many go to the UK to work, and state sector teachers generally hang on to a job for dear life once they have one. Employment in the public sector, with its some-times arcane systems of competitive entry exams (*oposiciones*) and its excellent terms and conditions, is all but unobtainable for foreigners.

You will *find* work in Spain if you really want to. The historically low birth-rate means the country is a labour shortage waiting to happen. In many areas of the economy, immigrant labour is now essential. This can only help foreigners from whatever nation in their search for employment.

Looking for Work

Ideally, anyone planning to live and work in Spain should go with a job already fixed up, but this is not always possible and there is nothing to stop you taking the plunge and going on spec. It all depends on your circumstances and whether you have enough of a financial cushion between arriving and finding work. Either way, there are various ways of searching before heading off for Spain and plenty more once there. If you are claiming unemployment benefit in your home country, you may arrange for this to be paid to you in Spain while searching for work there.

In any EU country you can visit your local employment office and look at the database of the EURES scheme (**http://europa.eu.int/jobs/eures**, 'The European Job Mobility Portal'), on which job vacancies are posted Europe-wide. It also has other useful information such as a labour market overview, nationally or by Autonomous Communities, giving you an idea of what skills are in demand in any given place. In addition, you can place your CV on the site for potential employers to see. There is an exhaustive list of Spain-specific job-seeking resources as well as links to useful sites such as **www.cedefop.eu.int/transparency/cv.asp** where you can download sample CVs.

While on the Internet you can sign up to any of the following websites:

- **www.infojobs.net**
- **www.trabajo.org**

- **http://jobera.com** (tips on writing CVs and cover letters, interview techniques, etc. in several languages)

- **www.monster.es**

- **www.anyworkanywhere.com/jobsearch.html** (most jobs currently offered on this site are with tour operators in the Balearics and the Canaries)

- **www.eurojobs.com**

A more traditional source is the printed press. Not many Spanish jobs come up in the UK press, but it always pays to keep an eye on the job pages of the major British dailies or the *International Herald Tribune*, particularly for high-flying jobs. If you are looking in the field of education, then there is really no substitute for the *Times Educational Supplement*. Major Spanish newspapers have job ads galore but you cannot expect to understand them, still less apply, if your knowledge of the language (Castilian principally) is not up to scratch. Advertisements do occasionally appear in English, usually when the company is looking to recruit a high-flyer and does not want to limit the search to Spain. *El País*, *El Mundo* and other Spanish newspapers are distributed in larger UK cities or may be found at local libraries. The pink, finance and economy supplements on Sundays carry many job ads.

The English-language press in Spain (*see* **Spain Today**, 'Major Media', pp.68–9) can also be useful, although the jobs section is limited and much of the work advertised is for people with a trade or skills. On the other hand, most ads are aimed at English-speakers, as servicing the expat population has become an industry all of its own. You can of course always place an ad of your own.

Apart from the general press, if you are looking for a job in a given sector it is a good idea to look for trade magazines. In Spain itself there are other jobseekers' publications. The weekly *Mercado de Trabajo* has over 1,200 job ads, features on emerging markets for aspiring entrepreneurs, job fairs, training and work expeience opportunities. Some people also recommend *Segundamano*, the thrice-weekly Spanish equivalent of *Exchange & Mart* which has a substantial classifieds section. *Laboris* is another weekly tabloid-format publication with many job ads.

Another way is to target potential companies where you would like to work or where you think you might find a job. Selling yourself is the point here, and the target companies are most likely to be British or North American multinationals operating in Spain. It may seem like a shot in the dark, but remember that a good, well-presented CV that arrives on a personnel manager's desk unsolicited may attract more attention than one sent in reply to an advertised post (where it will be just one among many). Some companies actually prefer to recruit this way.

There are far too many foreign companies operating in Spain to list here, but chambers of commerce can be helpful in this respect (British Chamber of

Commerce, **britchamber@britchamber.com**; **www.britishchamberspain.com**).
For €25 you can also insert your profile on the site for 10 weeks.

Any newly arrived EU citizen has the right to sign on as a jobseeker (*demandante de empleo*) with the **INEM** (Instituto Nacional de Empleo), the equivalent of the UK Job Centre. Remember, as pointed out in **Red Tape**, pp.112–17, you no longer need to produce a residence card in order to be able to sign on; your passport will suffice. Whether the functionary dealing with you knows this is another matter! To find out where your nearest office is, look in the telephone directory or **www.inem.es**.

Alternatively, check out private agencies, of which there are basically two types in Spain. One is the Private Placement Agency (**Agencia Privada de Colocación**), whose role is that of intermediary in the job market. They normally charge a fee, which should by law be limited to reasonable costs. The other type of agency, also an 'intermediary', but with certain differences, is the Temporary Work Company (**Empresa de Trabajo Temporal – ETT**). These companies contract workers and then assign them to companies by means of service contracts. ETTs tend to specialise in certain areas, for example catering, secretarial or construction personnel. Workers are usually hired out during times of exceptional demand or when seasonal backlogs occur. Adecco, Manpower and Randstad are big players in this field, but the *Yellow Pages* will throw up many more.

Once you have been in Spain for a while and got to know a few people, word of mouth is one of the best ways of all of finding work. Networking, schmoozing, crawling – call it what you will, getting friendly with potentially useful people is extremely common in Spain. Business cards are frequently exchanged – get your own made, and give it out with abandon. The system of *enchufe* is not exclusive to locals; expats can take advantage of it too.

Job Interviews

Interviews are usually one-to-one, but for high-flying jobs you may have to face a panel and be called back for a second or third 'roasting'. Arrive early, dress formally (suit and tie for men, dress/suit for women) and bring all useful documents such as written references and certificates of qualifications. Above all, be prepared. Make sure you know what the job will require and what questions you may expect to be asked. The first impression is *importantísima*.

During the first interview, shake hands with everyone you are introduced to, looking them in the eye and presenting your business card if appropriate. Use the '*usted*' form, be attentive to everything said to you and reply appropriately but do not speak out of turn. Avoid monosyllabic answers wherever possible. Show interest in the job and what may be expected of you but be careful not to mention your salary expectations until asked (which you probably will be in the final stage).

If you get past the first hurdle, you will probably be asked back for psychological and psychometric tests and maybe more interviews. Be prepared for all manner of questions regarding your motivation, reasons for wanting this particular job, etc. Recruiters will also be looking at your human qualities. Good luck.

CURRICULUM VITAE

Henry Davidson
t 914 482 309/656 131 229
h_davidson@yahoo.co.uk
C/ Espiritu Santo 22, 2° izq.
28012 MADRID
NIE: X-03020846-C
Fecha de nacimiento: 04/06/78

FORMACIÓN ACADÉMICA
2001   **Licenciado en Informática.**
Universidad de North East London

FORMACIÓN COMPLEMENTARIA
2003   **MBA en Negocios en Internet y Comercio Electrónico.**
London Business School, Holborn, Londres

EXPERIENCIA PROFESIONAL
Sep 2001 – Ene 2002   **Administrador de Sistemas y Redes.**
Datasystems and Applications plc
Funciones: Encargado de instalar y mantener operativas las redes de varios clientes

Ene 2002 – Jun 2002   **Consultor Informático (freelance)**
Walthamstow Borough Council
Funciones: Encargado de elaborar y administrar la página web oficial de la Junta de Walthamstow así como de instalar la intranet utilizada por los distintos departamentos de la misma

Sep 2003 – Ago 2005   **Profesor de Informática e Inglés**
ANFP – Academia de Negocios y Formación Profesional, Madrid
Funciones: Impartir cursos de informática, ofimática e inglés a alumnos que preparaban Masters en Administración de Empresas (MBA)

IDIOMAS
Inglés: nivel de nativo, leído, escrito y hablado
Español: leído, escrito y hablado, nivel avanzado
Alemán: leído, nivel intermedio, escrito, nivel intermedio bajo, hablado, nivel avanzado

OTROS DATOS DE INTERÉS
Disponibilidad total, incorporación inmediata en cualquier empresa dedicada al comercio electrónico

Your Curriculum Vitae

Spanish employers prefer brief CVs, maximum two pages. Information about your hobbies and interests is not usually included but, as the Spanish place a lot of emphasis on paper qualifications, all courses attended and diplomas

CURRICULUM VITAE

Henry Davidson
t 914 482 309/656 131 229
h_davidson@yahoo.co.uk
C/ Espiritu Santo 22, 2° izq.
28012 MADRID
NIE: X-03020846-C
DOB: 04/06/78

EDUCATIONAL BACKGROUND
2001   BSc in Information Technology (IT)
University of North East London

FURTHER TRAINING
2003   MBA in Internet and e-business
London Business School, Holborn

WORK EXPERIENCE
Sept 2001 – Jan 2002   **Systems and Networks Administrator**
Datasystems and Applications plc
Functions: In charge of installing and maintaining operative the internal systems and networks for various customers

Jan 2002 – June 2002   **IT Consultant (freelance)**
Walthamstow Borough Council
Functions: Employed as a freelancer to design and maintain Walthamstow Borough Council's official website as well as installing the internal intranet system used by different council departments

Sept 2003 – Aug 2005   **IT and English Language Teacher**
ANFP – Academia de Negocios y Formación Profesional, Madrid (Business and Professional Training Academy)
Functions: Teaching MBA students to use computer applications and English language

LANGUAGES
English: native-speaker level, reading, writing and verbal
Spanish: Reading, advanced level; writing, advanced level; verbal, advanced level
German: Reading, intermediate level; writing, low intermediate level; verbal, advanced level

ADDITIONAL INFORMATION
Available to work immediately in any company specializing in internet and e-business

obtained should be mentioned. It is now common practice to attach a recent photograph. Few companies write back acknowledging receipt of the CV and application letter unless they are desperate to recruit you.

Being Employed

Employment Contracts

Contracts may be made between an employer and any person over the age of 18 (or 16 if the worker in question is legally emancipated or has parental consent to work). There is no distinction made in the legislation governing working contracts entered into by Spanish or EU workers, but non-EU citizens are subject to the limitations outlined elsewhere in this guide.

Contracts are usually written but may also be verbal, the latter being less common nowadays except in the casual labour field, but they are **binding**. Contracts for work experience (internships), for training, for the carrying out of a specified service, for part-time work, for short-term renewable labour, for the temporary replacement of a worker on leave, to work for a Spanish company abroad or for a determined period greater than four weeks must all be made on paper. Either contracting party may demand a written contract, either before or after it has been entered into. Written contracts must also be registered at the INEM (Instituto Nacional de Empleo) by the employer.

The law allows for **trial periods**, which are not obligatory but are common. Trial periods that are part of the terms of the contract must also be stated in writing. For qualified workers or graduates the maximum trial period is six months; for other workers it may not exceed two months. At any point during the trial period workers may be dismissed without notice and without the reasons being stated unless there is a written agreement to the contrary. Workers on their trial period are otherwise subject to the same rights and obligations as all others on the payroll, and the period counts towards their seniority (*antigüedad*) when calculating holidays, severance pay, etc.

Contracts may be indefinite (*temporal*) or for a fixed period (*fijo*). All contracts are full-time and indefinite unless stated otherwise – the latter is almost invariably the case nowadays; it is ever harder to get *fijo* status. One-year contracts, renewable after each year, are common in many professional areas. On reaching three years and a day of employment, the employer is obliged to make you fijo (if he has not already), although it is a frequent practice not to renew when the third contract is up. This is because it is expensive to get rid of workers once they have been made *fijo*.

A written contract must state the following:

- **the identity of both parties.**
- **the date of commencement of employment and the foreseen duration.**

- the address of the company and/or the workplace.
- the professional category to which the worker belongs or a proper job description.
- the basic salary and anticipated complementary payments as well as their frequency (weekly, monthly, etc.).
- the duration of the normal working day and starting and finishing times (a 40-hour week is the norm).
- holidays and the criteria by which these are determined.
- the notice of termination or, if this is not possible, the criteria to be used to determine the period of notice.
- the collective agreement applicable to the contract entered into.

Current employment legislation encourages the employment of persons from groups more affected by unemployment, such as the disabled, young people, women, the long-term unemployed, those over 45, etc. Employers are given tax breaks and relief on social security contributions in return for hiring people from these groups.

Terms of Employment

What Do Your Wages Consist of?

The wage (*el salario*) constitutes the total of your earnings whether in cash or in kind in return for your services as an employee, either for work performed or rest periods counted as working time. **Payment in kind** may never exceed 30 per cent of your income.

The wage structure is usually established by collective bargaining or, failing this, in the individual contract, and must comprise a basic wage plus bonuses. The basic wage is established on a time or project basis. Bonuses are payments established according to your personal circumstances, the work performed, the company's position and results. Bonuses normally agreed upon in collective bargaining take into account seniority in the company and may foresee profit-sharing or be for transport and travelling, special jobs, heavy, toxic or dangerous work, shift work, night shifts, etc. Productivity and quality- or quantity-linked incentives may also be paid as bonuses. Money paid as compensation for expenses, social security benefits and contributions, relocation or compensation for suspensions or dismissals is not considered to be part of the wage.

Your employer must pay you as and when specified in the contract and give you a **wage slip** (*nómina*) which must conform to the official Ministry of Labour format. Your periodical and regular earnings must be paid at intervals of no greater than a month and you are also entitled to 10 per cent interest on wages paid late. It is the responsibility of the employer to deduct, on your behalf, **tax**

and social security contributions. Most wages these days are paid by direct bank transfer into your account.

Most employees in Spain are entitled to a minimum of two **bonus payments** per year (*pagas extraordinarias*). These are normally paid at Christmas and during the summer. The *paga* may also be on a pro-rata basis. Remember this is not an 'extra', given generously by your employer, but is your agreed annual salary divided by 14. You could argue that you would rather have the difference, bank it and get interest (which employers do anyway).

Spanish employment law also makes provision for wage guarantee in case of employers going into liquidation. All employers must contribute an amount equivalent to 0.4 per cent of wages to the **Wage Guarantee Fund** (Fondo de Garantía Salarial – FOGASA), an independent body attached to the Ministry of Labour whose function is to ensure that wages and compensation are paid to workers when companies go bankrupt. You are advised to contact specialist employment lawyers if such a situation is foreseen.

Working Hours, Overtime, Leave and Holidays

The standard full-time **working week** is 40 hours. By law, nobody may be obliged to work more than nine hours per day unless this is provided for in the collective agreement; longer shifts must be compensated for with rest periods. In theory, rest periods between the end of one working day and the beginning of the next must be at least 12 hours. Any shift of six hours or more must include at least a 15-minute break. Workers must also be given a minimum of one and a half days free each week. There are 14 paid public holidays.

Overtime is not compulsory, may not exceed 80 hours in one working year and must be paid at least at the normal hourly rate. It is also forbidden on night shifts except in certain sectors where the work is by its very nature nocturnal. Unfortunately, with so many people on temporary contracts these days, the reality is that 'extra' hours are often worked without compensation.

Paid **annual holidays** (*vacaciones anuales*) are subject to a collective agreement or an individual work contract but for full-time workers may never be less than 30 calendar days (or 20 working days). Holidays may be taken as agreed between the employer and the worker in accordance with the provisions in collective agreements. In the past, most companies (and most of Spain!) shut down for a whole month in the summer. If this is the case, you will be obliged to take all of your holidays in one go. This is changing and many companies now stay open, with minimum staff, throughout July and August. Many employees take just two or three weeks in the summer and save days to take at other times. Public holidays never count as part of annual leave. Workers on 9- or 10-month contracts (e.g. teachers) usually receive the proportional part as holiday pay (that is, either 9/12 or 10/12 of the salary) even though their 'forced' holidays amount to three months.

Leave of absence is also given for various reasons, usually compassionate or personal. This includes one day for moving house, two days for the death of a close relative, two days for the birth of a child (in the case of the father), 15 natural days – as opposed to working days – for marriage and the number of hours necessary for pregnant women to attend ante-natal classes.

Maternity leave is more generous in Spain than in the UK. Recent mothers, regardless of the length of their employment contract, are entitled to 16 weeks, which may be taken up to six weeks before the birth and 10 weeks after or spread over a different time span. Where the latter stages of the pregnancy are not complicated, many women work until as close as possible to the birth. Two of the 16 weeks may be transferred to the husband, and until the child is nine months old the mother is entitled to an hour a day 'feeding time' (*lactancia*) which may be taken in two sessions. The father, if employed, may substitute for the mother if the baby is not being breast-fed.

Health Insurance

Since the social security system includes practically all employed workers in Spain and covers healthcare, workplace accidents, sick leave, unemployment, invalidity and retirement, not many companies provide health insurance for their employees. The exceptions, perhaps, are multinationals employing large numbers of foreign workers. It is quite common, however, for larger companies to have an agreement with a private health insurance company such as Sanitas (belonging to BUPA; *see* p.208) which employees may join at a discount.

Sick Leave and Disability Pay

Generally speaking, 'taking a sickie' does not cause problems in Spain. Your word is considered good when calling in with a cold or 'flu and being absent from the workplace for one to three days. From the fourth day you should produce a doctor's note.

For all affiliates to the social security system, visits to doctors or hospitals and most prescribed medications are free. If you are absent owing to common illness or a non-industrial accident for between four and 20 days, you are entitled to 60 per cent of your salary, and from the 21st day this goes up to 75 per cent. If the reason for your absence is work-related, sick pay is 75 per cent from day one.

If you are self-employed, you may be entitled to some sick pay (75 per cent of the minimum legal salary, a pittance if you normally earn well but better than nothing) if you can show that your ailment impedes you from carrying out your normal activity.

For information on the social security system, *see* **Living in Spain**, 'Social Services and Welfare Benefits', pp.209–10.

Pensions

As in most countries, workers in Spain may retire and qualify for state pensions on reaching 60 (women) and 65 (men). The amount payable depends on the number of years' contributions made by the worker and his employer(s), from a minimum of 15, and on earnings over the eight years prior to retiring. Contributions made during periods of work in other EU countries also count towards entitlement in Spain. Like many other western economies, Spain's pensions industry has really struggled recently and the system has been on the point of collapse, needing urgent cash injections. It is not unfeasible that the pension age will be raised at some point, although few politicians dare to include that in their electoral programmes! For more on pensions, *see* **Living in Spain**, 'Retirement, Pensions and Investments', pp.210–11.

Losing Your Job and Signing On

The Spanish system covering unemployment is fairly generous but less all-embracing than in certain other EU countries. There is no real equivalent of the UK Jobseeker's Allowance, and **unemployment benefit** (*prestación del desempleo*) as such is contributory. Therefore, many people who have never worked or have only worked for a few short periods are left not covered, since they have not accumulated sufficient contributions to the system.

If you have worked and lost your job, your entitlement to unemployment benefit (also known as *el paro*) is determined by the number of days worked (and daily contributions made – *días cotizados*) during the six years prior to the situation of 'legal unemployment' arising. You need upwards of 360 *días cotizados* in order to claim dole. Entitlement to a full year's payment requires 1,080+ days, and the maximum period possible for which you may receive *paro* is 720 days, for which you need 2,160 days' accumulated contributions. Contributions made in other EU countries may also count towards your entitlement, though you may have to fight for this. The amount that the unemployed can receive depends on the contributions they have made within the last 180 days.

The amount of money to which you are entitled depends on your basic salary and contributions – known as the regulated base (*base reguladora*) – over the six-month period prior to becoming unemployed (overtime is not included). For the first 180 days you receive 70 per cent; after that it drops to 60 per cent. Allowances are made for *parados* with children and there is a top limit – executives cannot expect to get anything like their previous salary! While you are in receipt of *paro*, the INEM makes your social security contributions, and benefit is understood as taxable income, to be declared with your annual tax returns.

Self-employed persons may never claim benefits as they cannot lay themselves off, so if there is a drop in demand in your chosen field, start thinking about branching out in other directions!

To claim benefit you must be in a 'legal situation of unemployment', which means having been made redundant (owing to bankruptcy of the employing company), laid off as part of staff cuts, unfairly dismissed (this must be ratified by a labour court) or not rehired after completing a temporary contract. You must then register as a jobseeker at the local office of the INEM within 15 days of your unemployment beginning, produce the documents necessary to prove your situation (in most cases this is a certificate from the former employer plus a labour court ruling in cases of unfair dismissal), provide ID, fill in a benefit application form, sign an authorisation for the INEM to check your tax situation, and where applicable fill in a declaration if you have dependant relatives.

In cases of collective dismissal, workers who would like to form a co-operative (Sociedad Anónima Laboral, SAL) with other co-workers may apply for lump-sum payment of benefit in order to finance the venture.

General Information

For all questions relating to the world of work in Spain, you can look at the INEM's website, if your Castilian is up to it (**www.inem.es**) or acquire a copy of the *La Guía Laboral y de Asuntos Sociales 2006* (*2006 Guide to Labour and Social Affairs*) published by the Labour Ministry. Costing €15, this guide is available from the Ministry's shop in Calle Agustín de Betancourt, 11, 28003 Madrid or from many bookshops or news stands. A reduced version is also on the Ministry's website (**www.mtas.es/Guia2006**).

Teaching

Many native English-speakers survive in Spain by teaching English. Spanish state schools are still not producing competent English-speakers, and Spanish businesses that operate within the EU increasingly need linguistically competent employees. The gap between these two realities means there is a large English-teaching industry.

Virtually any reasonably educated native speaker should find work, although better schools will require a university degree as a minimum and preferably some training in teaching English as a foreign language (TEFL). Experience also helps. A TEFL course is recommended if you plan to teach for any length of time. Although there are various qualifications, the most internationally recognised is the Cambridge CELTA certificate, courses for which are offered at 286 centres in 54 countries. There are many in the UK and Ireland − check the website, **www.celta.org.uk**. It is also offered in Spain through International House and other centres. It consists of 109 hours of training which can either be completed through an intensive four-week course or part-time, spread over 12 weeks.

There are several ways of searching for work. Language schools regularly offer jobs in newspapers, especially *El País*, in the classified *Enseñanza* (teaching) section. The Sunday edition, particularly, has many offers, especially at the beginning of the academic year. Job offers can also be found in publications aimed at expats (*see* **Spain Today**, 'Major Media', pp.68–9). Often overlooked are the *Yellow Pages* (**www.paginasamarillas.es**), which list most language schools.

Some English teachers supplement their income with private classes; others only teach privately. Private classes are often paid in cash, but finding them means advertising yourself. This can be done by placing ads in newspapers, which costs money. Alternatively, publications like the thrice-weekly *Segundamano* have sections for people offering services and do not charge for ads. However, dozens of people advertise here and responses may be limited. Word of mouth is another useful source of work. However, even if you find work in a school, many require teachers to be freelancers (*autónomos*) nowadays.

Although most teaching is with businesses, it still follows the academic year. Classes begin in September or October and continue until late June or July. Given this, language schools generally offer nine-month contracts, and you will have to fend for yourself in the summer months. There may also be work teaching in universities, although as a rule this is found through private schools or institutions such as the British Council that have reached an agreement with a university to provide on-campus English classes. There is work to be found teaching at summer camps for children, mostly in July, some in August. Many business people also sacrifice part of their holidays to take a week or fortnight's intensive course.

Some language schools offer courses on the premises to the general public so that teachers can work blocked hours in morning and/or afternoon shifts. Mainly, though, they send teachers out to companies, where classes are usually given outside working hours. Thus, you teach 8–9.30am, 2–3.30pm and after 6pm. In between you may be travelling from one company to another and killing 'dead hours' drinking coffee or reading the newspaper. It is not unusual to spend almost as much time travelling as you do teaching. Travelling from class to class can also affect the amount of teaching you can do. Some language schools do pay a travel supplement if your classes take you far from the centre, or out of town to an industrial estate.

There are different types of contracts and different conditions.

• **Some schools change contracts monthly. For example, if you are scheduled for 15 hours a week, you will be paid for them whether students cancel classes or not. However, if a class of, say, three hours a week cancels definitively and no replacement is found, your contract for the following month will be for 12 hours.**

• **Some larger schools offer 12-month contracts with a month's paid holiday. You will be guaranteed the same pay for the same number of hours each** month whether you teach them or not (though you may have to spend 'spare hours' developing materials or doing administrative tasks).

• Private (*autónomo*) teachers make their own arrangements with their students. Most are paid only for the classes given. Autónomos working through a school are usually paid if the class is cancelled with less than 24 hours' notice, and some private teachers insist upon a retainer fee guaranteeing a minimum amount each month, regardless of cancellations. This is not a bad idea, since private students are notorious for cancelling.

Freelancing or Part-Time Work

It is becoming increasingly common in Spain to work as a freelancer. Since a freelancer is responsible for his or her own social security payments and is not eligible for unemployment benefits (to which the employer would contribute), more and more employers prefer to outsource and take on freelancers either for ongoing employment or on a one-off basis.

A self-employed worker is referred to as working *cuenta propia* – on his own account – or as a *trabajador autónomo*.

Freelancers can ply just about any trade in Spain. Language teachers, translators, photographers, artists, painters and decorators, singers, writers, models, etc. do not necessarily have to be qualified, as their professions are not 'regulated'. Their challenge is just getting out there and finding the customers. Doctors, vets, dentists, midwives, architects, lawyers and other professions, on the other hand, must not only be qualified but also may have to get their qualifications recognised before setting up in business. This can be a lengthy process. Qualifications from EU institutions are more readily accepted than pre-1992, which is when the European Court ruled that similar qualifications were to be considered equal Europe-wide. *See* 'Getting Recognition', p.247, for some helpful contacts for checking yours.

Social Security

A freelancer must register as an *autónomo* with social security and make monthly contributions to the system. The scale varies, with the minimum being around €250 per month. You may choose to make larger payments, which will be reflected in the retirement benefits you will eventually receive.

Taxes

Freelancers have to worry about two taxes: IRPF (*impuesto dobre la tenta de las personas físicas* – Income Tax) and IVA (VAT).

Case Study: From Derbyshire to the Madrid Mountains

David Weston, 49, from Long Eaton in Derbyshire, graduated in French from City of London Polytechnic in 1988 and came to Madrid the following autumn. He started working as an English teacher. A talented linguist, David learned Castilian quickly and is now a freelance translator and sports journalist.

How does working here compare to at home?

Working hours tend to be later than in the UK (in all types of jobs). When I was teaching I regularly got home at 10 or 11pm, but often wasn't working between 2 and 6. Now that I write and translate, generally working from home, I set my own hours, but late supper is the norm.

What is good and bad about living in Spain?

In general, a friendly, relaxed working atmosphere and long lunches! Lots of public holidays and a lively atmosphere: bars, street life, *fiestas* and evening strollers. The downside is that, for freelancers like me, bills often take a long time to process, especially in summer. I always seem to be chasing up clients for payment! Also, a lack of punctuality and general seriousness in the area of work (but it works both ways). Red tape is better than it was when I first came, but queues for officialdom are long. This is also the case in banks, which are inefficient and not user-friendly.

Are you integrated into Spanish society?

My girlfriend is Spanish and I live in a village 50km from Madrid, so I mix with a lot of Spaniards. When I go to Madrid it's usually to see British or Irish friends, playing/watching football, music, etc. I've had no problems mixing with Spanish people. I find them open, friendly, hospitable and generous.

How do you find the prices?

Spain is generally cheaper than most European countries for basic, everyday things. Hotels and B&Bs are still cheap but prices are rising. Consumer goods like IT equipment or musical instruments aren't any cheaper, and the range on offer is smaller. Watching live football is cheaper. Telephone charges are high. Prices have gone up considerably since the introduction of the euro.

Any tips for would-be residents?

Drivers and pedestrians should be ultra-defensive on the road, because the chances are that other road-users will take risks. Don't yawn and stretch in public, and don't make jokes about Spaniards' mothers or families in general. Don't leave big tips.

Everyone is liable for **IRPF** but you can choose between having 7 or 15 per cent withheld. If you choose seven per cent you will probably have to pay the difference when you file your return. IRPF is withheld by those you invoice and it is their responsibility to pay it to the Agencia Tributaria.

The other tax is **IVA**. Whether you must charge your clients this depends on what your activity is. It can be rather complicated, so be very sure whether your activity requires it to be charged. For example, if you are a translator, your liability to pay IVA depends on which type of translating you do. Texts to be published commercially, for example, usually carry IVA, but an academic paper written for publication may not. Consult the Agencia Tributaria (or a private *gestor*) to find out what your IVA obligations are.

If you are liable for IVA, you charge it directly to your client and are then responsible for declaring, and paying it directly to the Agencia Tributaria. IVA must be declared every three months, as opposed to IRPF which you declare once a year.

See **Living in Spain**, 'Taxation', pp.180–90.

Double Taxation

Spanish income tax regulation offers provisions for relief in cases where double taxation can occur. Spain has agreements with many countries (including the UK and Ireland) to avoid double taxation. Essentially this means,

---

Getting Recognition

Finding your way through the maze to get your qualifications recognized may be a lot easier if you look at some of the following contacts.

On the European Mobility Portal **http://europa.eu**, find the section 'Living and Working', select 'Spain' and click on 'Recognition of Diplomas and Qualifications' in the 'Working Conditions' box. This gives good guidance on which professions are or are not subject to the recognition process. It also directs you to the Castilian-only page of the Spanish Ministry of Education, Culture and Sports. Don't bother with this: go instead to the website of NARIC (the National Academic Recognition Information Centre, **www.naric.org.uk**). This agency is the official source of information and advice on the comparability of international qualifications from over 180 countries worldwide with those in the UK, and also promotes UK qualifications abroad. They offer advice and information about academic recognition, the comparability of qualifications and their use in education and training, professional registration and international employment. On the site, explore the 'recognition and evaluation services' section. The contact address is:

- **UK:** NARIC ECCTIS Ltd, Oriel House, Oriel Road, Cheltenham, Glos GL50 1XP, **t** 0870 990 4088, **f** (01242) 258611; **naric@naric.org.uk**.
- **Spain:** Lorena Gonzalez Olivares, Head of NARIC Spain, Federico Curto Herrero Nieves Trelles Cansejeria Técnica de Titulos de la Unión, Europea Paseo del Prado 28–4a planta E, 28014 Madrid, **t** 915 065 593, **f** 915 065 706; **lorena.gonzalez@educ.mec.es**.

in the case of a British citizen living in Spain, deducting the taxes you have paid to the Inland Revenue from your Spanish tax declaration, and deducting the taxes you have paid to the Agencia Tributaria from your UK tax declaration. You are liable for Spanish tax on any income earned in Spain. In this case, you may be taxed in Spain and will have to apply for relief when you pay income tax in your home country. British citizens are required to reside abroad for a full tax year before no longer being liable for British income tax. Since UK and Spanish tax years overlap, a UK citizen could be liable for taxation both in the UK and in Spain during his first year in Spain. Afterwards, however, a non-UK resident will not be liable for UK tax on any foreign income. You will, however, normally remain liable for UK tax on your UK income. For more information see the Inland Revenue publication IR20 'Residents and non-residents – liability to tax in the UK', and also pp.180–90.

Some useful websites are:

- **www.taxsites.com/international.html**: Access to the tax websites of governments and other organisations for a wide range of countries.
- **www.hmrc.gov.uk/cnr/index.htm**: Selection of tax guides, including IR20.
- **www.dwp.gov.uk/lifeevent/benefits/social_security_agreements.asp**: UK government website with details of social security agreements between the UK and other countries.
- **www.aeat.es**: Website of the Spanish tax authorities.
- **www.seg-social.es**: Website of the Spanish social security authority.

Starting Your Own Business

Many foreign residents in Spain are attracted by the idea of starting their own business. You may have come to Spain with the express idea of opening a bar or shop, or perhaps, after a couple of years, the country's long working hours lead you to the conclusion that your quality of life would be improved if you were your own boss. Whatever your motivation, it is worth remembering that, while many contemplate launching their own business, relatively few ultimately succeed. Preparation is everything.

Assuming that you have done your research and identified the market for your business (don't even think about setting one up if you haven't), then you can begin your adventure with officialdom. As in many other areas of Spanish life, it is essential that you make contact with a *gestoría* that can guide you through the necessary steps to set up your business in accordance with the law. It may also be advisable to seek the advice of a separate tax consultant (*asesor fiscal*) to help avoid financial problems with the authorities further down the line.

When looking for **premises** for your new business there are three basic options. You can buy your premises, rent them, or take a longer-term lease. A lease is still widely referred to as a *traspaso*, although it is now officially known as a *cesión*. A *cesión* may be bought or sold either by the owner of the premises or by the previous leaseholder. If you buy the *traspaso* or *cesión* of a going concern, it is likely that the seller will not be the owner of the building. In this case, when the original term of the lease expires, the building's owner has the right to renegotiate the terms and conditions of the lease. If, however, you lease directly from the owner you will have the right to renew your *cesión* when the original term expires. If at any point you wish to sell a business which is housed in a leased property then you are obliged to offer the *cesión* for sale to your land-lord at the same price as you may have agreed with any potential buyer. While buying premises outright or renting space may provide less opportunity for misunderstandings to arise, you still will need professional advice. In cities and resort areas there should be no problem in locating an English-speaking *gestor*.

Once you have located your premises you will need to apply for a **permit** to open your business (*licencia de apertura*). This will be issued by the local town hall (*ayuntamiento*). The cost of the *licencia* varies from around €60 for a permit to open a small retail outlet, to around €120 for a bar and as much as €4,000 for a financial institution such as a bank. Depending on the nature of your business there will be technical and/or health and safety **inspections** carried out before you can go ahead. There can be considerable delays in the process of issuing the *licencia de apertura*, so you should apply as early as possible.

Many Spanish-owned businesses do open their doors without the necessary paperwork. For expats this is highly inadvisable. First, as a foreigner your shop or bar or whatever will attract more attention than a small Spanish-owned enter-prise and therefore you would run a greater risk of provoking punitive action from the authorities. The last thing you want is to be closed down a couple of days after starting trading!

If your business is a small-scale enterprise then you will probably operate as a *trabajador autónomo* (*see* 'Freelancing'). You should remember that *autónomo* status involves paying a minimum monthly **social security contribution** of around €220. You must also enter your details in the **economic activities register** at your local *ayuntamiento*.

Before you open for business and once you are up and running, you should keep detailed **records** of all business expenditure and make sure that all **receipts** you are given display your Número de Identificación de Extranjero (**NIE**) – your tax identification number. As in the UK, you will be able to set your business expenses against your own tax bill providing you have supporting paperwork.

For small enterprises there are two usual **ways of paying tax** on your company's earnings: modules (*módulos*) or direct estimation (*estimación directa*). It is normal for a new business to begin on the *módulos* system. This involves paying business tax on a quarterly basis based on an estimation of your earnings. In the first instance this may be based on the size of your prem-ises, the nature of your business and the number of staff you employ. You then submit your full business accounts at the end of the year, and if the estimate of your income exceeds the real figure then you should receive a refund.

After the completion of a full year under the *módulos* system of taxation, you have the option of switching to *estimación directa*. This also involves quarterly payments of tax, but in this case based on detailed quarterly accounts. The key difference here is that you are only paying tax on your real income rather than an official estimate.

If you need to **employ staff** you should also consider the costs involved. Employment of one full-time worker is likely to cost a minimum of €800 per month. This estimate assumes a low basic wage and social security payment of just under a third of the total cost to the employer. There are established minimum wages, which may vary depending on the type of business, and employers are obliged to pay social security for all their employees. You will see businesses that flout all types of employment regulations but again, as a foreigner in Spain, you cannot afford to risk cheating the system. There are numerous examples of employers who have been landed with heavy fines for failing to stick to the letter of Spanish employment law. Neither is it unknown for employees to seek to capitalise on a foreigner's ignorance of Spanish law. One English-owned company on the coast had their bank accounts raided by an employee, only to be sued for wrongful dismissal by the same ex-staff member.

If you intend to undertake any larger economic activity you will probably set up a **Spanish company**, or a Spanish branch of a UK company. Both residents and non-residents have the right to form a company in Spain, and there are two basic forms which incorporation can take: **Sociedad Anónima (SA)** or **Sociedad Limitada (SL)**. Although the names may suggest otherwise, it is actually a Sociedad Anónima (SA) which is closest to a British public limited company or plc. To form an SA you need to have approximately €60,000 capital. In return you have the benefit of limited liability for all investors should the business fail. A Sociedad Anónima must have its accounts audited each year and must register those accounts in the public domain. You are unlikely to consider setting up an SA unless you are creating a Spanish wing of an existing UK company or already have considerable business experience in Spain. In either case you must have access to specialist advice (*see* below). Less is demanded in terms of capital and shareholder structure to establish a Sociedad Limitada (SL), but you will still have to have your Articles of Association signed before a Spanish notary. All Spanish companies are liable for **corporation tax** on 35 per cent of their profits.

There are no golden rules for making your business succeed in Spain, just a need for reserves of patience and cash. If you are competing directly with Spanish-owned businesses you will find that many small enterprises are family-owned and -staffed. Unless you have a large extended family that you intend to bring to Spain, this may mean that the odds seem to be against you. After all, employees who have a stake in a family business will put up with

Case Study: The Self-Employed Electronics Engineer

David Fillmore, 45, originally from London and a graduate in Electronic Computer and Systems Engineering at Loughborough University, arrived in Madrid 16 years ago. He started out working at INISEL SA and now runs his own electronics engineering consultancy, Fillmore Systems.

How did you find your first job? Was it easy?

Actually my first job found me. I was contacted by a consulting company and asked if I would like to come for a job interview here in Spain. I came, and I got the job.

How do you find working here compares with working at home?

Things have changed over the time that I have been here. At first I found the atmosphere much more relaxed, though with longer hours (40 per week); people definitely worked to live and not lived for work. However, with the telecoms crisis companies have put much more stress on the employees and expect them to work even longer hours for no extra pay.

What are the pros and cons of working and living here?

The advantages for me are the climate, the open, friendly people, and the food, which is relatively inexpensive and very varied. The main disadvantage for me is living in a flat, with no private garden to enjoy the good weather. Unless you move 50–60km outside Madrid, buying a house is too expensive. Prices have tripled since I arrived.

Do you live mainly in the expat community or have you integrated? Or is your life a bit of both?

Mine is a bit of both. As my wife is Spanish I'm fairly integrated, as the majority of my friends are Spanish or mixed-nationality couples like ourselves. I am also involved in the expat life. In my free time I am part of an English-language amateur theatre group.

How easy or difficult did you find mixing with Spanish people?

I've found no problems mixing with Spanish people, though it was quite difficult in the beginning when I didn't speak Spanish, which I learned first by going to classes, then through English–Spanish exchanges and then just by living the language socially and through work.

What tips would you give to any would-be residents?

Learn Spanish and mix with the local people, it's the only way to truly enjoy your time here and understand the country. Have plenty of patience when doing bureaucratic tasks – they are complicated and take time.

poorer pay and conditions in the interests of profitability. A foreign-owned business in Spain must be that extra bit more innovative and dynamic than a Spanish-owned equivalent. You may, for example, find yourself having to advertise where the Spanish might rely on word-of-mouth (*boca a boca*) trade.

However, if you have done your research and found the right location for your business, then being your own boss is one of the best ways of getting the most from the Spanish way of life.

Where to Find Advice

While all the red tape can seem daunting, especially if you only have a smattering of Spanish, there are some places where you turn to for help. First, before leaving the UK, look at the UK government websites that deal with trading in Spain. The website of the British Embassy in Madrid (**www.ukinspain.com**) offers general information about moving to Spain and has links to other sites which may be of interest to anyone thinking of setting up a business. Another government website (**www.uktradeinvest.gov.uk**) lists a range of publications offering advice about doing business with and in Spain.

The local Spanish authorities also have services designed to help new small businesses. Your local *ayuntamiento* should have a chamber of commerce (*cámara de comercio*) which can offer free advice and information on any incentives to help you get going. The Spanish Ministry of Economy also publishes a series of useful pamphlets in English, *A Guide to Business in Spain*, designed to help people contemplating launching their business in Spain. These are available from the Spanish consulate in the UK. The Ministry's website (**www.mineco.es**) lists all publications, and, although it is not currently available in English, an alternative government site (**www.interes.org**) offers English language advice on all areas of trading in Spain.

The British Chamber of Commerce in Spain provides advice for businesses starting up in Spain, although the annual membership fee of €1,500 may make it expensive for small businesses. See **www.britishchamberspain.com**.

Much of the best advice available on the internet is to be found on independent sites dealing with moving to Spain. The contributors are people who have made their businesses work in Spain and have practical experience of how the theory translates to practice. See, for example, **www.spain-villas.info/start-business-spain.htm**.

In a similar vein, consult the English-language press in Spain for local business clubs or for individuals who may be willing to offer you advice.

Volunteering

In principle, nobody should find problems getting voluntary work. You are, after all, offering your services and skills in return for nothing, other than maybe some experience, plus a sense of gratification from doing something worthwhile or whatever else you are looking for. Although you may come up against the same language barrier faced by those looking for paid work, this should be less of a problem as you are offering yourself free. And what better way to learn another language?

While most Spanish volunteers work on projects in developing countries, there is still a great demand for willing hands, particularly young ones, within Spain. The country's massive architectural and archaeological heritage is in constant need of conservation and upkeep. Similarly, declining agriculture and changes in land use have brought about a need for willing people to work on rural regeneration projects. There are also large pockets of poverty affecting many people, both in rural and urban settings, and organisations exist to bring relief. The *Prestige*, the oil tanker that sank in November 2002, was still leaking its foul contents which contaminated beaches in northern Spain throughout the summer of 2003. Plastic-clad volunteers were to be seen continuing the cleaning-up work among bathers and beach-volleyball players.

Before leaving for Spain, contact the **British Council**, in particular their Information Centre, which now handles all education and training enquiries (**education.inquiries@britishcouncil.org**; **www.britishcouncil.org**). The British Council Information Centre is based at Bridgewater House, 58 Whitworth Street, Manchester M1 6BB, **t** (0161) 957 7000, **f** (0161) 957 7111; while the London offices of the British Council are at 10 Spring Gardens, London SW1A 2B, **t** (020) 7389 8466, **f** (020) 7389 6347. This organisation publishes two useful books: *Working Holidays* and *Volunteer Work*. See also the *International Directory of Voluntary Work*, published by Vacation Work.

In Spain, a branch of the Labour Ministry, the **Instituto de la Juventud** (Youth Institute), based at Calle José Ortega y Gasset 71, 28006 Madrid, **t** 913 637 700) promotes and co-ordinates cultural exchange programmes for young people. For the English-language pages go to **www.programajuventud.mtas.es**.

Madrid's regional government (Comunidad de Madrid) has the **Servicio del Voluntariado Social**, Calle Espartina 10, 1ª, 28001 Madrid, **t** 900 444 555. This service co-ordinates voluntary programmes related to conservation projects, work with the elderly, the disabled and other disadvantaged groups within the Madrid region, but can also put you into contact with projects elsewhere. If your Castilian is up to it, go to **www.madrid.org/voluntarios**.

An NGO called **Solidarios para el Desarrollo** (Solidarity for Development) is also based in Madrid, but has links all over Spain. If you want to work with this organisation, you will need a reasonable level of Castilian as it carries out voluntary projects in the social work field. You must also be prepared to undergo training. Targeted groups are the homeless, AIDS and cancer victims, the mentally ill, old-age pensioners, convicts, children, the physically and mentally handicapped, prostitutes, drug addicts, immigrants and refugees. If you contact their Madrid offices(Calle Donoso Cortés 65, 28015 Madrid, **t** 913 946 425, **f** 913 946 434; **www.solidarios.org.es**) they will be able to put you in touch with similar groups elsewhere in Spain.

NGOs abound in Spain. They are called ONG (*organizaciones no-gubernamen-tales*) in Castilian. There are plenty of opportunities to get involved with them on a voluntary basis. This may well be a way of getting a foot in the door for a paid job, though these are not frequent and, if anything, harder to get than 'normal' jobs. If you access the website of the **CONGDE**, Coordinadora de ONG para el Desarrollo España (Coordinating Committee for Development NGO's Spain), **www.congde.org**, you can click on the *ofertas de trabajo* link. Many more are to be found on **www.canalsolidario.org**, where a click on *bolsa de trabajo* takes you to **www.hacesfalta.org**.

Finally, if you want sunshine while learning about accessible, low-tech methods of agriculture suitable for semi-arid environments, contact Shirley Savage, booking administrator at Sunseed Desert Technology, Apdo 9, 04270 Sorbas, Almería, **t** 950 525 770, **sunseedspain@arrakis.es**; **www.sunseed.org.uk**.

References

08

Spain at a Glance

Capital city: Madrid

Official name of country: Reino de España (Kingdom of Spain)

Type of government: Constitutional monarchy

Head of government: José Luis Rodriguez Zapatero, President of the Executive

Area: 504,782 sq km

Length: Distance from San Sebastián to Cádiz (far north to far southwest): 1,132km; from Girona (northeast) to Huelva (southwest): 1,240km

Maximum width: Distance from Lugo (far northwest) to Girona (northeast): 1,120km

Geographic highlights: Picos de Europa in Asturias; the Pyrenees, on the French border; the Sierra Nevada, south of Granada; rolling plains with big skies in La Mancha and with the addition of cork trees and bulls grazing in Extremadura; striking landscapes of the *meseta* in Castilla y León; deserts once used as locations for 'spaghetti westerns' in Almería; green, fertile and hilly Galicia, complete with dramatic (if oil-stained) coastline; many other mountain ranges throughout the country such as the Sierras de Madrid, Cazorla (in Jaén) and Cádiz

Independent states within Spain: None, but the country has 17 'Autonomous Communities' (Comunidades Autónomas), each with its own assembly, plus the North African enclaves of Ceuta and Melilla. Some have had a greater range of powers devolved than others. They are: Andalucía; Aragón; Asturias; Ceuta (an enclave in Morocco); Canarias (Canary Islands); Cantabria; Castilla-La Mancha; Castilla y León; Catalunya (Catalonia); Comunitat Valencià (Community of Valencia); Extremadura; Euskadi (the Basque country's name in Basque, referred to in Castilian as País Vasco); Galiza (Galicia in its own language); Illes Balears (Balearic Islands in the dialect of Catalan spoken there); La Rioja; Madrid; Melilla (an enclave in Morocco); Murcia; Navarra

Languages and dialects: Castilian Spanish (*Castellano*); Catalan (*Català*); Galician (*Galego*) and Basque (*Euskera*)

Bordering countries: France, Portugal, Gibraltar, Andorra, Morocco

Surrounding seas: Mediterranean, Atlantic

Population: 44,708,964 (2006 census)

Religion: Roman Catholic 76 per cent, 19 per cent identify as non-believers or atheists; other 5 per cent follow other religions

GDP purchasing power parity: USD$1,089 billion (2006 estimate).

GDP growth rate: 3.6 per cent (2006)

GDP per capita: USD$26,855 (2005)

Unemployment: 7.6 per cent (October 2006)

Further Reading

Travel Guides

Andrews, Sarah et al, *Lonely Planet: Spain* (Lonely Planet Publications).

Baskett, Simon, *Madrid (Rough Guide Directions)* (Rough Guides).

Ellingham, Mark, *The Rough Guide to Spain* (Rough Guides).

Facaros, Dana and Michael Pauls, *Spain* (Cadogan Guides); *Andalucia* (Cadogan Guides); *Northern Spain* (Cadogan Guides); *Bilbao and the Basque Lands* (Cadogan Guides); *Madrid* (Cadogan Guides); *Barcelona* (Cadogan Guides).

Garvey, Geoff, et al, *The Rough Guide to Andalucia* (Rough Guides).

Lloyd, Chris, *Costa Brava (Rough Guide Directions)* (Rough Guides).

Noble, John and Susan Forsyth, *Lonely Planet: Andalucia* (Lonely Planet Publications).

Roddis, Miles, et al, *Lonely Planet: Walking in Spain* (Lonely Planet Publications).

Sawday, Alastair, *Special Places to Stay: Spain* (Alastair Sawday Publishing).

Simonis, Damien, *Lonely Planet: Barcelona* (Lonely Planet Publications).

History

Brenan, Gerald, *The Spanish Labyrinth* (CUP).

Carr, Raymond, *The Spanish Tragedy* (Weidenfeld).

Fletcher, Richard, *Moorish Spain* (Phoenix).

Gibson, Ian, *Federico García Lorca: A Life* (Faber & Faber).

Orwell, George, *Homage to Catalonia* (Penguin).

Preston, Paul, *Franco, a Biography* (Harper-Collins).

Beevor, Antony, *Battle for Spain: The Spanish Civil War 1936-1939* (Weidenfeld & Nicolson).

Vilar, Pierre, *Spain, a Brief History*.

Modern Spain

Carr, Raymond, *Modern Spain* (Opus).

Elms, Robert, *Spain, A Portrait After the General* (Mandarin).

Hooper, John, *The New Spaniards* (Penguin Books).

Hughes, Robert, *Barcelona* (Harvill).

Preston, Paul, *The Triumph of Democracy in Spain* (Routledge).

Travel Literature

Ball, Phil, Morbo, *The Story of Spanish Football* (When Saturday Comes Books).

Borrow, George, *The Bible in Spain* (Century [Travellers Series]).

Brennan, Gerald, *South from Granada* (Penguin Books).

Cawley, Joe, *More Ketchup Than Salsa: Confessions of a Tenerife Barman* (Summersdale Publishers)

Cervantes, Miguel de (translation Rutherford), *Don Quixote* (Penguin Classics).

Graves, Lucía, *A Woman Unknown*.

Jacobs, Michael, *Between Hopes and Memories* (Picador).

Lalaguna, Juan, *Traveller's History of Spain* (Interlink Publishing Group).

Lee, Laurie, *As I Walked Out One Midsummer Morning* (Penguin Books).

Noteboom, Cees, *Roads to Santiago: Detsours and Riddles in the Lands and History of Spain* (Harcourt Brace).

Sands, George, *A Winter in Majorca*.

Stewart, Chris, *Driving Over Lemons* (Sort of Books).

Stewart, Chris, *A Parrot in the Pepper Tree* (Sort of Books).

Thomas, Hugh, *Spain: The Best Travel Writing from the New York Times* (New York Times).

Food and Wine

Aris, Pepita, *Spanish Cooking* (Lorenz Books).

Casas, Penelope, *Tapas, The Little Dishes of Spain* (Alfred A. Knopf).

Floyd, Keith, *Floyd on Spain* (Penguin Books).

Mendel, Janet, *Traditional Spanish Cooking* (Frances Lincoln).

Read, Jan, *The Wines of Spain* (Mitchell Beazley).

Bullfighting

Douglas, Carrie, *Bulls, Bullfighting and Spanish Identities* (University of Arizona Press).

Kennedy, A.L., *On Bullfighting* (Anchor Books/Doubleday).

Marvin, Gary, *Bullfight* (Illinois University Press).

Shubert, Adrian, *Death and Money in the Afternoon: A History of the Spanish Bullfight* (Oxford University Press).

Major Films

No list of Spanish films can claim to be definitive, less still be to everybody's taste. The 20 listed here were judged by a panel of actors and directors to be the best ever.

Atraco a las Tres: Director **José María Forqué** (1962). Comedy about a group of bank workers who plan a robbery.

Bienvenido Mister Marshall: Director **Luis García Berlanga** (1952). This satirical look at how American 'aid' passed normal folk by in 50s Spain surprisingly passed censors.

Bilbao: Director **Bigas Luna** (1978). A masterpiece that combines terror and eroticism, a truly 'dirty' film.

Calle Mayor: Director **J. Antonio Bardem** (1956). A bitter portrayal of small-town life in the provinces in which a bunch of youngsters play a cruel joke on an innocent girl.

El Cochecito: Director **Marco Ferreri** (1960). Large helpings of black humour in this story of an old man who wants a wheelchair in order to go out with his friends.

El Espíritu de la Colmena: Director **Victor Erice** (1973). The story of a child growing up in Spain after the Civil War.

El Extraño Viaje: Director **Fernando Fernán-Gómez** (1964). A portrait of deepest Spain around a plot involving a sordid crime.

El Sur: Director **Víctor Erice** (1983). Portrait of the sordid atmosphere after the Civil War.

El Verdugo: Director **Luis García Berlanga** (1963). Spain's 'dark side' is treated comically in this movie. An employee at an undertaker's marries the daughter of an executioner and ends up taking over his father-in-law's profession.

El Viaje a Ninguna Parte: Director **Fernando Fernán-Gómez** (1986). Fernán-Gomez's tribute to his life and the persons he loved through a comic portrayal of two travellers.

Furtivos: Director **José Luis Borau** (1975). A powerful, crude, incestuous drama premiered just before Franco's death, still relevant.

La Caza: Director **Carlos Saura** (1965). A subtle metaphor of the Civil War.

La Tía Tula: Director **Miguel Picazo** (1965). This story of the relationship between a widower and his spinster sister-in-law reflects on sexual repression.

Los Santos Inocentes: Director **Mario Camus** (1984). Based on the eponymous novel by Miguel Delibes, this film looks bitterly at social injustice in rural Spain.

Muerte de un Ciclista: Director **J. Antonio Bardem** (1955). Successful abroad, this movie, a fine example of Spanish neo-realism, showed that not all cinema in Francoist Spain was Francoist in spirit.

¿Qué he hecho yo para merecer esto?: Director **Pedro Almodóvar** (1984). Halfway between wacky comedy and tragedy, Almodóvar's first hit and most original film.

Surcos: Director **José Antonio Nieves** (1951). A neo-realist portrayal of the rural exodus.

Tristana: Director **Luis Buñuel** (1969). Buñuel's personal take on the eponymous Pérez Galdos novel also sneaked past the censors.

Viridiana: Director **Luis Buñuel** (1961). Winner of a Palme d'Or at Cannes, Buñuel's film was slammed by Franco's government, who thought it sacrilegious and blasphemous.

Volver: Director **Pedro Almodóvar** (2006). Highly acclaimed screenplay about the rich culture that surrounds death in the region of La Mancha; seen through various female characters from different generations.

Dictionary of Useful Words and Phrases

For useful vocabulary relating to accommodation *see* **Living in Spain**, 'Housing Jargon', pp.134–5. For some warnings on 'false friends' see 'With friends like these...', pp.128–97. For reasons of space we have concentrated on Castilian (or 'Spanish' as it is most commonly known) to the detriment of Catalan, Galician and Basque.

Everyday Words and Phrases

Hola	Hello
Adiós/hasta luego	Goodbye
Buenos días/Buenas tardes	Good morning/afternoon
Buenas noches	Goodnight
Por favor	Please
(muchas) gracias	Thank you (very much)
De nada	You're welcome
Con permiso/¿Me permite?	Excuse me
Disculpe/Perdón	I am sorry (apologising)
Lo siento (mucho)	I am sorry (expressing regret)
No importa	It doesn't matter
De acuerdo/Está bien	All right
Vale	Okay
Sí	Yes
No	No
Nada	Nothing
No (lo) sé	I don't know
No hablo español (castellano)	I don't speak Spanish (Castilian)
Hablas/Habla usted inglés?	Do you speak English?
¿Hay alguien que hable ingles?	Does anyone here speak English?
Por favor, hable más despacio	Please, speak slowly
¿Me puede(s) ayudar?	Can you help me?
¡Socorro!	Help!
¿Cómo estás/está usted?	How do you do?
Bien, gracias, ¿y tú/usted?	Well, and you?
¿Como te llamas/se llama?	What is your name?
Yo me llamo ...	My name is ...
¿De donde eres/es usted?	Where are you from?
Yo soy de ...	I am from ...
¿Qué es esto/eso?	What is this/that?
¿Qué?	What?
¿Quién?	Who?
¿Dónde?	Where?
¿Cuándo?	When?
¿Por qué?	Why?
¿Cómo?	How?

¿Cuánto/a?	How much?
¿Cuántos/as?	How many?
Me he perdido	I am lost
Tengo hambre/sed	I am hungry/thirsty
Estoy cansado/a	I am tired
Me siento mal	I am ill
Bueno/malo	Good/bad
Despacio/rápido	Slow/fast
Grande/pequeño	Big/small
Caliente/frío	Hot/cold

Los Números   ## Numbers

Uno/una	1
Dos	2
Tres	3
Cuatro	4
Cinco	5
Seis	6
Siete	7
Ocho	8
Nueve	9
Diez	10
Once	11
Doce	12
Trece	13
Catorce	14
Quince	15
Dieciséis	16
Diecisiete	17
Dieciocho	18
Diecinueve	19
Veinte	20
Veintiuno	21
Veintidós	22
Treinta	30
Cuarenta	40
Cincuenta	50
Sesenta	60
Setenta	70
Ochenta	80
Noventa	90
Cien	100
Ciento uno	101
Doscientos/as	200
Trescientos/as	300

Cuatrocientos/as	400
Quinientos/as	500
Seiscientos/as	600
Setecientos/as	700
Ochocientos/as	800
Novecientos/as	900
Mil	1,000
Un millón	1 million

La Hora — The Time

¿Qué hora es?	What's the time?
¿Tienes/llevas la hora?	Have you got the time?
Es la una	It's one o'clock
Son las dos/tres/cuatro etc...	It's two/three/four etc. o'clock
Son las ... y cinco/diez/veinte/veinticinco	It's 5/10/20/25 past ...
Son las ... menos cinco/diez/veinte/veinticinco	It's 5/10/20/25 to ...
Son las ... y cuarto/media	It's quarter/half past ...
Son las ... menos cuarto	It's quarter to ...
El amanecer	Dawn
La madrugada	The early hours
(La) mañana	Morning
(El) mediodía	Noon
(La) tarde	Afternoon
(La) tarde/noche (before/after sundown)	Evening
La noche	Night
Ayer	Yesterday
Mañana	Tomorrow
La semana pasada/el mes/año pasado	Last week/month/year
Anteayer	The day before yesterday
Ahora	Now
Más tarde	Later
Temprano/pronto	Early
Tarde	Late
La semana/el mes/año que viene	Next week/month/year

Los Días — Days

Lunes	Monday
Martes	Tuesday
Miércoles	Wednesday
Jueves	Thursday
Viernes	Friday
Sábado	Saturday
Domingo	Sunday

Las Estaciones

La primavera
El verano
El otoño
El invierno

Seasons

Spring
Summer
Autumn
Winter

Los Meses

Enero
Febrero
Marzo
Abril
Mayo
Junio
Julio
Agosto
Septiembre
Noviembre
Octubre
Diciembre

Months

January
February
March
April
May
June
July
August
September
November
October
December

De Viaje

Avión
Aeropuerto
Reservación/Reserva/Reservar un billete
Autobús/Autocar
Estación de autobuses/trenes
Aduana
Vuelo
Viaje
Andén
Asiento
Barco
Billete
Viaje de ida/ida y vuelta
Tren
Consigna
Horario
¿Dónde está el/la ...?
¿Cómo puedo llegar al/a la ...?
¿A qué hora sale el próximo ...?
¿A qué hora sale/parte?
¿De dónde sale/parte?

On the Move

Aeroplane
Airport
Booking/to book a ticket
Bus/coach
Bus/railway station
Customs
Flight
Journey/trip
Platform
Seat
Ship
Ticket
One way/return trip
Train
Left luggage
Timetable/schedule
Where is the ...?
How can I get to the ...?
When is the next ...?
What time does it leave/arrive?
Where does it leave from?

Quiero un billete a/un billete de ida y vuelta a ...	I want a single/return ticket to ...
¿Cuánto cuesta el billete?	How much is the fare?
Aquí/allí/allá (the last one means 'even further')	Here/there
Cerca/lejos	Near/far
A la izquierda/derecha	Left/right
Todo recto/directo	Straight on
La primera/segunda a la izquierda/ derecha	First/second left/ right
Calle	Street
Plaza	Square
Esquina	Corner

En el Camino

On the Road

Coche	Car
Bicicleta	Bicycle
Moto	Motorbike
Gasolina	Petrol
Aceite	Oil
Gasolinera	Garage (for petrol)
Taller (mecánico)	Garage (for car repairs)
Carretera	Road
Autopista	Motorway
Autovía	Main road/highway
Carretera comarcal	Back/country road/lane
Permiso de conducir	Driving licence
Salida	Exit
Entrada	Entrance
Peligro	Danger
No aparcar/estacionar or *estacionamiento prohibido*	No parking
Limite de velocidad	Speed limit
Reduzca su velocidad	Slow down
Ceda el paso	Give way
Obras	Roadworks
Alquiler de coches	Rent (cars)

De Compras, Por la Ciudad, Servicios y Personas Utiles

Shopping, Around Town, Services and Useful People

Banco	Bank
Grandes almacenes	Department store
Tiendas	Shops (of all types)

Mercado	Market
Centro comercial	Shopping centre/mall
Correos	Post office
Sellos	Stamps
Abierto/a/cerrado/a	Open/closed
Farmacia	Chemist's (for prescriptions)
Ambulatorio	Health centre
Urgencias	Emergency ward/out patients
¿Cuánto es/son ...?	How much is/are ...?
¿Dónde está el/la ... mas cercano/a?	Where is the nearest ...? or Is there a ... near
Or ¿Hay un/a ... cerca de aquí?	here?
¿Puede cambiar un billete (de cincuenta euros?)	Can you change a (€50) note?
¿Tiene/Me puede dar cambio para el teléfono/tabaco etc.?	Have you got any change (for the telephone/cigarette machine, etc.)?
Comisaría	Police station
Bomberos	Fire service
Museo	Museum
Teatro	Theatre
Cine	Cinema
Oficina de turismo	Tourist office
Taquilla	Box/booking office
Agencia de viajes	Travel agency
Servicios/aseos	Toilets
Hombres/Caballeros	Men
Mujeres/Damas	Women
Fontanero	Plumber
Electricista	Electrician
Mecánico	Mechanic
Carpintero	Carpenter
Albañil	Builder/bricklayer
Abogado	Lawyer
Gestor	'Administrative service provider' (no real translation exists, see p.113)
Trámites	Red tape/bureaucratic procedures
Agencia pTributaria (Hacienda)	Tax office
Oficina de Empleo (INEM)	Employment office
Ministerio de(l) educación/justicia/ interior etc. ...	Ministry of education/justice/the interior (home office), etc. ...

Comer Fuera

Eating Out

Restaurante	Restaurant
Restaurante chino/italiano/mexicano/ tailandés/hindú etc. ...	Chinese/Italian/Mexican/Thai/Indian etc. ...restaurant
Comedor	Dining room/area (often at the back of a bar or cafeteria)

Menú del día	Fixed-price set menu
Carta	Menu
Lista de vinos	Wine list
Comer a la carta	To eat *à la carte*
Camarero/a	Waiter/waitress
Entradas/primer plato	Starters
Segundo	Main course
Verduras	Vegetables
Ensalada	Salad
Carne	Meat
Pescado	Fish
Mariscos	Seafood
Postre	Sweet
La cuenta	Bill
¿Tiene una mesa para una/ dos persona(s)?	Have you got a table for one/two?
¿Me puede dejar la lista de vinos, por favor?	Can I see the menu/wine list?
¿Me trae la cuenta, por favor?	Can you bring me the bill please?
¿Puedo pagar con tarjeta?	Can I pay by credit card?
Or *¿Admiten/Aceptan tarjetas?*	Do you take credit cards?
¿Admiten/Aceptan Visa/Amercian Express, etc.?	Do you accept Visa/American Express, etc.

Internet Vocabulary

Base de datos	Database
Borrar/Suprimir/Cancelar	Delete
Arroba	@
Descifrar	Decode
Barra barra/doble barra	//
Dos puntos	: (colon)
En línea	Online
Dirección de correo electrónico/correo-e/e-mail	E-mail address
Guión bajo	_ (underline)
Punto	. (dot)
Red (La red)	Network
Reiniciar	To restart
Seleccionar	To select
Buscar	To browse
Barra	/ (forward slash)
Apagar (el equipo)	Shut down
Guión	- (hyphen)
Usuario	User
Uve doble, uve doble, uve doble/tres uve dobles	www

Public Holidays and Celebrations

Days celebrated nationwide are asterisked; others are celebrated almost everywhere:

1 January*	New Year's Day (*Año Nuevo*)
6 January	Epiphany or Kings' Day (*Reyes Magos*)
19 March	San José (*Día de San José*)
March/April*	Good Friday, *Viernes Santo*
	Easter (Holy Week)*, *Semana Santa*
1 May*	International Labour Day (*Fiesta del Trabajo*)
May/June	Corpus Christi, on the 2nd Thursday after Whitsun
	Ascension Day (*Ascensión*) 40 days after Easter
15 August*	Assumption of the Virgin (*Asunción*)
12 October*	Virgin of Pilar, National Day (*Día de la Virgen del Pilar*)
8 December*	Immaculate Conception (*Inmaculada Concepción*)
25 December*	Christmas (*Navidad*)

Spain's *fiestas* are rightly famous worldwide. Every city, town and village has *fiestas* in honour of its patron saint while many others are national events. Local tourist offices provide full information of *fiestas* in every town. Some major celebrations are:

31 December	New Year's Eve: a large family dinner, everyone eats a grape with each chime of the clock just before midnight to bring good luck for the new year.
1 January	New Year's Day is quiet but is a public holiday.
5 January	In most of Spain processions celebrate the coming of the *Reyes Magos* (the Three Kings), who will bring children presents the next morning.
6 January	*Reyes* or *Epifanía*. More important than Christmas for many; children receive their 'big' presents, and naughty children are threatened with just a piece of coal, usually made of sugar (few really go without presents).
January–February	Carnival, *Carnaval*, an occasion for dressing up and revelling. Most spectacular in Cádiz and Tenerife, the latter considered second only to Rio de Janeiro's.
March or April	Easter, *Semana Santa*, a major *fiesta* throughout Spain. The most spectacular processions are in Andalucía.
19 March	*Fallas*, in Valencia, during the week before San José (19 March) paper-maché caricature statues of celebrities adorn the streets and are then burnt. Impressive fireworks.
April	*Feria de Abril*, Seville. The April Fair is a week-long party. Womenfolk wear traditional flamenco dresses, singing, dancing and sherry-drinking into the small hours.

23 April	*Sant Jordi* (Saint George in Catalan). Men give their loved one a rose, she (or he) responds with a book. Now common throughout Spain.
Whitsuntide	Fifty days after Easter Sunday this colourful mass pilgrimage goes to the shrine of El Rocío in the village of Almonte, Huelva. Traditional Andalucian garb and two days of merry-making in Doñana park.
1 May	International Labour day, less significant politically nowadays but large union-organised marches throughout Spain.
June	Corpus Christi is celebrated nationally, but the processions and other festivities are especially colourful in Andalucía, Salamanca, Toledo and Barcelona.
June	*San Juan*, the shortest night of the year, celebrated throughout Spain. People jump over bonfires three times (an act of purification). Most spectacular in Alicante.
6 July	*San Fermín*, a week-long *fiesta* in Pamplona. The main attraction is bull-running (*encierros*). Bullfights every afternoon plus dances, processions and copious eating and drinking.
July–August	During the summer practically every village in Spain celebrates its local *fiestas* with concerts and dances in the main square.
15 August	The Assumption of the Virgin, *Asunción*, is celebrated nationally.
12 October	A national *fiesta*, known as *El Día de la Raza* (Day of the Race) or *El Día de la Hispanidad* (Day of the Hispanic World). The Virgin of Pilar is venerated, particularly in Zaragoza.
1 November	All Saints' Day, *Día de Todos los Santos*.
2 November	All Souls' Day, when people take flowers to the tombs of their dead relatives.
8 December	Immaculate Conception, *La Inmaculada Concepción*.
25 December	*Navidad,* Christmas. Celebrated with gifts and, more recently, a tree, but tradition calls for a *Belén*, a Nativity scene with handmade figurines. The big family meal is on Christmas Eve, *Noche Buena*, roast lamb is preferred to turkey. Boxing Day is not a holiday.

Regional Climate Chart

Average monthly temperatures °Celsius (average daily maximum and minimum) and rainfall (monthly mm)

	Jan	Feb	Mar	Apr	May	June	July	Aug	Sept	Oct	Nov	Dec
Malaga												
Max	17	15	18	20	24	27	30	30	28	23	20	17
Min	11	7	12	11	14	17	20	20	18	16	13	10
Rainfall	8	8	7	9	6	3	1	1	3	8	9	9
Alicante												
Max	18	19	22	26	28	31	34	31	24	24	18	17
Min	7	8	13	15	19	20	21	22	18	14	12	8
Rainfall	9	6	9	9	6	6	3	5	7	8	10	7
Majorca												
Max	17	10	17	18	23	25	31	32	29	22	19	17
Min	4	0	7	7	8	14	16	18	18	13	8	7
Rainfall	13	11	9	11	5	5	3	4	9	11	11	10
Madrid												
Max	9	11	15	18	21	27	31	30	25	19	13	9
Min	2	2	5	7	10	15	17	17	14	10	5	2
Rainfall	8	8	10	9	7	6	3	3	4	7	8	9
Las Palmas												
Max	13	14	16	18	21	25	28	28	25	21	16	13
Min	6	7	9	11	14	18	21	21	19	15	11	8
Rainfall	7	7	9	8	6	6	4	5	7	8	6	6
Tenerife												
Max	21	22	23	22	23	23	27	28	27	26	24	22
Min	16	16	16	16	17	17	21	22	22	21	19	17
Rainfall	3	3	4	3	2	2	0	1	2	2	5	4
Barcelona												
Max	13	14	16	18	21	25	28	28	25	21	16	13
Min	6	7	9	11	14	18	21	21	19	15	11	8
Rainfall	31	39	48	43	54	37	27	49	76	86	52	45
A Coruña												
Max	13	13	15	16	18	20	22	23	22	19	15	13
Min	7	7	8	9	11	13	15	15	14	12	9	8
Rainfall	118	80	92	67	54	45	28	46	61	87	124	135
Santander												
Max	12	12	14	15	17	20	22	22	21	18	15	13
Min	7	7	8	10	11	14	16	16	15	12	10	8
Rainfall	119	88	78	83	89	63	54	84	114	133	125	159

Regional Calling Codes

To call Spain from abroad, dial the international code (from the UK oo), then 34 and then the 9-digit number of the subscriber. The subscriber's number incorporates the regional code so is the same wherever you are dialling from in Spain, even from within that province. Thus all numbers in Madrid (and its surrounding province) begin with 91, followed by seven more digits. In the list that follows you will notice that some provinces' codes comprise three digits. This is because they actually coincide in the first two with a larger or more important province and the third digit is a 'sub-code' of that one. Thus 95 is the code for both Málaga and Seville, in Andalucía, but other Andalucian provinces take 95, then another number, plus six digits. Almería is, by this logic, 950, etc.

To call Gibraltar from within Spain, dial 9567 and the subscriber's number.

A Coruña	981 (may be referred to as La Coruña in some publications)
Álava/Araba	945 (includes the city of Vitoria, Gasteiz in Basque and capital of the Basque Autonomous Region, Euskadi)
Albacete	967
Alicante	96 (the city is also called Alacant by Catalan speakers. Note that the code is the same as that for Valencia)
Almería	950
Asturias	98 (includes both the cities of Gijón and Oviedo)
Ávila	920
Badajóz	924
Barcelona	93
Burgos	947
Cáceres	927
Cádiz	956
Cantabria	942
Castellón de la Plana	964
Ceuta	956 (North African enclave)
Ciudad Real	926
Córdoba	957
Cuenca	969
Girona	972
Granada	958
Guadalajara	949
Guipúzcoa/Guipuzkoa	943 (includes the city of San Sebastián, Donostia in Basque)
Huelva	959
Huesca	974
Illes Balears	971 (the name of the Balearic Isles in Catalan, which is spoken there)
Jaén	953
La Rioja	941 (includes the city of Logroño)
Las Palmas	928
León	987

Lleida	973 (this city is referred to as Lérida by Castilian speakers)
Lugo	982
Madrid	91
Málaga	95
Melilla	95 (North African enclave)
Murcia	968
Navarra	948
Ourense	988 (may be spelt 'Orense' in some publications)
Palencia	979
Pontevedra	986
Salamanca	923
Santa Cruz de Tenerife	922
Segovia	921
Seville	95 (note it is the same as Málaga)
Soria	975
Tarragona	977
Teruel	978
Toledo	925
Valencia	96 (note it is the same as Alicante)
Valladolid	983
Vizcaya/Bizkaia	94 (includes the city of Bilbao, Bilbo in Basque)
Zamora	980
Zaragoza	976

Post Codes

All Spanish post codes consist of five digits. The first two of those are present in practically all codes in a given province and are then followed by three more digits. Thus, all Madrid post codes begin with 28 (+ three more digits), all Barcelona codes begin with 08 (+ three more digits) etc. In larger cities and provincial capitals, a code in which the first two digits are followed by a zero usually indicates an address within the provincial capital, and the first two followed by a number greater than one onwards usually indicates locations outside the provincial capital. Some provinces, for reasons of proximity, have a few outlying villages with a code corresponding to the neighbouring province. In the following table, the first two digits only are given and the more important exceptions are indicated.

Names in co-official languages are indicated in italics.

Province	Provincial Capital (*where different from the province name*) and other main cities	First two digits in provincial code:
A Coruña	This province also includes the city of **Santiago de Compostela**	**15---**

Province	Provincial Capital (*where different from the province name*) and other main cities	First two digits in provincial code:
	which is the capital of the Galician Autonomous Community.	
Álava/*Araba*	Vitoria/*Gasteiz*	01---
Albacete		02---
Alicante/*Alacant*		03---
Almería		04---
Asturias	Oviedo/Gijón/Avilés	33---
Ávila		05---
Badajoz	This province also includes the city of **Mérida** which is the capital of the Autonomous Community of Exremadura.	06---
Barcelona		08---
Burgos		09---
		(Plus some beginning with 26---, 34---, 39--- 42---, villages bordering on the provinces of La Rioja, Palencia, Cantabria and Soria respectively).
Cáceres		10---
Cádiz		11---
Cantabria	Santander	39---
Castellón de la Plana/ *Castelló de la Plana*		12---
Ceuta (North African enclave)		51---
Ciudad Real		13---
Córdoba		14---
Cuenca		16---
Gerona/*Girona*		17---
Granada		18---
Guadalajara		19---
		(plus one, 28190, bordering on Madrid province)
Guipúzcoa/*Guipuzkoa*	San Sebastián/*Donostia*	20---
Huelva		21---
Huesca	Jaca	22---
Islas Baleares/*Illes Balears*	Palma de Mallorca/Mahón (*Maó*)/Ibiza (*Eivissa*)	07--- (*Maó*) 077---
Jaén		23---
La Rioja	Logroño	26---
Las Palmas de Gran Canaria		35---
León		24---

Lérida/*Lleida*		25--- (except several villages bordering on Barcelona province, beginning **08**---).
Lugo		27---
Madrid		28---
Málaga		29---
Melilla		52---
Murcia	Murcia/Cartagena	30---
Navarra	Pamplona	31--- (plus one, **50686**, a village bordering on Zaragoza province).
Orense/*Ourense*		32---
Palencia		34---
Pontevedra	Pontevedra Vigo	36---
Salamanca		37---
Santa Cruz de Tenerife		38---
Segovia		40---
Sevilla		41---
Soria		42---
Tarragona		43---
Teruel		44---
Toledo		45---
Valencia		46---
Valladolid		47---
Vizcaya/*Bizkaia*	Bilbao/*Bilbo*	48---
Zamora		49---
Zaragoza		50--- (Plus some beginning with **22**---, **42**--- and **44**---, villages bordering on Huesca, Soria and Teruel provinces respectively

Index